UNDERSTANDING EQUAL OPPORTUNITY POLICIES

KEN BLAKEMORE
and
ROBERT F. DRAKE
University of Wales, Swansea

PRENTICE HALL
HARVESTER WHEATSHEAF

London   New York   Toronto   Sydney   Tokyo   Singapore
Madrid   Mexico City   Munich

First published 1996 by
Prentice Hall Europe
Campus 400, Maylands Avenue
Hemel Hempstead
Hertfordshire HP2 7EZ
A division of
Simon & Schuster International Group

Typeset in 10/12pt Baskerville
by Dorwyn Ltd, Rowlands Castle, Hants

Printed and bound by
T. J. Press (Padstow) Ltd, Padstow, Cornwall

Library of Congress Cataloging-in-Publication Data

Blakemore, Kenneth, 1948–
    Understanding equal opportunity policies / Ken Blakemore and
Robert F. Drake
        p.   cm. — (Contemporary social policy series)
    Includes bibliographical references and index.
    ISBN 0-13-433319-5
    1. Discrimination in employment.   2. Discrimination in
employment—Great Britain.   I. Drake, Robert F.   II. Title.
III. Series.
HD4903.B55   1996
331.13'3—dc20   95–47285
                                                              CIP

British Library Cataloguing in Publication Data

A catalogue record for this book is available from
the British Library

ISBN 0–13–433319–5

---

1 2 3 4 5   00 99 98 97 96

UNDERSTANDING
EQUAL OPPORTUNITY
POLICIES

CONTEMPORARY SOCIAL POLICY

Series Editor: Michael Sullivan, University of Wales, Swansea

A series of concise and accessible introductory guides to key topics and issues in contemporary social policy.

Also available in the series:

Ian Law, *Racism, Ethnicity and Social Policy*

Future volumes in the series will cover topics such as:

Welfare Pluralism
Social Policy in Europe
Community Care
Health Policy
Education Policy
Housing and Homelessness

CONTENTS

v

SERIES EDITOR'S PREFACE

The restructuring of the welfare state is gathering pace. But paralleling this general restructuring is an equally rapid restructuring of work and of relations between employers and employees. These changes are stimulating a dramatic increase in interest among academics, managers and professionals in the connections between welfare, opportunity and work. As Blakemore and Drake ably show, the belief, firmly held during the 'golden age' of the welfare state, that lifelong and permanent employment would remain the bedrock of social welfare and insurance-based benefits is now open to question.

However as Ken Blakemore and Robert Drake observe in their introductory chapter, there is a dearth of empirical or theoretical studies in the field of social policy that address these important questions. While there has been a steady flow of publications in the fields of industrial relations and management on equal opportunities in the workplace and the changing nature of work and while ideas of equality and equity are at the core of the discipline of social policy, few other social policy studies concern themselves with the relation between equality, equity and work.

It is therefore timely and significant that one of the first books in the *Contemporary Social Policy* series should be concerned with bridging the gap between social policy, equality strategies and employment.

The value of this book lies firstly in its consideration of the social context of equality policies. There has been a growing interest in the future of the welfare state and alongside it concerns about the 'state of the nation' (see, for example, Will Hutton's masterly polemic *The State We're In* (Cape, 1995)). We have also seen a burgeoning of studies about how economic restructuring can devastate the social fabric and severely limit opportunities for 'excluded' social groups, now conveniently seen by some as an underclass. Blakemore and Drake address these questions but go further than reviewing the social and economic context. This volume supplements contextual issues with a careful and even-handed analysis of how far equality policies have made, or could make, a difference.

Understanding Equal Opportunity Policies also makes a significant contribution by including discussion of the impact of equality policies in all the major social dimensions: gender, 'race' and ethnicity, disability, age and, to a lesser extent, social class, sexual orientation and religion. The inclusiveness of the book fulfils one of the primary aims of the series – to provide vantage points on a range of current developments in social policy. This is particularly important in the area of equality and opportunity, where there is a danger that discussion about any one dimension of inequality can become introspective, over-theoretical and disconnected from policy concerns.

The book is, then, an admirably disinterested review of the area which will be of immense help to undergraduate students and teachers of social policy, sociology and industrial relations. But it is more than this. I believe that this book will also make a contribution to enabling the change process. This is not to suggest that it is a 'how to do it' book for managers and practitioners. Rather, one of the aims of this book and of the series is to inform practice and to sharpen the concepts and definitions used by those working within the public and private sectors. In that sense, Chapter 3, which surveys and prompts further questions on models and principles of equality policy, is as applied to practice and policy as the penultimate chapter of the book which reviews the outcomes of different management approaches in 'real-world' companies and public sector organisations.

Michael Sullivan
Swansea
October, 1995

ACKNOWLEDGEMENTS

We first wish to acknowledge the contributions of colleagues and students at the Department of Social Policy, University of Wales, Swansea: Mike Sullivan struck the first spark of the idea for this book; Anthea Symonds provided cheery encouragement throughout; Jeni Chamberlain and fellow students very helpfully submitted to the punishment of reading early drafts of chapters; and Eryl Evans at the administrative hub was crucial in keeping chaos at bay.

Secondly, Ken Blakemore and Robert Drake acknowledge the contribution made by Rob Behrens at the Civil Service College, Sunningdale, who provided us with insights and experience which were immensely valuable in writing Chapter 8 and in helping us to reflect on the international context of equal opportunities. We are also grateful to Julia Johnson and Bill Bytheway for reading and commenting upon a draft of Chapter 8.

Thirdly, formal acknowledgements are due to: the OECD, Paris, which gave permission to reproduce Figure 2.1; the Office for Official Publications of the European Communities, Luxembourg, for permission to use (in Table 4.4) data on employment from the Eurostat Publication, *Europe in Figures*; *Equal Opportunities Review* (published by Industrial Relations Services, Eclipse Group Ltd) for permission to reproduce statistical material used in Table 5.2; Macmillan Ltd for permission to use data in Table 4.7 from A. H. Halsey's *British Social Trends Since 1900*; and the Employment Department for permission to reproduce, in Chapter 5, statistical material from the *Employment Gazette* (May 1994) on employment, gender and race/ethnic origin.

Robert Drake also wishes to acknowledge his debt to three mentors: Professor Emeritus Maurice Broady, gentleman and scholar, whose academic integrity is matched always by his unfailing courtesy and generosity; Dr Ralph White, a historian whose passion for his subject and encouragement of his students enabled so many of them to fulfil the adjuration of their University: *altiora petamus* (let us seek higher things); and Dr David Owens, a sociologist and PhD supervisor of infinite patience, wisdom and sound judgement. I am also grateful to Ken Blakemore for sharing with me his much wider experience as an author and for providing gentle and erudite guidance throughout this endeavour.

Finally, as completion of the book drew near, we were able to snatch unequal opportunities from our families and our partners, Dilys Blakemore and Gillian Drake, to finish it off. Without their tolerance and positive support this book would not have been written, and we warmly acknowledge their help in these respects.

1
INTRODUCTION

Conversations about equal opportunities turn, as often as not, into heated discussions. Our aim in this book is to promote continued interest in and concern about equal opportunities, but in a way which questions value-laden assumptions and which aims to replace flag-waving with a more critical and objective approach.

Two contrasting images are often used to portray equality policies and their impact. First, there is the image of equal opportunities as a powerful and pervasive set of influences on people's lives. According to this image, equality policies have been taken too far. They are seen as a baneful influence, effectively promoting the interests of people who do not deserve a job or promotion on grounds of merit. They are also associated with 'political correctness' and with having to conform to bureaucratic *diktats* about how to address people or how to behave with them.

The second image, also a negative one, depicts equal opportunities quite differently. Rather than representing a growing force in work and public life, equality policies are seen as a sham, serving only as a skimpy and threadbare mantle to disguise deep and continuing inequalities. People who are supposed to be helped by equality policies, for example people in minority ethnic communities, women, disabled people and older workers, find policy achievements derisory. Equality policies may be a hair shirt for the socially concerned or an attempt to whitewash discrimination, but in neither case do they have any practical impact on the world of work or the status of the disadvantaged.

The point is that both these images cannot be correct, or even close to the truth, at the same time. Equality policies cannot be both deeply pervasive and cosmetic. One important task in the following pages is therefore to examine which image, if either, is closer to the truth. Another is to examine other possibilities, because there are more positive images of equal opportunities than the first two: there is the real prospect of introducing greater fairness in education and training, and of opening up talents in the workplace that would otherwise remain underused or unemployed.

Taken together, all the images or perceptions of equal opportunity prompt the same basic question: *How much difference, if any, do equal opportunities policies make?*

The scope of the book

This, then, is the focus of our book. We are not setting out to prove a case, willy-nilly, for all equal opportunities policies; nor are we grinding the axe of those who wish to dismantle all of them.

There is no single principle of equal opportunity either to die for, or to oppose to the death. Rather, there is a variety of equality strategies which can be considered, rejected or accepted on their merits. The relative value of one kind of equality strategy can be compared to another in terms of economic, social, political and ethical considerations.

In sum, much depends upon:

1. the social and economic context in which equal opportunities policies are to be developed;
2. the concepts or definitions of equal opportunity one is working with;
3. the nature and degree of inequality experienced by different groups such as women or minority ethnic groups, and the outcomes of equality policies in each case; and
4. the effectiveness of strategies of change and management of equality policies.

The content of the book reflects these points.

The first part (this chapter and Chapter 2) examines the *context* of equal opportunities policies. The aim is to set the scene by looking at key concepts of equal opportunity and discrimination; at developments in employment and in the nature of work; and at the cultural, social and economic factors which affect acceptance of equality policies. The legal context, and in particular the context of European Union laws on equality, will also be discussed.

Chapter 3 outlines and assesses *models* or principles of equality and how these are interpreted in practice. Concepts are examined in greater depth and we evaluate the justifications that have been used to defend different kinds of equality policy.

The third part (Chapters 4–7) evaluates the *outcomes* of equal opportunities policies, each chapter focusing in turn upon a particular dimension or aspect of inequality and exclusion: gender, 'race' and ethnicity, disability and age.

And finally the fourth part (Chapters 8 and 9) concludes our survey by examining the *implementation* of different kinds of equality strategy, chiefly at the level of the organisation or the firm.

A variety of factors and circumstances affect outcomes: for instance the state of the employment market, the effectiveness of equality laws, and the role of attitudes towards the various excluded or disadvantaged groups. Towards the end of the book, however, we assess the impact upon outcomes of different implementation strategies.

□   □   □   □   □

To further clarify the scope of the book, three more points should be made. The first is that this is a study of equality strategies in *employment*. These strategies are highly relevant to social policy for a number of reasons, not least because traditional approaches to the discipline have tended to neglect connections between the employment market, public policy and human welfare. Traditionally, social policy and social administration were 'all about' the great public welfare services such as the health service and social security system, but these were usually considered in isolation from the changing face of work and fundamental shifts in patterns of opportunity or unemployment.

Work itself can be seen as a form of welfare. Though it may be alienating, stressful and exploitative, employment can provide identity, social integration and other sources of wellbeing. Unemployment and discrimination prevent access to work, and thus in one sense access to a source of welfare.

A second major point about the book is that it is based on the United Kingdom's experience of developing equal opportunities policies. However, where relevant we draw comparisons between the United Kingdom and other countries, or make reference to the international dimension in equal opportunities, particularly

3

with regard to Europe-wide influences on equality strategies and to the impact of multinational companies (see Chapter 2).

In their respective ways, Sweden (and other Nordic countries) and the United States are countries which have ploughed perhaps the longest and deepest equal opportunities furrows, and consequently it is these examples which are referred to most often (see Chapters 4, 5 and 6). This is not to denigrate the achievements of other countries, however, and where space permits other examples are mentioned.

The British case represents one of the most contradictory examples of equal opportunities strategies. Equality strategies in the United Kingdom are in some respects more evident than in other European countries (for example anti-discriminatory and equal opportunities legislation specifically on 'race' – see Chapter 5). Yet in terms of implementation, acceptance among employers and general willingness in the majority culture to consider equality issues, the United Kingdom often seems to be characterised by at best a lukewarm and often a hostile response, especially where European Union legislation is concerned. Thus for comparative purposes Britain offers a highly pertinent example of the prospects for equal opportunities, representing a range of both positive and negative features.

A third point about the scope of the book relates to the topics to which separate chapters are devoted (gender, 'race', disability and age) and other topics (sexual orientation, religious affiliation and social class) which we have not covered in chapters of their own, but to which we do refer where appropriate.

We do not wish to deny the significance of the latter three topics or groups. Discrimination on grounds of sexual orientation, for instance, is important and has had a significant and blighting effect upon the opportunities and careers of large numbers of people. There are references to sexual orientation and equal opportunities in both Chapters 2 and 4; in the latter we outline the examples of recent tribunal rulings on discrimination against gays and lesbians (for instance personnel in British military forces).

Religious discrimination is also of great significance, overlapping in some ways with patterns of ethnic discrimination (as demonstrated in extreme forms by current conflicts between ethnic nationalist groups in the south-east of Europe) but worthy of study in its own right. In the United Kingdom laws against religious discrimination are restricted to Northern Ireland (see Chapter 5). The relatively tough approach to religious discrimination in the Northern Ireland Fair Employment Act, and the introduction of more active policies to ensure fairer outcomes, provides a good comparative example of the effects of innovative legislation. We return to this particular case in Chapter 3, which compares models of equal opportunity policy.

The examples of inequality and sexual orientation, religious affiliation and social class illustrate the enormous practical tasks facing equality policies. Yet we also found that, in comparison with questions of gender, 'race', disability and age, the research base dealing with these topics is relatively undeveloped. We therefore concluded that more research needs to be done before we could fully do justice to discrimination and sexual orientation, religion and social class in the form of separate chapters on each.

Of the three, the absence of social class from much contemporary discussion of equal opportunities is perhaps the most striking. For instance the pages of *Equal Opportunities Review*, a flagship journal covering employment in the United Kingdom, reveal relatively few explicit references to social class as a discrete category of inequality or discrimination compared to 'race' and racism, or gender and sex discrimination (though class-related issues such as inequalities in pay or pensions are often discussed with reference to other social categories or minority groups).

Class identity, though not an ascribed status in the same way as gender or disability, is nevertheless often extremely important in influencing opportunities. As children and adolescents, our parents' and families' class positions strongly affect educational opportunities, material advantages, aspirations and 'cultural capital'; and as adults, our inherited class position will often continue to affect career expectations, mastery of 'middle-class' patterns of communication and access to financial resources.

However, sufficient class mobility occurs in British society (Halsey, 1978) to draw attention away from the ascribed characteristics of social class. The presence of significant numbers of men and women of working-class origin who have 'made it' to higher positions strengthens the popular notion that each individual's opportunities are largely his or her own making. This, perhaps more than anything else, may explain why managers and employees alike would balk at the idea of incorporating social class into an equal opportunities strategy, and why commentators have steered away from the subject in research on equal opportunities.

Research on the dimension of social class in equal opportunities policies therefore represents an important but underdeveloped area of study. The significance of class-related equality issues is highlighted in Chapter 2, in relation to changing patterns of work and the rise of low-paid, part-time work. In Chapters 4 and 8 we also examine some of the relationships between gender, social class and managing equality policies.

Equal opportunities: nightmare or necessity?

At the outset we suggested that equal opportunities policies are surrounded by controversy and sometimes by extremes of opinion. At one end of a spectrum there is a strongly negative image or 'nightmare' view of equal opportunities policies as a pervasive, illiberal and stifling set of influences. At the time of writing, these views are becoming increasingly evident in both political and cultural expression.

Before we begin to look at various kinds of equality policy, it therefore seems important to begin to examine these 'backlash' views: how do they originate, and how credible or justifiable are they? First, as an example, there is a gathering movement of opposition to racial equality 'affirmative action' policies in the United States. In June 1995 the Supreme Court's verdicts on two separate cases sharply curtailed the right of federal government to continue with affirmative action policies.

One case resulted in a judgment which will greatly restrict the granting of contracts to minority businesses. The racial classifications used by federal government will now 'come under the same "strict scrutiny" that applies to the states, to show that white firms are not disadvantaged' (Walker, 1995: 9). The other judgment put limits on racial desegregation policies in schools. The Supreme Court decided (in the case of Kansas City vs. the state of Missouri) that measures to achieve a racial mix in the schools (for example by busing) are no longer justifiable on grounds of previous racial discrimination and disadvantage.

As Walker observes, the Supreme Court 'fulfilled the old proverb that it "watches the election returns", echoing the new Republican claims that affirmative action programmes can amount to reverse racism'. The Republican Party needs to consolidate support among white men, as 62 per cent (of those who voted) supported Republican candidates in the 1994 congressional election (Reed, 1995: 12). As Reed adds, the backlash occurred despite the reality that

> Among doctors, lawyers, scientists, and university teachers, fewer than one in 20 is black. The ratio is only slightly higher in the construction trades. The plain truth is that the number of blacks at the professional or skilled worker level is simply too slight to produce much competition, let alone discrimination against white men. (1995: 12)

In both the United States and the United Kingdom, 'backlash' sentiments have also been widely expressed against policies to counter sex discrimination and sexual harassment. David Mamet's stage play, *Oleanna*, and a 1995 film by Michael Crichton, *Disclosure*, both portray men as the victims of unjust charges of sexual harassment in which women exploit anti-harassment policies for their own ends.

However, objective assessments of the problem show first that 'fewer than one per cent of sexual harassment cases prove to be based on false accusations' (Feinstein, 1995: 14); secondly, very few men are the victims of sexual misconduct. According to an Industrial Society review, for example, fewer than 7 per cent of those who are harassed are men (Collier, 1995: 9). And thirdly, survey evidence shows that over half of women in paid work experience at least one incident of sexual harassment, though many choose not to report what happens to them for fear of further victimisation or worries about job security (Coussey and Jackson, 1991: 172).

This is not to say that the injustices illustrated in dramatic form by Mamet and Crichton do not exist, nor to deny that they are occasionally a serious problem for individual men. Our point is that genuine concerns about the occasional misuse of anti-discriminatory measures seem to have been seized upon by those who are critical of the wider goals of equality policies. A deeper unease has been triggered, reflected in growing uncertainty about how relations between men and women, or between majorities and minorities, should be conducted. Thus negative images of equal opportunity policies may not just be a backlash against the policies themselves but also against more fundamental changes in social relations.

How far backlash attitudes and political initiatives will succeed in reversing equality and anti-discrimination policies is an open question; it is a question which should be borne in mind throughout the book and to which we will return in the concluding chapter. What we are anxious to stress at the outset is the sheer scale of the task facing equal opportunities policies. Backlash sentiments seem to be completely out of proportion to the limited changes actually achieved.

Lack of change or opening up of opportunity is noticeable at the very top as well as lower down the social scale. Inequalities extend into the most prestigious or elite institutions and often combine together to exclude women, minorities and people from the 'wrong' regions or social class backgrounds. For example, in the senior ranks of the British civil service 35 permanent secretaries share ultimate Whitehall responsibility for services employing more than 500 000 people with a budget currently standing at £20 billion. As Purnell points out,

> Permanent secretaries are all white and in their late 40s or 50s, two-thirds went to Oxbridge, almost all are male [there were only three women permanent secretaries in 1994, of whom only one held a top tier post] and from the South. 'Haven't heard a rich northern voice round the table for a long time', says one. 'Southerners know their place . . .'. (1994: 11)

Not only are few women promoted to high office, but there is also continuing evidence of discouragement of women in other areas of work traditionally seen as the province of men (see for example, S. Milne, 1995).

Harsh forms of discrimination are also frequently experienced by members of black and Asian communities in the United Kingdom, both at work and in the community. A report on a House of Commons Home Affairs Select Committee's discussion of 'race' relations notes, for instance, that 'about 140,000 racist attacks [were] estimated in 1992'. This spate was partly linked with the extreme right and increased neo-fascist activity (*Independent*, 1994b: 19). Yet in the police service itself there are 'unacceptable levels of prejudice, sexual harassment, and racist exchanges, frequently unchecked by supervisory staff' (Campbell, 1994: 5) and as a result the recruitment of black officers is low.

Many other examples of inequality and discrimination, affecting people at both the personal and the group level, could be cited. However, at this stage our point is simply to highlight both the seriousness of problems of discrimination and the scale of underrepresentation of women and minority groups in certain occupations and social positions. Inequalities and disadvantage are widespread, affecting people in all walks of life and not an isolated few in clearly demarcated minorities.

Before we discuss these central questions in the following chapters, though, it may be helpful to establish some preliminary definitions of the main concepts to be used: direct and indirect discrimination, positive action and affirmative action.

Concepts of discrimination and equal opportunity policy

Concepts of discrimination and disadvantage on the one hand, and of equality strategies on the other, are closely related. Just as theories of disease shape our ideas about appropriate treatment, so theories about the nature and causes of discrimination lead to competing ideas about what the best anti-discrimination or equal opportunities strategies might be.

For example, a definition of discrimination as *direct* suggests particular remedies. Direct discrimination occurs when someone, or a whole group, is treated differently (either positively or negatively) from others solely or mainly because they belong to a particular social category: a woman or a man, disabled or non-disabled, gay or straight, for instance.

Negative direct discrimination occurs because those who discriminate share erroneous or stereotypical beliefs about the people they wish to exclude or victimise. In short, the people who are discriminated against are *categorised* and are no longer treated as individuals with their own talents or personalities. Above all, direct discrimination, though it may be hidden from public view, is an observable action based on conscious intentions.

With this definition in mind, a corresponding equal opportunities remedy is that of *fair or like treatment*. That is, equality is seen to consist of treating everyone in the same way, irrespective of gender, 'race', religion, etc. The emphasis in such equality policies is upon sanctions, legal or otherwise, against behaviour which is defined as discriminatory: for example, racist or sexist behaviour.

The basic reference point in this model of equality policy is the individual. It is assumed that guilt or innocence can be established. The actions of individuals can be examined to judge whether they were discriminatory or not. Also, a central aim of this kind of policy is preventative: laws and sanctions against discrimination aim to stop certain behaviours happening, but they are not designed to take special steps or provide extra resources to improve the position of minorities, as in the form of education or training for instance.

Though ideas of fair or like treatment still form the backbone of most equality and anti-discriminatory policies, they have been criticised over the years because they are limited in scope. They do not necessarily address subtler forms of *indirect discrimination.*

In practice the latter is harder to define than direct discrimination. This is because most interpretations of indirect discrimination stress the significance of in-built or institutional *patterns* of inequality rather than the particular actions of individuals. With patterned inequality, discrimination may occur even when everyone is treated the same way. Thus, 'like treatment' will not solve the problem.

What kinds of institutional practice lead to indirect discrimination? One example, cited by Coussey and Jackson (1991: 190), is of a health authority which was found to have indirectly discriminated against an applicant for a nursing job because it required all applicants to have 'demonstrated progression' in their careers. This requirement had the effect of disproportionately reducing the number of nurses from minority ethnic groups who could be considered eligible. It treated everyone in like fashion, but was actually unfair because it ruled out other ways of assessing candidates who were able to do the job and who could have demonstrated their competence in other ways.

Other examples of indirect discrimination can be found in localised patterns of recruitment to work. Thus it might be claimed that all applicants are treated equally, irrespective of gender, 'race' and other characteristics, but if there is a tendency to draw employees from a particular area and minority applicants, for instance, find it harder to meet that requirement, indirect discrimination may occur.

Note that this is different from an intentional prejudice or pattern of discrimination against a particular neighbourhood or minority group (which would be a form of direct discrimination). In cases of indirect discrimination, neither those who discriminate nor those who are disadvantaged need be aware of the problem. Not surprisingly, as a result of this, it has proved difficult both to investigate and to substantiate patterns of indirect discrimination (see Chapter 5).

However, at least some of the criticism of 'like treatment' policies or anti-discrimination laws seems to be justified. As we demonstrate in later chapters, not much will change unless the institutional practices which cause indirect discrimination are challenged. For these reasons concepts of *positive action* (in the United Kingdom) and *affirmative action* (in the United States) have been developed.

Here the emphasis is less upon 'like treatment' or procedural justice and more upon *outcomes*. The argument is that the earlier 'like treatment' model of equal opportunity is too individualised: that is, anti-discrimination laws may help individuals to gain redress if they are mistreated or suffer injustice, but each successive generation of women, black people, older workers and so on must re-fight the same battles to win their place in society.

To bring lasting and more fundamental change, the argument runs, steps should be taken to encourage more representative numbers of people from previously excluded or underrepresented groups to be considered for all occupations and positions; positive action also means taking positive steps to make sure that employees from previously excluded groups are not neglected once they are in post, and that they continue to have a fair share of opportunities for training and promotion.

How are these aims to be realised? 'Positive action', as it is usually defined in the United Kingdom, will entail, for example, wider advertising of opportunities, scrutiny of selection procedures and the provision of additional training or career opportunities (for instance, career-break schemes which encourage parents to resume their careers after absences to look after children or other dependent relatives).

Note, however, that the concept of positive action can be distinguished from *preferential treatment* or *'positive discrimination'*. Although positive action focuses on group outcomes (for instance, representative proportions of men and women), the emphasis is still upon individual merit or capabilities. Positive action is not intended to be a policy of placing people in jobs or educational institutions *because* they are women or members of various minority groups.

In effect, members of overrepresented groups have enjoyed 'positive action' of their own, being favoured for selection or being considered for promotion because they belong to the 'right' groups or have well-established connections with those who are dominant in decision-making circles. Equal opportunity positive action aims to redress the balance. It can be seen as a goal to encourage the previously disadvantaged to the starting-gate for jobs, promotions and other opportunities. But once at the starting-gate the race should be on equal terms between all competitors.

In the United States, affirmative action has been defined in much the same way as positive action in Britain. However, the American judicial system has a more significant role in policy development and amendment than the law has in the United Kingdom. Also, American courts permit 'class action' judgments which, in addition to giving redress or compensation to individual complainants, also force employers to compensate all employees in the same category if it has been decided that they too have suffered discrimination. As a result equality policies in many American states have been noticeably tougher than in the UK, and in some circumstances affirmative action has gradually shifted in meaning to incorporate an element of preferential treatment or preferential hiring. As we have already shown, this subject is now surrounded by renewed controversy, though even in earlier days supposed preferential policies have been successfully challenged in American courts.

American examples raise a fundamental question: how justifiable are policies which begin overtly to discriminate in favour of previously underrepresented groups? What are the arguments for and against what would be termed 'reverse discrimination' in the United States and 'positive discrimination' in the United Kingdom? In Chapter 3 we return to these questions and examine, for example, how far individual rights and the principle of merit may be compromised by tougher kinds of equality policy. However, as far as the United Kingdom is concerned this is largely a discussion of principle rather than concrete policy; in the United Kingdom even the relatively weak model of positive action has yet to gain a secure foothold.

2
EQUAL OPPORTUNITIES
IN CONTEXT

Introduction

To make comparisons between different types of policy, to evaluate their impact and to work out why policies have taken the particular shape they have in different countries or settings, we need to know something about context: for example, political factors and the relative strength of parties or governments which support equality legislation; the cultural context and its impact on attitudes to gender roles or sexual orientation; the economic context and the impact of economic policies on the supply of jobs.

However, it is not only the economic, political or social background that forms the context for equal opportunities policies. Previous equality legislation itself becomes part of the context. In Britain, for example, there have been discussions about the need to amend and improve the 1976 Race Relations Act (CRE, 1991). The 1976 Act and its impact form part of the context.

There is also an international policy context, with possibilities of policy learning by one country's government or institutions from others. Again, Britain's legislation provides an example in the case of both the 1965 and 1976 Race Relations Acts, which were substantially influenced in their design by the American laws on racial equality. Roy Jenkins, Home Secretary in the mid-1960s, was much influenced by American developments and his team's exposure to them proved to be of crucial importance (Solomos, 1989: 73).

The context of previous legislation and the influence of other countries' policies might be summarised as the 'regulatory framework' of equal opportunities policies. It is important to consider, under this heading, not only the legal system itself and the effectiveness of the legal sanctions that can be imposed upon those who break equality laws, but also the work of equality commissions, tribunals and similar semi-autonomous bodies: for example, the 'quangos' set up to oversee equality legislation such as the Equal Opportunities Commission in the United Kingdom or the Equality Ombudsmen in Sweden.

Above all there is the significant influence of European law and jurisdiction. Member governments respond to European laws with varying degrees of enthusiasm. However, as a result of a series of binding agreements made well before the Treaty of European Union at Maastricht in 1992, the recommendations and directives of the European Commission and the judgments of the European Court of Justice have come to represent a legal framework to which individuals and groups seeking justice will increasingly refer. In Britain, for example, much publicity attended cases of wrongful dismissal of women from the armed forces on grounds of pregnancy (see discussion below).

To sum up, we will look at the context of equal opportunities policies in three ways:

1. The context of the labour market and of fundamental changes in the structure and nature of employment in the past few decades.
2. The context of social, political and cultural change. Striking changes in these spheres rival economic change in their importance for equality policies.
3. The context of law in a European framework.

The employment and labour market context

As the theme of this book is employment and equal opportunities, it is of central importance to have an overview of both the supply of jobs and demand for them in recent times. In broad terms, the second half of the twentieth century can be seen in two phases: an initial post-war phase of employment boom, which lasted for 20 to 25 years, followed by a phase which featured the arrival of mass unemployment in market economies.

The latter phase began in the mid or late 1970s, though its timing depended on the relative success or failure of different economies in weathering the economic crisis of that decade. In Sweden, for example, unemployment remained at a low level of a few per cent of the labour force through the 1970s and 1980s, and only since 1991 reached comparable European levels of 10 per cent or more. And in the former Communist or state-planned economies of eastern Europe and Russia, underemployment and inefficiency substituted for unemployment; only recently, with liberalisation and market reforms, did outright unemployment first appear and then soar to very high levels.

With some exceptions, though, the first phase was a time of economic reconstruction and of booming demand for workers. Qualifications were relatively unimportant as a basic requirement for obtaining work, if not for climbing the career ladder. In Britain, for example, strong demand for labour meant that in the 1940s and 1950s most employees could afford to leave a job with a fair degree of certainty that another could easily be found. Heath refers to the majority of school-leavers completing their education with no formal qualifications as one of the 'most striking features of British society, mid-century' (1981: 155).

This legacy had implications for perceived need for anti-discriminatory legislation. Refusal by an employer to employ someone mattered less, at least for the white majority and the non-disabled, when there was a plentiful supply of comparable jobs.

While educational attainments did improve in the first phase, it was the expansion of the job market itself which provided most of the opportunities for upward social mobility and better wages. The 'class gap' in relative educational achievements, especially entry to higher education, at first remained as wide as it had been in pre-war years. Much of the growth in student numbers in the 1960s was accounted for by the steady increase of middle-class *women* in higher education (Halsey, 1992).

In the initial post-war period, the dramatic increase in the supply of jobs meant that categories of workers who might otherwise have been excluded from the workforce were incorporated: for example, Phillipson (1982) has shown how for a brief period older (post-retirement age) workers were written about in government reports as a valuable source of skills and experience. It was argued that for such older workers to retire 'too early' would not only be a loss to the nation's economy but would also hasten their own decline and loss of vigour. In 1951 in Britain, almost a third of men aged over 65 continued to be economically active (Laczko and Phillipson, 1991: 21).

It was also during this period that labour migration from poorer, less industrial parts of the world to Europe, North America, Australia and other rich countries began to affect the social composition of the workforce and to combine racial inequalities with those of class.

Not all black, Asian or southern European migrant workers entered the industrial workforce at the bottom and remained at the lowest levels of pay and conditions. In 1960s Britain, for example, a majority of Afro-Caribbean and Indian men (though not Pakistani men) in work were in occupations above unskilled and semi-skilled levels (Westergaard and Resler, 1976: 356–7).

While they did not form an underclass, however, a disproportionate number of immigrant workers took the lower-paid and less-desired jobs. Migrants from ex-colonial countries to France, the Netherlands and Britain, or southern European and Turkish 'guestworkers' in Germany and other countries, facilitated upward social mobility among the majority by replacing white indigenous workers in the lower occupational positions.

One might also include disabled workers among the categories of people who were temporarily favoured by strong demand for labour in the initial post-war period. As Oliver says of the Disabled Persons (Employment) Act (1944),

> This legislation was not uninfluenced by the shortage of labour at the time or the collective guilt of seeing ex-servicemen, disabled while fighting for their country; but economic and social climates change, and these rights have never been enforced. (1990: 89)

The case of the 1944 Act is particularly significant for equal opportunities because it was an early and highly unusual example of the use of a quota: a requirement that organisations or companies over a certain size employ a minimum percentage of an historically disadvantaged group. However, despite clear legal requirements and a plentiful supply of work in the initial post-war period, the example of disability shows how the barriers of prejudice can prove to be yet stronger influences.

Social attitudes were also relatively slow to change with regard to the employment of women. The period of 'full' employment from the 1940s to the late 1960s was actually a period of full *male* employment. Following a large-scale mobilisation of women into the workforces of Britain, Germany and other combatant countries during the Second World War, it was largely assumed that women would relinquish their emergency wartime roles in the economy to revert to either full-time domestic work or part-time paid employment. However, even during the initial 20-year period after the war, but especially in the last quarter of the twentieth century, the percentages of women in paid employment have risen substantially in all industrial countries and very markedly in some. For example, women are now taking over half the new jobs created in the European Union. In some northern European countries, notably Sweden and Denmark, about four-fifths of all women of working age are in paid employment (see Chapter 4).

The second main phase in the development of the labour market, marked principally by the arrival of mass unemployment, contrasts quite sharply with the first. There were, however, some harbingers of what was to come, even during the first phase. For example in Britain in 1957, the 'stop' phase of 'stop-go' economic policy resulted in a slowing in the growth of demand for labour; in turn, this fuelled public disquiet about immigration and perceptions of a threat to majority white workers from immigrant labour. The first notable post-war racist disturbances took place in Notting Hill, London, in 1958 (Solomos, 1989: 48).

In all, though, the first phase was one in which there would have been a favourable economic or employment climate for the development of equal opportunities policies had legislation and other policies been in place. In fact the first wave of equality and civil rights legislation, typified for example by laws against sex and race discrimination in the United Kingdom and the United States in the 1960s, took place in the employment boom of the initial post-war period, but had to be implemented on the eve of economic recession.

Unemployment increased across the board, but particularly rapidly among those social groups already somewhat marginalised in the labour force and in need of equal rights: for example, older workers. Among men over 60 in Britain, the unemployment rate reached 20 per cent by mid-1982 following the profound economic problems and large-scale lay-offs of labour in the first government led by Mrs Thatcher (see Chapter 7).

Unemployment has also been unequally shared in terms of 'race'. Taken as a whole, people in minority ethnic groups are still much more likely to experience unemployment than people in the white majority. As Jones (1993) points out with reference to Britain, this basic inequality is complicated by a number of other differences: first, the 1980s saw the continuing emergence of differences among the minority communities. Unemployment among those of 'East African' Asian and Indian descent was only marginally higher in 1988–90 than among the white majority, while people of Pakistani and Bangladeshi origin had 'higher rates of unemployment than any other racial group' (Jones, 1993: 113).

These differences are further explored in Chapter 5. They do not deny the importance of racial discrimination in the labour market but they do point to the growing significance of economic and status differences among minority communities.

Another complication is the question of how far rates are higher among the minorities because black and Asian people tend to live in the more economically depressed areas and inner city districts. However, racism does have a distinctive effect: in 1988–90, for example, Afro-Caribbean men in non-manual occupations experienced double the rate of unemployment of white men in non-manual jobs. Among non-manual Pakistani men the rate was four times greater (1993: 114). There are similarly large differences in unemployment among manual workers, between whites on the one hand and Afro-Caribbean, Pakistani and Bangladeshi men on the other.

'Racial' differences in the unemployment rate are also complicated by differences in the economic roles of minority communities in different places. Thus at the local level we may not find the same inter-ethnic contrasts as have been observed nationally. In Birmingham in 1991, for example, unemployment among Indian men and women was *not* appreciably lower than among Afro-Caribbean men and women (see Table 2.1), and this contrasts with the national picture. The summary of Birmingham's unemployment rates in Table 2.1 also bears out the point that white people who are economically active are significantly less likely to be unemployed than black and Asian people in the same city or local labour market.

The main exception to the trend of higher unemployment among less advantaged groups is found in the experience of

Table 2.1   Unemployment by ethnic group in Birmingham (1991)
(percentages)

Ethnic group	Unemployed (as % of economically active)		
	Men	Women	N
White	14.8	8.2	405,818
Black Caribbean	21.0	15.8	32,784
Black African	27.6	19.6	1,586
Black other	32.2	21.3	3,463
Indian	18.2	16.5	26,106
Pakistani	35.0	44.8	23,779
Bangladeshi	41.5	44.0	3,983
Chinese	15.4	14.3	1,508

Source: OPCS, 1992: 117.

women. Male unemployment has risen steadily in recent years, mainly as a result of the decline of manufacturing industries. In Britain in 1993 for example, unemployment among men of working age stood at 14 per cent. Among women, however, unemployment was only 5.6 per cent, a drop of over a third since the mid-1980s (Cohen and Borrill, 1993). The local example above (see Table 2.1) also illustrates a significantly lower unemployment rate among women in most ethnic groups. For young men, though, the idea of plentiful work has become a distant memory in some of the more economically depressed and run-down parts of industrial Europe.

To summarise, the late 1970s and the 1980s were in retrospect one of the most testing times in which to have introduced equal opportunities policies, at least in Britain and much of Europe. However, we must beware of overgeneralisation. Different world regions have had varying degrees of success in generating employment.

Employment in Europe and a changing world

According to an OECD survey (OECD, 1994), Japan and the United States have created many millions more jobs in their economies than have countries now in the European Union. In North America, for example, employment growth almost doubled between 1960 and 1994, while in Japan it increased by 50 per cent. In the European Community, employment hardly grew at all (see

19

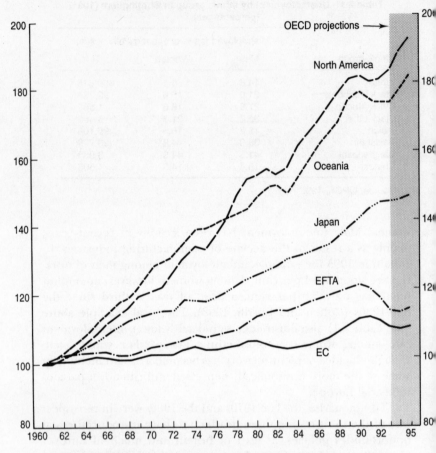

Figure 2.1 Employment growth in OECD regions, 1960–95. © OECD, 1994, *The OECD Jobs Study: Facts, Analysis, Strategies*. Reproduced by permission of the OECD.

Figure 2.1). Most of Europe's limited employment growth took place in the public sector: there were absolute falls in private sector jobs in the 1970s and mid-1980s.

There has been much discussion of the reasons for Europe's relative economic failure and inability to supply employment on the scale of other faster-growing world regions. At the time of writing, Conservative politicians in Britain were seizing upon extracts of the OECD survey which appeared to support their

contention that 'burdensome' welfare spending and 'overprotec-
tive' social and employment legislation, including equal opportunities policies, are the chief reasons for Europe's
uncompetitiveness.

However, the OECD report itself presents a more balanced
view. Much depends on the ability of social and economic policy to
increase the productivity and the flexibility of the labour force.
Thus educational and training investments which result in demonstrable productivity gains were seen as desirable. And though
the OECD report played down questions of equity in the labour
market, there was implicit if not very strong acceptance of equality
policies if they enhance flexibility. Widespread and publicly subsidised child care provision, for example, can be a way of enabling
both men and women to adapt to changing requirements in terms
of availability or hours worked.

However, there are some hard lessons to learn in Europe from
the OECD report (1994) and from international employment
trends generally. The lessons are not simple, and do not necessarily entail 'US-style labour market deregulation' (Bassett, 1994:
29). The OECD report does however argue that the inflexible
application of protective legislation, for example on minimum
wages, will make the regeneration of employment difficult.

Sweden is again a pertinent example, for although that country
did appear to combine high social expenditure and equality policies
with economic growth, it has become increasingly apparent that the
old formula of the 'Swedish model' cannot be sustained. This is not
simply a reflection of political choice or changing social values, but
of changing international economic realities which are affecting all
industrial countries: for instance the relative decline of the manufacturing sector as a source of employment; technological changes
which encourage the shedding of labour even in times of economic
growth; the globalisation of capitalist enterprise and an increasingly
international division of labour.

Multinational companies seek out the best locations for their
operations and base their decisions on, among other things, key
characteristics of the labour force: wage costs, skill levels, productivity and flexibility. There is an ever-present danger that European
countries will be seen as relatively inefficient, restrictive and unproductive locations in which there are labour 'rigidities' such as
protective employment legislation and union rights. As a

consequence millions of jobs have been exported to other countries in which wage costs are appreciably lower.

However, it is important to note that multinational companies are not inevitably drawn by the logic of basing their operations in countries with low wages and a laissez-faire approach to social policy or employment rights. As Elson and Pearson point out in relation to the employment of women,

> There is no generalised tendency for multinationals to relocate *all* female-labour intensive operations away from the EEC countries . . . . The European market remains a vital attraction, not only encouraging European multinationals to keep much female-labour intensive production at home, but also encouraging American and Japanese multinationals to set up new plant in Europe. (1989: 8–9)

Much depends on the nature of the multinational company's business and the skills that are required. Multinational companies often seek locations in which there is a degree of social stability, some public investment in terms of welfare benefits, health services and education, as well as a degree of flexibility in the workforce. At the same time the development of new technologies, though often leading to redundancies or de-skilling in manufacturing, does create new opportunities, especially in the growing services sector. As we have already seen, many of these new jobs are being taken by women.

Thus the growth of the multinational corporations has both negative and positive consequences. Quoting International Labour Office (ILO) survey evidence, for example, Elson and Pearson suggest that multinational companies tend to have a record which is usually no worse, often better, 'than uni-nationals as "good employers" in terms of wages and conditions of work' (1989: 1).

However, their record is little different from uni-nationals as far as breaking down established divisions of labour between men and women is concerned, to say nothing of other marked patterns of discrimination affecting disabled people, workers in minority ethnic or racial groups, older workers, and other excluded groups. Therefore, while multinationals cannot be blamed for stripping Britain and other European countries of jobs, much remains to be done to improve equality of opportunity within multinationals' workforces.

Changes in work organisation

The changes in the employment market mentioned above are profound enough, but they are not the only changes in the nature of work which will have serious implications for equal opportunities policies. There are also significant trends in the organisation of businesses and work environments. These may be summarised as:

- The rise of 'new managerialism'.
- The decentralisation of business operations combined with centralisation or standardisation of performance targets.
- The rise of a 'culture of insecurity' in employment.

All these changes are connected with what Lash and Urry (1987) portray as 'the end of organized capitalism': that is, the end of an era in which employers, unions and governments were organised into a corporate system which controlled wage and price policies, and which balanced the conflicting pressures of economic growth and social welfare.

Among the clearest examples of 'organised capitalism' were Sweden and Germany, neither of which have ever been fully free market economies. Rather, they have been tightly run capitalist economies in which the state and corporate business interests have traditionally worked closely together. More recently, however, and especially in Sweden, some of the centralised machinery for deciding wage agreements, working conditions, etc. has been jettisoned. Thus according to Lash and Urry, even the most corporatist or centrally organised examples are beginning to enter the 'disorganised' phase, while other countries such as the United Kingdom have already moved a considerable way along the road.

Thus the employment context is shifting from one in which working patterns are controlled by centralised bureaucratic organisations (whether in the private or public sector) to one in which work is performed in local units which are more loosely controlled from the centre than they once were. Devolution of management and the creation of localised cost centres have brought about a new kind of managerialism, in which line managers are encouraged to take an enterprising and flexible approach to meet performance and profit targets.

In public sector institutions which have become self-governing (for example, NHS Hospital Trusts, Colleges of Further

Education), the new managerialist style can sometimes be perceived by employees, and particularly by professionals in organisations, as 'macho management' or as a clash between older, more bureaucratic forms of management and a newer approach which seems less accountable to other institutions and to the public interest.

What might be the consequences of these kinds of change for the future development of equal opportunities policies? Mason and Jewson (1992) suggest that at first sight the consequences would seem to be mainly negative. Despite their flaws, large bureaucratically organised corporations would seem to have the advantage of enforcing uniform policies, including those on equal opportunities. Once equal opportunities are formalised, or expressed as 'specified codes of rules and regulations expressed in documentary form' (Mason and Jewson, 1992: 100), the argument runs, centralised public institutions and private corporations can push equal opportunities policies into every layer and crevice of their organisations.

As Mason and Jewson point out, however, formalised and centralised equal opportunities policies can be circumvented in all sorts of ways. Also, even if they are implemented, they may not have been well-designed in the first place.

The impact of decentralising management upon equal opportunities is difficult to assess, though, because there is evidence that greater management discretion, together with a 'new managerialist' emphasis on personal qualities such as competitiveness or 'drive', can lead to greater discrimination against those who do not seem to fit the new ethos. This may affect women seeking jobs, older applicants or those who are disabled (see Chapters 6 and 7).

Notwithstanding these concerns, Mason and Jewson suggest that there is potential in the new management context to implement equal opportunities policies. Much depends on either winning over senior managers or making them comply with equal opportunities requirements. Once this is done, Mason and Jewson argue, equal opportunities policies can be made to work in devolved units. But they must be adapted in ways which take account of new management practice: for example by incorporating equal opportunities targets into reviews of local managers' performance, or into the business plans of local units. Indeed, as the decentralisation of some management functions has gone hand in hand with the *centralisation* of certain indicators of performance, and with a general policy of setting clear objectives for businesses and public sector organisations, there is perhaps added scope for the incorporation of equal opportunities goals into many fields of employment.

This brings us to back to the earlier point about the increasing scarcity of full-time, relatively permanent jobs. Some argue that advances in equal opportunities are unlikely in a climate of job insecurity. But again, this might not necessarily be the case. The OECD report (1994), referred to above, states that while traditional forms of protective legislation often seem to be job-inhibiting, equity objectives can be pursued 'through other instruments'.

There is the possibility that equal opportunities policies might become *increasingly* important in a period of increasing job insecurity if they are brought into the process of rationing access to the scarce resource of work or, more cynically, are used by employers as ways of legitimising the rejection or demotion of employees, or would-be workers. It is significant, perhaps, that the United States, the industrial country which has one of the most deregulated labour markets, 30 million working poor (Torday, 1994) and considerable job insecurity, is also one of the most advanced in terms of equal opportunities legislation and the application of equal opportunities codes and practice in management and recruitment practice.

Whatever the impact of increasing insecurity at work upon equal opportunities, there is no doubt that it is now one of the most important elements of the social and economic context. The 'culture of insecurity' can be summed up in a number of increasingly familiar developments: for example, short-term employment contracts; the spread of local wage and working conditions 'agreements' which reflect the dismantling of minimum wage protection and national pay scales; employers' expectations of 'flexibility' among their employees, which may amount to working longer hours or at weekends; and the encouragement of a more competitive, individualistic approach to work than in the recent past.

Reporting on an international survey of attitudes towards unemployment, Lansley (1994) shows that alarmingly high proportions of full-time workers are very concerned about losing their jobs: in Britain and Spain, over 60 per cent report serious concern, and these countries are second only to the former East Germany in this respect; in the former West Germany and the Netherlands the percentages concerned about losing their jobs are much lower, but still above 25 per cent of workers in both cases.

A central feature of recent social and economic change, and of the current context, is rising affluence among those fortunate enough to have full-time work and considerable gains in terms of material consumption. But these trends are combined with widening income inequalities, rising crime rates, increasingly strained welfare systems and, above all, feelings of insecurity about work.

The context of social and cultural change

These observations sound a pessimistic note, but not all aspects of recent social change have negative implications for the development of equal opportunities. For one thing, Britain and other industrial societies are undergoing significant demographic changes. Among these changes is the ageing of the workforce. Employers who have traditionally recruited young people will find a decreasing pool of job-seekers in the younger age groups, and some may increasingly turn to other previously underrepresented categories: for example women aged over 30 and older workers.

In Britain, according to the Central Statistical Office, 'in 1986 almost one in four of the labour force was under 25 – by 2001 this number will have fallen to less than one in six before increasing slightly by 2006' (1994a: 56). Thus the size of the labour force, and consequently the demand or competition among people for jobs, is not just affected by economic growth or the rise in economic activity rates among women, but also by the birth rate 15 to 20 years before the rising generation of employees enters the workforce.

Relatively high birth rates in the 1960s markedly increased the numbers of 16 year-olds entering the workforce in the late 1970s and early 1980s, since when the proportion of young people in the labour market has fallen (Central Statistical Office, 1994a). With the exception of Ireland, which still has a very 'young' demographic structure, all the European countries are to a greater or lesser extent experiencing a similar trend towards an ageing

Table 2.2   Civilian labour force, by age (percentages)

Estimates/ projections	16–24	25–44	45–59	60+	Total	All aged 16+ (millions)
1986	23	46	26	5	100	26.9
1996	20	50	28	2	100	28.2
2006	17	48	30	5	100	29.6

Source: Central Statistical Office, 1994a. Adapted from Table 4.4, p. 56.
Note: Percentages have been rounded.

workforce (see Table 2.2). At the same time as demographic changes are reducing the supply of young entrants to the workforce, at least in the foreseeable future, other changes of a cultural nature have been affecting attitudes towards minority groups.

These changes might be summarised as a growing awareness of minority rights and a tendency among minority groups themselves to assert their rights more actively than in the past. Minority rights activism has been part of a wider cultural critique of postindustrial society: a critique which challenges not only the distribution of work but also the way work is organised and how authority and personal relations in work settings are managed.

So in the first place there are increasingly assertive claims by 'minority' groups that they have been neglected or discriminated against and have never received a fair share of employment, particularly of the more creative, well-paid or responsible jobs. Secondly, especially with regard to feminist discussions of the labour market (see Chapter 4), the critique goes beyond querying 'Who finds work?' to other questions relating to the nature of employment itself. For example, working part-time has often been interpreted in some organisations as signalling a lack of commitment or ambition. 'Structural' feminist critiques (see Chapter 4) challenge such assumptions and seek changes in work culture which would give a more understanding view of part-time working, as well as a more positive attitude than typically exists towards the idea of increasing men's commitment to their domestic or family responsibilities.

The crucial message in feminist and other cultural critiques of established work settings is that the *majority's* need to change should be put on the agenda. They are not merely seeking modifications to existing work practices but also a radical review of the way those presently in full-time work perceive those who have been marginalised in the past.

To say that such critiques have become more evident in recent years is not to claim that sweeping cultural changes have actually affected everyone or that minority rights have been successfully pushed to the front of debates about the nature of work. However, there is no doubt that in many cases minority rights have at least been put on the agenda.

While even today one may come across job advertisements which are redolent of the prejudiced attitudes of former decades, and openly negative attitudes about the supposed unsuitability of women, disabled workers and others for certain kinds of work, there is now at least a case to be answered. Current unease about 'political correctness' in part reflects a certain defensiveness among the majority about 'unreconstructed' and intolerant attitudes. General opinion now at least has to take account of, or respond to, questions of discrimination and inequality which had previously been ignored.

Nowhere is this better illustrated than in the case of the disability movement and the campaign by disabled people to change the cultural climate in which their position and needs are judged. Writing about the period which preceded the passing of the first significant legislation for disabled people in Britain, the Chronically Sick and Disabled Persons Act (1970), A. Morris argues that

> It seems incredible and outrageous now, but from 1945–1964 there was no mention in party manifestos of anything specific to help disabled people. Between 1959–64, there was not one debate in the Commons on disability. . . . No one even knew how many disabled people there were in Britain. They were treated not even as second-class citizens, more as non-people: seen or heard only by their families or, if in institutions, by those who controlled their lives. (1994: 7)

So although the full potential of the 1970 Act has never been realised, and though much of its initial momentum has been lost as a result of financial stringency and deliberate attempts to obstruct its full implementation, Morris makes the point that the climate of opinion was irrevocably changed for the better by this legislation. More concretely, 'far more was spent on cash benefits and services. . . . In the first decade [after the Act] public spending on related benefits and services went up from £330 million to £3.03 billion' (Morris, 1994: 7).

Without this earlier advance, it is difficult to see how subsequent growth in awareness of the rights of disabled people could have developed even to its relatively limited extent in Britain (see Chapter 6 for a discussion of recent developments). The unacceptability of unfair discrimination against disabled people is now at least recognised by the more progressive employers, even if others continue to ignore the problem or to refute its existence.

Another example of the changing cultural context can be found in attitudes towards gays and lesbians in employment, and in the history of the modern gay and lesbian movement for public recognition and tolerance. Again, though, this is not to argue that tolerance is now widespread or that discrimination and prejudice have disappeared. It is to suggest that as a result of a more visible and assertive stance than before, the gay and lesbian movement has, like the disability movement, at least established the idea that discrimination is widespread and that the problem often lies in the majority rather than the minority.

For example, recent debate in Britain about the unfair dismissal of people from the armed forces, on grounds of their sexual orientation, was significant because it focused upon the size of compensation awards to those wrongfully dismissed and upon whether European laws should take precedence over British law. There were some exceptions: in the main, die-hard traditionalists who saw a conflict of interests between serving in a military role and being homosexual. But the basic principle that people should not be victimised because of their sexual orientation was in the main assumed in public debate.

In parts of the United States, acceptance of the public role of gays and lesbians in the forces and in other services, for example serving as police officers, has progressed farther than in Britain and some other European countries. As with other minorities and marginalised groups, this cultural change has been preceded by conflict and struggle, and by lengthy court cases involving the unfair treatment of gays and lesbians in employment.

The following description sums up the American experience. It is about a three-day riot at the Stonewall Inn in New York on 28 June 1969, when the mainly gay clientele reacted violently to police harassment:

At one point, the police barricaded themselves in the bar and were pelted with bricks and bottles. A dozen police and civilians were injured.

Though the number is trivial compared with those injured or killed in the black civil rights marches and the protests against the Vietnam war, the event is accepted as the start of gay people's resolve to fight for public tolerance. After Stonewall, the police ended their raids on gay bars and stopped their policy of entrapment of homosexuals. Gays launched themselves into politics and social activism. It was the birth of the modern gay and lesbian movement. (*Independent*, 1994a: 23)

It is significant that this discussion of gay activism refers to the civil rights movement among black people in the United States, for this was the example above all others which transformed public thinking about an oppressed and discriminated-against minority. As with the previous examples of the disability and gay movements, however, the point is not that such demonstrations and conflicts inevitably resulted in positive policy changes or the end of historic injustices. Unfortunately the material inequalities poorer black people experience today in the United States and elsewhere are in some ways as sharp as they were before the 1960s civil rights campaign (see Chapter 5).

In terms of thinking about the position of black people in society, however, the mould was broken. Racism and racial disadvantage still permeate American and other western industrial societies but despite this the nature of the conflict and of awareness of it have moved on a stage. In Britain, for example, some noticeable differences are appearing between first, Indian and 'East African' Asian, secondly, Afro-Caribbean, and thirdly, Pakistani and Bangladeshi communities. These are not only in relation to employment and unemployment, as noted above, but also as far as education, housing and other important indicators of well-being are concerned (Jones, 1993).

Not surprisingly, as this happens, changes are occurring in the attitudes of the white majority to the achievements of the different minority communities. Across Europe, continuing problems of racial violence, neo-fascist activity and anti-Islamic sentiment sit uneasily with signs of acceptance of at least some members of minority ethnic communities, or at least some aspects of minority cultures. Taking Britain as an example, marriages or stable relationships between black (Afro-Caribbean) men and white women, and of black women and white men, have become increasingly common. They now involve over 30 per cent of British black people aged under 25, and this in turn will lead to a sizeable 'mixed descent' generation in the coming decade (Nanton, 1992).

The example of race relations and the changing nature of racism summarises many of the other changes in the cultural context of equal opportunities. There has been a fundamental shift from a time in which majority attitudes towards minority groups and the disadvantaged were either paternalistic or unthinking and uninformed. In that era, and in the main before the 1960s, either it was unthinkable that the marginalised groups (women, black people, disabled people, and so on) could do certain jobs, or, if they were 'allowed' into the labour market, it was on the understanding that they would have to integrate to white, male 'majority' norms or to 'able-bodied' definitions of the workplace. Now, the rights and needs of the historically discriminated against are better known. However, they are also strongly contested. So while the fragmentation of cultural attitudes has opened up the debate about equality of opportunity and in that sense will facilitate the introduction of equality policies, at the same time there is a polarisation of opinion which is likely to lead to many more disputes about the legitimacy or fairness of such policies.

The context of law in a European framework

The European Union represents an important set of influences on member states whether in the economic, political or legislative field. However, the United Kingdom often seems to stand out from other member states because of her resistance to some of these influences. Britain's best-known 'achievements' in Europe have been almost entirely negative. In recent years Britain has sought either to opt out of European social legislation or to oppose what are seen as federalist European policies.

Despite this, and notwithstanding Britain's allegedly semi-detached approach to European affairs, leading economies in Europe, particularly the German economy, will continue to play a central role in Britain's economy. To take a single example, the interest rates set by the Bundesbank are arguably of more significance in determining British interest rates (with all the consequences for mortgage rates, investment, inflation, economic growth and job creation) than the actions of a British Chancellor.

When the Treaty of Rome was signed in 1957 between the original six member states of the European Community, the countries with higher wage costs and greater labour market regulation, especially Germany and France, realised that they would be at a disadvantage compared with a country such as Italy, where wage costs were then relatively low and the labour market has remained a comparatively unregulated affair. The 'Common Market' was set up, as its name implies, very much as a customs union in which tariff barriers would be dismantled and in which the free flow of capital, goods and workers would be promoted. The dilemma or contradiction of substantially different labour costs in different parts of the Community is therefore an old problem. To avoid 'social dumping', a free-for-all flow of investment and industries to countries with the lowest standards of social protection, a 'social dimension' in a basically economic union was needed. Myles gives an illustration of this when referring to Article 119 of the Treaty of Rome, on Equal Pay, which was 'inserted into the Treaty mainly for economic reasons, in particular to protect French industry against unfair competition due to lower-paid female labour in the other Member States' (1992: 3-199). These concerns have become particularly prominent in the recent economic recession in Europe. As Cable argues,

> The impression has somehow been created that the Social Chapter is the intellectual property of the . . . socially caring wing of European politics. Nothing could be farther from the truth. Its most eager advocates include the German and Benelux Christian Democrats, who are deeply concerned that as Europe moves towards monetary union the main burden of adjustment in the EU should not fall on their own employers and high-cost labour. (1994: 19)

These points raise important implications for Britain's perception of European labour and equality legislation. First, British interpretations, at least in some quarters, tend to overestimate the socialistic nature of European equality legislation. The European drive to regulate employer–employee relations should be kept in perspective. Though Germany and other member states may wish to extend legislation in various ways, the Community's commitment to social policy and social action programmes has always been chronically underfunded (Cunningham, 1992: 178). The proportion of Community funds devoted to agricultural subsidies and other agricultural policies, for example, has been far higher.

British anti-European views of a socialistic Brussels juggernaut need to be taken with a pinch of salt for another reason: a lot of rhetoric has been created in the European Union about citizens' rights and equality but, according to Cunningham (1992: 178) and others, much of this has been for the primary purpose of trying to legitimise the EU's existence. Substantive change has been achieved, particularly in the area of improving women's rights and opportunities, but the ambitious goals outlined in EU policy documents should not be interpreted too literally. In practice, according to Cable, 'governments of the right (France, Italy) and of the left (Spain) are quietly undermining [the Social Chapter] through the deregulation of their labour markets' (1994: 19).

To sum up, there is probably as much concern about the costs and rigidities of some of the EU's labour legislation among industrialists and political leaders of other European states as there is in Britain. It is also likely that the southern European countries – Italy, Greece, Spain and Portugal – will continue to find much EU social legislation unenforceable because in each of these countries there are weak traditions of public sector welfare and labour market regulation, and casual low-paid labour in the informal sector is an important feature of their economies.

This does not mean, however, that the European legislative framework will necessarily become a less important or weakening influence on equal opportunities policies in the United Kingdom. European legislation does have substance and can make a real difference. The above points are made in order to qualify some of the more stereotypical views of the EU, held on both the left and the right, which sometimes exaggerate the aims and scope of European equality legislation.

Has the United Kingdom opted out of European legislation?

The United Kingdom stepped out of commitments to European labour and equality policy on two notable occasions in recent years: in December 1989 the European Council in Strasbourg approved the Social Charter (the Community Charter of the Fundamental Rights of Workers), but with the UK dissenting from it, and in 1991 the Treaty of Maastricht was concluded with a compromise which allowed the United Kingdom to decide whether or not to join a single currency and to block the implementation in Britain of the Treaty's clauses on employees' rights and employer–employee relations – the hived-off 'social chapter'.

The Social Charter was more a symbolic statement of intent by member states than a binding commitment to a precise set of regulations. The subsequent action programme (COM (89) 568) became the substantial basis for equality and labour policies. These include provisions on the right of men and women to equal treatment, on health and safety at work, rights to training, freedom of movement and employment, social protection and social security, improvement of living and working conditions, rights to consultation and worker participation, and protection for groups excluded from the workforce such as older and disabled people.

As Collins (1991) notes, the adoption of the Charter by the 11 member states was the beginning of a road rather than the end. Reactions to implementation among the 11 have been mixed, especially bearing in mind the costs of the various action programmes to poorer countries such as Ireland.

The Treaty of Maastricht in 1991 signified, however, that all the member states of the EC – except Britain, which opted out of the social chapter – wished to continue along the path of social legislation outlined in the 1989 Charter. Thus the treaty on European union reaffirmed the commitments to improving working conditions, equal pay for men and women (where pay means the basic wage and other payments in cash or kind that workers receive), promoting worker consultation, etc. The broad objective, in social and labour policy terms, was to begin to create a cohesive Europe by advancing the rights and interests of nationals in member states to a stage when common citizenship of a European Union can eventually become a reality.

But the 11 signatories' agreement did not bind them to either a uniform or strictly timetabled process of implementation of social legislation. The European Council of Ministers will be able to issue directives on minimum standards in areas of labour law and social protection, but only in ways that will allow for gradual implementation.

Safeguards for small and medium-sized businesses have been written into the agreement because of widespread concern at Maastricht that the costs of social protection could threaten competitiveness. And while the 11 member states at that time agreed that the European Council may act by majority vote in some major areas of social legislation, it cannot do so in the following equally important areas: establishing contractual rights for workers when they are made redundant; social security and social protection; requirements that member states introduce employment generation schemes; and the introduction of 'codetermination' schemes, whereby management and employees are expected to work out together their contractual agreements on pay and working conditions. All of these provisions can only become binding upon member states following a unanimous vote among the 11 original signatories and consultation with the European Parliament.

As before the Treaty of Maastricht, then, the bold objectives of the European Community are still shrouded by mists of legal complexity and by differences of opinion among member states about the scope of social legislation and the speed with which it is to be introduced. Therefore one view is that Britain only opted out of requirements for equality and labour protection that are rather minimal, at least in the foreseeable future, and which are anyway met by the majority of British employers. However, the difference which opting out makes will depend on how far British policy continues to deregulate the labour market or whether, on the other hand, political change will lead to the reinstatement, if only in diluted form, of such protective measures as a minimum wage.

Of much greater importance is the point that Britain will continue to be affected by two sources of European influence: first, the authority of the European Court of Justice (ECJ) to amend or even override judgments reached in British courts and, secondly, pre-Maastricht legislation on equality.

The European Court of Justice

The ECJ in Luxembourg has served as a 'court of appeal' in the Community since the Treaty of Rome was signed in 1957. It gives rulings and interpretations of the laws agreed by member states and has become a kind of final arbiter and tribunal. In fact the ECJ has jurisdiction at a number of levels, hearing cases brought on behalf of individuals, private companies and organisations, and nation states.

According to Brewster and Teague (1989), there is 'no un-equivocal answer' to the burning question of whether European Community law is superior to, or always takes precedence over, the national laws of a member state such as Britain. Though British courts have challenged the ECJ's rulings from time to time on this matter, the ECJ has tended to be able to establish the principle that it does have precedence in those matters and policies which are specifically Community responsibilities – such as European equal pay legislation.

Much depends, of course, upon whether the ECJ is dealing with legal questions arising from *regulations*, which are directly applicable to all member states and binding upon them in the form that has been mutually agreed, or *directives* – these are also binding upon member states, but are applied in a form which takes account of the shape of existing national laws – or *recommendations*, which are policy goals and attempts to influence member states in other ways. Recommendations, such as the equality recommendation on Positive Action, are usually thought of as having no legal force (Meehan, 1993: 55). However, as Meehan points out in relation to such voluntary codes, a recent ECJ ruling 'may mean that measures that were thought to be non-binding might have effects in national courts' (1993: 58).

To sum up, the influence of the ECJ is at once strong and weak. It is strong in the sense that European laws are in general regarded as supreme: 'the special and original nature of EC treaty law could not be overridden by national law without depriving the Community of its very foundations' (Meehan, 1993: 57). The ECJ does not formally occupy the role of a constitutional court, but in practice it has established a central role in developing the framework of Community laws, and in making rulings upon cases where there seem to be inconsistencies between national and EC laws. This is so even in Britain, where in theory no law can be above the authority of Parliament to repeal or reverse it, but where in practice Parliament's European Community Act accepts the supremacy of those Treaty laws and obligations to which Britain has subscribed.

The strength and importance of the ECJ is also illustrated by the number of times cases on sex equality from Britain have been taken before the Court, though this may be as much to do with the willingness and effectiveness of the Equal Opportunities Commission, which has sought to improve British law on sex equality, as it is to do with Britain's actual record on equality compared with other countries.

However, the ECJ has legal limitations, and must itself broadly act within EC laws and restrict itself to the definitions of rights and equality laid down by those laws; it cannot freely develop laws or rulings in areas that the Council of Ministers has not agreed upon. Also, within the framework of European law, the ECJ can only enforce principles which are first and foremost geared to individuals' rights as employees in a labour market. In other words, it cannot impose sweeping judgments on every aspect of equal opportunity or create positive action policies, though the Court's powers should not be underestimated when it comes to dealing with cases of discrimination, especially in the area of sex discrimination.

To give some examples of the ECJ's influence in Britain, we may consider the recent (1993 and 1994) compensation awards to women unlawfully dismissed from the armed forces. While these awards have been decided by domestic industrial tribunals, compensation had been limited to £11,000 until August 1993, when the ECJ ruled in another case that such a limit breached European law (EOR, 1994a: 2). Thus the *size* of the awards has been directly increased by an ECJ ruling. In 1994, for instance, Nichola Cannock was awarded a record amount – £172,912 – because she was wrongfully dismissed from the Royal Air Force when she became pregnant.

The legal basis of this and other cases lies in the EC Equal Treatment Directive of 1976 (76/207), which came into effect in Britain in 1978. The Equal Opportunities Commission estimates that the Ministry of Defence 'could be facing a compensation bill totalling £50 million' (EOR, 1994a: 2) because thousands of women were unlawfully dismissed between 1978 and 1990, when the armed forces belatedly stopped the practice of dismissing pregnant women.

Other employers also face the implications of the ECJ's rulings on similar kinds of sex discrimination. For example, in July 1994 the ECJ decided that Carole Webb, a clerk employed by EMO Air Cargo, had been unfairly dismissed when she became pregnant in

1987. Mrs Webb's appeal to the ECJ had taken seven years in all, following unsuccessful appeals to an industrial tribunal, an Employment Appeal Tribunal, a Court of Appeal and the House of Lords, which finally referred her case to the ECJ.

To contain the rising costs of compensation for unlawful dismissal, the British government are considering changes to the industrial tribunal system. One way of doing this would be to require employers to re-employ unfairly dismissed workers, a practice which has been adopted in both France and Germany (Pilkington, 1994). This shows that, though the ECJ and European law may successfully establish the rights of individuals who have been unlawfully dismissed, member countries have considerable leeway in interpreting how justice will be restored.

Another example of discrimination, that of the dismissal of gay and lesbian service personnel from the armed forces, also shows both the potential significance and the limitations of the European court. Serious public concern has arisen about this matter in Britain, not only because it raises questions about the infringement of civil rights but also because of the economic waste involved in dismissing expensively trained and experienced officers.

Attempts to change British law on this matter have not been successful. Homosexual conduct or relationships still constitute a disciplinary offence in the British armed forces, and therefore dismissal of service personnel on grounds of sexual orientation is still permissible. According to one report, 259 people were discharged on these grounds between 1990 and 1994 (Travis, 1994: 1). At the time of writing, the scale of dismissals revealed by the Ministry of Defence was leading to speculation that successful claims for compensation could dwarf those payable to women service personnel dismissed on grounds of pregnancy.

However, it is not yet clear that the ECJ and European law will be as helpful to those wronged for their sexual orientation as it is in cases of gender discrimination against women. It may be possible to establish a case under the 1976 Equal Treatment Directive (see above), which outlaws discrimination 'by reference to marital or family status' (Travis, 1994: 1), although it is not specific about sexual orientation. Another possibility is that claims will be taken not to the ECJ but to the European Court of Human Rights in Strasbourg. Article Eight of the European Convention of Human Rights guarantees privacy, and the ways in which the British services have tried to establish the sexual orientation of their personnel breach this principle.

European equality laws

As we pointed out, the European Court is one source of influence on the development of equal opportunities policies in Britain; the other is the legislation itself, which predates Maastricht and is binding upon British employers in a number of ways.

First, in terms of women's rights to equal opportunity and equal treatment, the following are the key features of European legislation:

■ *Article 119* of the Treaty of Rome established the principle of *equal pay* for the same or similar work. This has since been extended by an Equal Pay Directive, which from 1976 required each member state to implement laws based on the principle of equal pay for work of equal *value*. The Equal Pay Directive also goes further in that it requires member states to demonstrate that measures have been taken to make employees aware of their equal pay rights; it also requires protection for employees who are dismissed because they have challenged an employer over unequal pay.

In 1979 the European Commission found that the United Kingdom's Equal Pay Act did not meet the above requirements, mainly because it only permitted claims for equal pay when women and men were engaged in 'like work' (Maes, 1990: 55). As a result, the United Kingdom had to modify its own legislation to take account of key notions of equal value, though the changes made have been the subject of various interpretations and criticisms (see Chapter 4).

■ The 1976 *Equal Treatment Directive* relates to sex discrimination in employment. It covers 'selection criteria . . . access to all jobs or posts, whatever the sector or branch of activity, and to all levels of the occupational hierarchy' (Myles, 1992: 3-215). It introduced the concept of indirect or institutional discrimination. However, discrimination on grounds of gender is permitted where the sex of the employee is seen as a 'genuine qualification': for example where personal or health services are to be provided. The directive also covers opportunities for training and vocational guidance, equal treatment in promotion procedures, and other aspects of terms and conditions of employment (for example, conditions governing dismissal). Myles notes that,

> As with the equal pay Directive, difficulties have been encountered with the application of the sex discrimination Directive in the Member States. Infringement proceedings were initiated in 1979 against Germany, Luxembourg and the Netherlands for not adopting all the necessary national measures. (1992: 3-218–19)

The Equal Treatment Directive can therefore be regarded as a significant change in that considerable efforts had to be made to bring several member states' legislation into line with it.

- The *Social Security Directive* extends equal treatment of men and women into the area of state pension schemes, other kinds of social security, and the benefits from such schemes. It was agreed by the Council of Ministers in 1978, and came into effect (as Directive 7) two years afterwards. The initial social security directive did not apply to company occupational pension or insurance schemes, or to other schemes based on collective agreements. However, it does apply to *state*-run schemes which are designed to protect people's incomes during old age, periods of illness or loss of earnings as a result of accidents or occupational diseases, and unemployment.

As a result of action programmes during the 1980s and later directives, equal treatment of men and women in social security and social protection matters has been extended to include equal pension ages for men and women (a measure which has now been planned for in the United Kingdom), equal access to family benefits, and rights to parental leave (though Britain has opted out of the latter – see Chapter 4).

Other directives followed the first social security directives: for example a 1979 directive extended the protection of equal treatment in social security to migrant workers in the Community (that is, member state citizens), while a 1986 directive (86/378) extended gender equality rights to private or non-statutory pension and insurance schemes.

- Finally, as far as gender equality is concerned, there are some important implications for Britain in European *Health and Safety* legislation. As Meehan points out (1993: 109), Britain is committed to agreements on health and safety even though the Social Charter does not apply. For example, pregnant women employees are given various rights under these agreements as well as being protected by the Equal Treatment Directive, as discussed above.

As can be seen from these examples gender equality has been given 'pride of place' in European legislation (Meehan, 1993: 108) and, by comparison, other areas of need and discrimination are relatively neglected. This is particularly noticeable as far as 'race', racism and discrimination on grounds of nationality and ethnicity are concerned. In a review of Britain's 1976 Race Relations Act, the Commission for Racial Equality suggested that 'even as it stands, the Race Relations Act is in advance of specific race legislation elsewhere in the European Community' (CRE, 1991: 5). However, we are brought back to the earlier point that the ECJ cannot easily widen its field of jurisprudence to include matters in which there is much less consensus among member states than in relation to gender equality.

While European legislation on gender and race equality could perhaps be seen as occupying the opposite ends of a spectrum from significant to minimal concern, the attention of European legislators to other groups – chiefly the disabled, older people, children and adolescents – can be portrayed as being somewhere in between.

As with racial discrimination, there are no European Community laws or directives dealing specifically with discrimination against disabled people, or on grounds of age. But as with sex equality, not inconsiderable Community funds have been devoted to action programmes which aim to improve the position of disabled people and older workers. And while directives have not been issued, there is a European Council recommendation on the employment of disabled people (Maes, 1990: 47).

The HELIOS programme, launched in 1981 and followed in 1988 and 1992 with a second and third stage, is the European Community's action programme for promoting the social and economic integration of disabled people. It includes measures to promote work-related improvements in the lives of disabled people: for example, vocational and technical training, encouraging member states to apply new developments in technology to promote the integration of disabled workers, and assistance with transport improvements (see Chapter 6).

The HELIOS programme also includes measures to improve the position of disabled people in general – that is, in non-work settings as well as in employment – and in this respect it is similar to the recommendations and action programme developed for older people, which has developed policy on such matters as an equitable retirement age and public transport for older people.

Because disabled and older people's actual and potential role in work has often been dismissed, however, the influence of European legislation on discrimination against these groups is rather weak. Though helpful to the extent that action programmes can put the needs of disabled people, older people and other disadvantaged groups 'on the map', and can add welcome resources and perhaps some progressive thinking to projects in Britain and other member states, another interpretation is to suggest that European policy is as much about compensating for continuing marginalisation (in the case of disabled people) or growing marginalisation (with regard to older workers) from the labour force.

In sum, British employers feel little pressure from European law to consider discrimination in the wider sense or with regard to sexual orientation, age, disability or 'race' and ethnicity. This does not mean that the domestic legal context is unimportant as far as these categories is concerned, and in later chapters we discuss the impact of domestic laws on equal opportunities policies in Britain and other countries. However, the 'European context' and the teeth of European Community law are almost entirely felt in the area of equal opportunities for women.

As the European Union develops, a 'lowest common denominator' effect may become more evident, weakening existing equality legislation and making it rather less likely than before that problems of 'racial' or religious discrimination will be addressed, or that equal rights for gay and lesbian, disabled and older workers will be promoted. However, we have tried in our review of the social and economic context to point out that the future for equal opportunities is an open one. The era of full male employment is over and unemployment is now affecting men much more seriously than women. But as the role of women in the labour force becomes more central than it was, and as the problem of finding reasonably paid or rewarding jobs intensifies, the pressure for a more equitable distribution of 'good' jobs may increase the pressure for equal opportunities policies (from men as often as women) rather than reduce it. At the same time, demographic changes, especially the ageing of the workforce, and cultural changes in attitudes towards stigmatised groups such as disabled people, also make the future of equal opportunities policies look uncertain rather than predictably gloomy or positive.

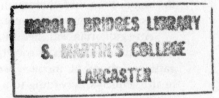

3
COMPARATIVE CONCEPTS
OF EQUAL OPPORTUNITY

Introduction

The policies that are the subject of this book aim for 'equality' and 'opportunity'. But what do these terms mean? To address this fundamental question we must also draw in other ideas which are inextricably bound up with equality: notably, concepts of inequality and freedom.

First, it is important to realise that no human society could be perfectly equal, or even approach near-equality between all individuals. There will be inequalities even in non-stratified societies (such as hunting and gathering communities which have no distinctions of class or other kinds of structured privilege), for example between the older and younger, the more or less socially integrated, the physically skilled and less skilled, and so on.

The significance of different *forms* of inequality varies from society to society (class, caste, gender, age, etc.), but experience of some inequality is an unavoidable human condition. Equality of opportunity policies may therefore, as a slogan, claim 'to be working towards equality' when in effect they are based on (i) reducing the *degree* or amount of inequality and/or (ii) changing the *bases* or justifications upon which inequalities rest.

An egalitarian will seek to reduce the gaps between the 'top' and 'bottom' sections of society as much as possible, whether the gaps are those of income, wealth, educational attainment, or health. Policies, according to this view, are instruments to achieve a more equal end-state or outcome.

Conversely, both conservatives and more 'radical' neo-liberal or 'New Right' thinkers celebrate inequality (Forbes, 1991). Conservatives put greater emphasis on the value of a traditional hierarchy (the wiser and better-off guide and 'protect' the poorer and less able). 'New Right' ideas stress the value of market competition in providing incentives and rewarding individual achievement. But their conclusions are broadly the same: policies which seek to level society by 'artificially' introducing equality are to be deplored, mainly because they are seen to reduce liberties and freedoms by an intolerable degree.

When we consider (ii), however, the picture changes. While there are sharp disagreements about the degree of inequality that is to be either tolerated or encouraged, there is at least a basic consensus that it is unjust to allow certain things to affect individuals' chances of employment or educational prospects. In particular, characteristics such as one's gender, sexual orientation, religion, 'racial' or ethnic identity are seen by many on the right as well as on the left as unfair and 'irrelevant' bases of discrimination. There may be more argument about other characteristics such as disability and age which, some contend, have a bearing upon suitability for employment or education.

Thus, as far as opinion on the right is concerned, there is not necessarily a contradiction between equality before the law and an end result which is highly unequal but based on fair competition between individuals. As Forbes puts it, 'equal opportunity is not rejected, just redefined' and becomes a 'vision of a perfectly competitive society' (1991: 27).

However, there are many shades of opinion about equality and yet more questions about the question of what are fair or relevant bases of *inequality*. As Jencks says,

> Attributes like skin color and ancestry ought to be 'irrelevant' and . . . distinctions based . . . on such characteristics are therefore incompatible with equal opportunity. But there is no such consensus about what characteristics we should consider 'relevant'. Conservatives usually assume that differences in past performance require us to treat people unequally. Liberals usually think that past *disadvantages* [our italics] require us to treat people unequally. (1988: 47–8)

The 'liberals' Jencks refers to place some importance upon an 'unequal' but favourable treatment of those who have been disadvantaged by former discrimination or lack of opportunity. Much depends upon how we interpret former injustices and inequalities and what weight we accord them. Egalitarian views would suggest that it is not enough to define equal opportunity as, for example, the same chance of success for two equally qualified job applicants. It would also consider whether certain individuals and groups have in the past been systematically discriminated against in the school system, or whether poverty played a part in preventing someone with talent from achieving their potential.

This expresses a need-based principle of justice. It goes beyond what Jencks has termed 'democratic equality' (1988: 50), the goal of treating every individual equally and, for example, devoting equal educational resources to all, to what some would see as a more humane approach. Extra educational resources, employment training and other assistance will be given to the disadvantaged according to need.

As Jencks reminds us, much has been said about the difficulty of defining need and the extent to which former disadvantages should be taken into account. Thus the 'humane justice' approach towards equality, despite its great potential, is beset with unresolved questions about how far the cause of equality should be taken by government and which inequalities the community and the state are responsible for.

Choice and freedom

The suggestion that government should attempt to maximise equality, for example by helping every individual to realise his/her potential to learn, or find a suitable job, carries with it assumptions about public responsibility. The community becomes responsible for setting right certain wrongs, as far as it can, or for compensating for certain disadvantages; at the same time, the disadvantaged may begin to claim certain rights to be helped or to have opportunities.

Fundamental questions, however, are raised by these assumptions. If individuals are provided with educational resources and opportunities but choose not to search for jobs, or for employment in occupations they have traditionally seen as 'not for the likes of us', is government responsible for that choice?

This question is well illustrated by gender segregation and the apparent preference for certain occupations among men and for other occupations among women. In Sweden, a very high level of participation by women in the paid labour force is combined with a surprisingly persistent degree of gender segregation (see Chapter 4). It is unlikely that discrimination of a direct or indirect nature accounts for *all* the job segregation. What of the remainder? One explanation is that women have freely chosen not to enter male-dominated occupations. Another is that they are constrained by traditional family and childrearing roles, or as a result of general social attitudes do not see 'male' jobs as fitting and are not motivated to apply for them.

Commentators on the right usually stress individual choice and responsibility rather than the second, more sociological view. For them, any in-built social tendency or tradition for men and women to adopt segregated roles in the family and at work would largely be a matter for individuals in each succeeding generation to negotiate, accept or reject; to involve the state in equalising such roles would according to them breach important principles of freedom (though conservatives in some countries are ready to lay aside 'laissez-faire' principles to support social policies which encourage 'traditional' family forms and values).

Similar controversies surround educational attainment among poorer social groups. For those who stress the importance of social structure, education outcomes suggest that children growing up in low-income homes are often, though not always, doubly disadvantaged by a lack of cultural capital. Poorer parents, even if they are strongly motivated or interested in educational success for their children, may find that their efforts to assist their children are discounted by the 'official' middle-class culture. But for those on the right,

> growing up in a home where studying is a low priority . . . does not mean that Johnny had less 'opportunity' than Mary to attend a good college. Conservatives usually reject this argument, insisting that Johnny's decision reflects lack of 'motivation', not 'opportunity'. (Jencks, 1988: 48)

One does not have to fully accept the conservative view of causes of inequality to recognise that there is *some* truth in this argument even if it is not the whole story. Human beings do exercise choices and preferences, and in some cases the disadvantaged can swim against the tide of discrimination and low expectations. For example, recent evidence shows that higher proportions of students from certain minority ethnic group backgrounds are entering British higher education than 'majority' white students (Jones, 1993), though we must beware of generalising this example to other social groups or examples of inequality. Nor does it conclusively demonstrate the truth of views on the right about the nature of equality and inequality, only that change does occur and that patterns of inequality are not immutable.

'Social' and 'natural' inequality

In this section we continue the debate by looking at human characteristics and qualities which appear to be immutable and unchangeable. For example, people have varying levels of physical strength, dexterity and intellectual capacity. Is government and society to be responsible for countering or reducing the inequalities generated by these differences?

Rousseau (1761) drew a distinction between 'natural' or 'physical', and 'political' kinds of inequality. The latter were, in some ways, to be viewed as artificial and constructed differences. Equality would be seen as a state in which such convention-based distinctions are swept away. However, Rousseau assumed that we cannot do very much with the 'natural' differences. If a society were to be successful in progressively removing its social barriers and privileges, the remaining 'natural' differences would become increasingly important. They would be distinctions of merit: intelligence, ability, skill and artistic talent.

At first, this seems quite acceptable. What could be more reasonable than an assumption that those with the most merit or talent are given recognition, irrespective of their social background, race, gender or age? Also there is a logic to the notion that government does not tinker with 'natural' differences but does take responsibility for countering the social causes of disadvantage (either because they are under its control and can be reduced, or because a government today may decide to compensate for the failures of previous governments).

However, there are serious weaknesses in the argument that we can distinguish sharply between 'natural' and 'social' differences or inequalities. It is wrong to assume that we can only 'do something' to alter the inequalities arising from socially caused disadvantages. It is also possible to 'do something' to affect the inequalities which result from genetic and other innate differences.

We should clarify at once that while making 'environmental' changes to take account of individual circumstances need not cause ethical problems (for example a schoolteacher who varies his/her approach with different kinds of students), fundamental moral questions are raised by the proposition that medical science can ameliorate individual disadvantages by using new techniques such as genetic manipulation.

At the time of writing, the discovery of a link between sexual orientation and genetic inheritance – the so-called 'gay gene' – was causing great interest and debate. Scientists have identified specific genetic dissimilarities between a significant proportion of homosexual men and the majority of men. It is only claimed, however, that this specific genetic configuration *predisposes* men towards homosexual behaviour; the claim was not that genetic inheritance determines sexual orientation in every case. It may be inferred from the reporting of this research that science may one day command the means to alter or eliminate this or any other behavioural or physiological predisposition.

Our example therefore raises at least two fundamental questions: first, for whom is sexual orientation (or any other personal attribute) a 'problem', and do any resulting disadvantages arise rather from the prejudicial impact of social norms, values and beliefs? Secondly, is there any ground upon which intervention at the genetic level could, in any case, be justified? If so, what are the wider ethical ramifications? These questions go beyond the scope of this book, but debate and moral concern about connections between specific genes and human behaviour is growing and may, in the future, become centrally important in the field of equal opportunity.

Note that this is a substantially different prospect from existing techniques of exercising choice over genetic inheritance: for example genetic counselling with prospective parents. With the latter, existing knowledge of particular conditions (for instance the transmission of sickle cell anaemia from one generation to the next) can be used to inform partners, who may then decide whether to have children or not. More recent genetic research, however, is leading towards much more sophisticated techniques of genetic alteration with the object of removing or changing a far wider range of human behaviour patterns.

We suggest that because the moral implications of such a step are enormous, the application of genetic manipulation techniques is unlikely ever to win widespread approval, especially as some scientists are urging humanity never to apply genetic discoveries in this way. It is more likely that we will continue to acknowledge (and value) the complex interrelationship between the 'natural' or genetic side of our makeup and the environmental or 'social' side, despite the growth of scientific knowledge about how these two sides of our nature combine and how the genetic contribution may be manipulated.

These debates are of particular concern to many disabled people. Members of the disability movement have argued strongly that the idea of genetic manipulation is based upon the false premise that disabled people 'deviate' from some 'able-bodied' norm. In direct opposition to such a view, these disabled people have expressed their pride in their status as disabled people (Hevey, 1992; J. Morris, 1991), and refute utterly the notion that they are in some way 'deviant' or 'deficient' human beings. For them, each person has differing capacities and aptitudes, and one state of being is as valid as any other. Accordingly, their concern lies not with physiological amelioration or 'rehabilitation', but with the construction of society in such a way as to facilitate and accommodate all citizens, rather than to compel some to adapt themselves to the social contours of the majority (Oliver, 1989).

Nevertheless, there is broad acceptance that since we all have differing physiological and cognitive competences, certain activities (cerebral or physical) will be beyond the reach of some individuals even in the most accommodating of circumstances.

The acknowledgement that people have different levels and kinds of ability is important because in seeking to effect change, equal opportunity policies have hitherto responded more readily to 'social' and environmental disadvantages than to physiological or cognitive inequalities, and we would question the assumption that equal opportunity policies may only be legitimately concerned with the 'social' side of disadvantage.

In the first place, it is difficult or impossible to disentangle the environmental from the cognitive causes of individual human differences, capacities and inequalities. Secondly, because social and innate factors are so closely linked, appropriate environmental and social changes may well offset or nullify some disadvantages resulting from physiological or cognitive impairments (see Chapter 6). Thirdly, in acknowledging that people have different intellectual abilities, it follows that we must examine closely what capacities are actually needed to carry out various types of work and whether particular individuals have those capacities; this is different from making generalised or stereotyped judgements about the capacities of whole groups or categories of people, such as older workers or disabled people.

To sum up, we have argued that the idea of trying to base equal opportunity policies on 'social' or environmental disadvantages alone is a weak one. It would seem as though policies must *either* (i) largely disregard former disadvantages and restrict themselves to forbidding discrimination at the point at which people are provided with education or jobs, *or* (ii) take into account a wide range of former disadvantages and lack of opportunity, as well as countering discrimination in the present.

If policies are influenced more by (ii) than (i), they will deliberately or otherwise compensate for an element of genetically caused inequality. Perhaps the reason for previous lack of discussion about this, especially in progressive or welfare-minded circles, is that there has been a reluctance to come to terms with the idea that *any* inequality has a genetically transmitted element.

The prospect of trying to equalise outcomes among people who are born with different levels of intelligence and ability is for some a totalitarian nightmare which seems to work against nature, while for others (and especially those who stress the social influences on intelligence) it represents a step towards a fairer society.

Minimalist definitions of equal opportunity

We have just made a basic distinction between (i) equality measures directed more at 'the here and now' and promoting fairness of procedures in employment or in education, and (ii) the broader, more far-reaching notions of equal opportunity and of the causes of inequality (see also Chapter 1). The first category of ideas may be summarised as follows:

Minimalist concepts of equal opportunity

Definition of equality
'Fairness' – the equal probability among equals, or the
equally qualified, of obtaining work or a selective educational
place.

Basic aim
To ensure fairness of *procedures* of selection and appointment; to forbid direct discrimination, or the use of 'irrelevant' criteria in selection.

Existing inequalities
Employers and educators must be 'blind' to gender, 'racial'
identity, etc. as these are normally irrelevant to job/
educational performance; however, equal opportunity policies cannot equalise society – unequal abilities and merit
mean the unequally qualified will end up in unequal
positions.

Model of society
A competition between individuals; competition is no less
fair than any other way of allocating jobs or education places.

Another term for the minimalist approach is 'prospect-
regarding' equal opportunity. This puts the emphasis on the practices (of selection or discrimination) which affect the prospects of
success: 'prospect-regarding equal opportunity requires ending
de jure segregation and ensuring equal citizenship rights'
(Hochschild, 1988: 93). Equal opportunity in this sense is

> a value asserting the primacy of the individual . . . neither [sic]
> sex, race, creed nor any other ascriptive characteristic should
> interfere with the possibility of individual achievement . . . every
> individual should have the opportunity to develop his or her
> capacities to the utmost . . . (Prager, 1982: 195)

The US Civil Rights Act of 1964 provides a famous example of
this approach. It established comprehensive powers for the federal
law to prohibit discrimination (Gregory, 1987: 107). Title VII, the
section of the Act dealing with employment, forbids employers

> (1) To fail to refuse to hire or to discharge any individual, or otherwise to discriminate against any individual with respect to his compensation, terms, conditions, or privileges of employment, because of such individual's race, color, religion, sex, or national origin; or (2) to limit, segregate, or classify his employees or applicants for employment in any way which would deprive or tend to deprive any individual of employment opportunities or otherwise adversely affect his status as an employee . . .

As mentioned in Chapter 1, however, there are substantial criticisms of the limitations of prospect-regarding definitions of equal opportunity. A key argument is that policies which aim to 'treat individuals in like fashion' take little or no account of historic patterns of inequality. These substantive inequalities (between social classes, the sexes, 'races', etc.) will almost always result in the historically advantaged gaining the most merit, as conventionally measured by educational qualifications or verbal skills in interview.

Another question often raised about the value of prospect-regarding definitions of equal opportunity is 'How level is the playing field?' Procedural justice may be the aim but the nature of the competition for employment or education (for example interviews, personality tests) can inadvertently disadvantage applicants from the groups who are traditionally underrepresented. For example, an intelligence test may contain cultural bias or an aptitude test may favour the young or not accurately reflect older applicants' abilities.

Positive action

Is the *concept* of positive action (see Chapter 1) really all that different from prospect-regarding concepts of equal opportunity? 1970s legislation in the United Kingdom and the United States did recognise both the impact of institutional discrimination and the need to take positive action to counteract historical patterns of inequality. But for some (see for example Gregory, 1987) the principles upon which much of the legislation rests do not represent a substantial change. Positive action still seems to be built upon ideas of *individual* disadvantage and injustice, or individual redress. Stronger policies, to bring about a more equitable distribution of jobs and education, would be based on notions of *group* disadvantage and group redress.

On the other hand there are some who argue that positive action policies do represent a significant departure from pre-existing principles such as treating individuals in like fashion. Glazer, for example, is particularly critical of the direction of American equal opportunity policy. He supports, from a traditional liberal position, earlier American legislation – notably, the Civil Rights Act of 1964 – which expresses the original meaning of affirmative action, which according to Glazer meant that employers should 'not only treat those who applied for jobs without discrimination' but also encouraged them to 'seek out those who might not apply' (1987: 58).

Change since then, according to Glazer, has been on a slippery slope towards a new definition of affirmative action, which 'assumes that everyone is guilty of discrimination' (1987: 58) and has shifted from specific examples of injustice to concepts of statistical underrepresentation. As a result, Glazer and others argue, job and education quotas are tacitly if not explicitly introduced in order to 'correct' these patterns of under- and overrepresentation. Rather than doing too little, these critics argue, government and equal opportunity agencies have gone too far.

Whether or not this is right, it is worth noting that outside the United States positive action strategies are still largely untried (Pitt, 1992: 297). Pitt concludes that tougher equal opportunity policies – in her terms, 'reverse discrimination' – should 'be deferred until it is clear that other measures alone will not work'.

Fair employment in Northern Ireland

One illustration of what could be achieved by somewhat 'tougher' policies based on a positive action model is provided by the 'fair employment' example of Northern Ireland. Here, the powers given to the Fair Employment Commission are stronger and distinctively different from other UK equality legislation, yet they do not go as far as reverse discrimination.

The 1989 Fair Employment (Northern Ireland) Act, which followed earlier legislation applicable to Northern Ireland (see McCrudden, et al., 1991: 30), aims to bring about an equitable distribution of employment and employment opportunities between the Catholic and Protestant communities. It established a Fair Employment Commission (FEC), which acts in many ways like the Equal Opportunities Commission (see Chapter 4) and the Commission for Racial Equality (see Chapter 5).

However, the Fair Employment Commission has rather stronger powers over employers than its mainland cousins to enforce compulsory monitoring of recruitment and employment. Under the Fair Employment Act all employers must carry out a detailed review within three years of registration and report to the Commission on whether or not they are managing to achieve fairer participation.

If improvements towards a more equitable distribution of jobs are not apparent, employers are then required by law to decide 'which affirmative action measures need to be taken and, in appropriate circumstances, decide on the goals and timetables for the required improvement' (Cooper, 1994: 18). As Cooper adds, 'The Commission has quite strong powers to ensure that employers take the appropriate actions' and 'when necessary, they will be used'.

By and large, though, effective compliance with fair employment goals seems to have been achieved through consultation with, and advice from, the Commission. As a result, modest but significant progress has been made towards a more equitable distribution of employment between Catholics and Protestants than before. For example, in 1990 Catholic men were about 7 per cent underrepresented in the workforce; by 1993 they were 5 per cent underrepresented (FEC, 1994). Cooper (1994) reports that while totals of all men employed had declined in the two years following the introduction of the new legislation, employment among Catholic men had risen by about 1000; among women, employment had risen but with no difference in increase between the two communities. As he concludes, these modest changes must be seen against a background in which an additional 12 000 Catholic men would need to have been employed in the same period to achieve equality of participation in the workforce.

These results say nothing about continuing inequalities in the rate of unemployment (significantly higher in the Catholic community) or in the patchy effects of fair employment policy among different occupational groups: for instance affirmative action has been most noticeable in its effect on recruitment of Catholics into managerial, administrative and professional positions (FEC, 1994). However, Northern Ireland's fair employment legislation is relatively recent and the Commission has had to work in a particularly polarised and hostile social climate. Its achievements, which are both noticeable and significant, highlight not only the potential of a stronger form of positive action but also, by contrast, the relative weakness of race and sex equality legislation and policies in the United Kingdom as a whole.

Maximalist definitions of equal opportunity

In Britain the term 'positive discrimination' has often been used to refer to the idea of bringing greater equality but, according to Edwards (1987), this does not necessarily mean that 'positive

---

Maximalist concepts of equal opportunity

Definition of equality
Degrees of equality and inequality are demonstrated by how far major social groups or categories (e.g. disabled people) are represented among various educational tracks/various types and levels of employment.

Basic aim
To break down entrenched social divisions and to bring equality of outcome: equality of educational opportunities and attainments; equality in the workplace and in employment patterns. The aim is to reserve jobs so that organisations become microcosms of the wider society.

Existing inequalities
Based on inherited structures of privilege, advantage and discrimination against the politically and economically weaker sections of society.

Model of society
Some inequality is acceptable if it reflects differences in ability, aptitude and personal choice. But fixed hierarchies tend to perpetuate the dominance of particular groups; each major social grouping (e.g. ethnic groups) should be fairly represented in each social rank or occupational grade.

---

discrimination' can be equated with maximalist ideas of 'reverse discrimination' or 'preferential treatment' of minority groups. For example, the Scarman Report on British inner city disturbances and policing (Scarman, 1982) refers to 'positive discrimination', but the meaning is closer to 'positive action'. Scarman did not advocate reserved jobs or quotas for black and Asian police officers, for example.

British commentators tend to use 'positive discrimination' to refer to any policy which is aimed at meeting additional or special needs, or which is to deal with deprivation. For instance, 'positive discrimination' was often quoted as the principle underlying the distribution of additional resources to inner city areas in the 1960s and 1970s, whether this was to improve schooling, housing or other aspects of the environment. But arguably this is not positive discrimination in the strict sense; it is simply varying the distribution of resources according to need. A child whose mother tongue is not the official language of the country may receive extra English tuition in school, but because s/he is identified as having a need, not because s/he happens to be a member of a minority ethnic group.

As outlined in Chapter 1, one definition of positive discrimination is when individuals receive benefits (payments, services), education or employment *because they are members of a group recognised as disadvantaged* and whether or not, as individuals, they are in greater need than others. As Edwards admits, policies based on this principle could have the appearance of unfairness at the individual level even if a broader equality was being achieved. For instance, qualified unemployed women seeking jobs in occupations in which women were underrepresented would *always* be given priority over unemployed men, even though some individual men might be judged to be in greater need of work than some individual women. Or, on the grounds that racial discrimination has traditionally caused injustice in the housing market, all black applicants for housing might for example be given priority in the allocation of public housing irrespective of individual income or needs.

There is at least one exception, as Edwards points out. Disabled people would qualify for preferential treatment on grounds of individual need as well as membership of a disadvantaged group, because having a severe impairment by definition implies certain needs in a way that being a woman or a member of a minority does not.

These are hypothetical and oversimplified examples but they underline the point that maximalist policies are all about the preferential treatment of *groups* identified as historically disadvantaged and discriminated against. Parekh eloquently defends preferential treatment, though is careful to distinguish between support for the general principle and the way in which any policy is to be implemented:

> Preferential treatment can be misused, and then it becomes counter-productive. But . . . in spite of its limitations it is one of the few policy tools capable of breaking through the self-perpetuating cycle of deeply entrenched inequalities, and weakening the visible and invisible walls the disadvantaged and weak often find almost impossible to scale. (1992: 278)

What merit do these arguments have? As we suggested at the outset, much depends on one's political values and outlook. Many would agree with Cunningham that fully to achieve equality in this way 'would require considerable intrusion on individual liberty and the family, and this is both unrealistic and impossible to enforce' (1992: 178). Yet one also has to question what meanings are attached to liberty or freedom in this context: *Whose* freedoms would be reduced by the operation of maximalist policies?

Are tougher policies justifiable?

To weigh these arguments, we will now explore in greater depth four main kinds of justification for equal opportunities policies. These are:

1. The goal of representative proportions of groups in the workforce.
2. The need to revise ideas on merit, desert and fairness.
3. Compensation or redress for previous injustice.
4. Utilitarian justifications.

In this section we will concentrate on arguments for and against the 'tougher' or maximalist forms of equal opportunities policies such as preferential treatment of excluded or disadvantaged groups. However, many of the arguments can also be applied to the case for and against less tough (but not minimalist) examples of positive action.

Equality and 'proportionality'

The fundamental argument behind maximalist definitions of equal opportunity is that a statistical underrepresentation of certain groups and an overrepresentation of others is clear evidence of injustice. However, the logic of tough affirmative action policies or preferential treatment does not *entirely* rest on the equal proportions argument. Even Parekh, who strongly argues the case for positive discrimination, suggests that 'Contrary to the general impression, positive discrimination is not committed to proportionality, that is, to ensuring that disadvantaged groups are represented in all, most or even major institutions in proportion to their number in the population at large' (1992: 270). For Parekh, the key goal of positive discrimination or preferential treatment is to give back to the disadvantaged their power to choose. In his words, 'If they then freely choose to confine themselves to certain areas of social life, including those devoid of power and prestige, there is no reason for concern' (1992: 270).

This is both an attractive and a rather confusing argument. First, there is a recognition of diversity and choice. Ethnic traditions might well result in a degree of ethnic specialisation in certain occupations. In a free pluralist society, and assuming minorities were not always relegated to low-status occupations, such differences might even be regarded as a healthy phenomenon.

A flexible approach to proportionality would certainly counteract the danger of overcentralised and dictatorial policies. If carried to its logical conclusions, strict proportionality would mean that each public organisation, business firm or profession would have to employ the 'correct' or centrally defined proportions of men and women, disabled people, age groups, different sexual orientations and ethnic groups. This would be artificial, as Parekh suggests, if people do not seek education or various kinds of work in equally proportioned groups.

Added to this are a host of practical problems: for example, does an employer have a representative workforce when the proportions of various minority groups match those in the local area, the local region or in the nation as a whole? All of these yardsticks will probably differ. What counts as the 'local' area (where is the boundary drawn, and who draws it?) or 'the country' (for example, the United Kingdom, or its constituent countries?) is also problematic and open to debate.

Moreover, is an employer failing to bring about proportionality when the representation of minority groups does not match that in the total population, or only when it does not tally with the percentage of *qualified* people in each minority, for example the number who qualify or enter a profession in a particular year?

Yet other thorny questions arise from the proportionality idea because of the ambiguous nature of population categories and the problem of deciding who belongs to which group. Apart from gender, which is almost always a clear-cut difference (but for a minuscule proportion of people whose biological sex identity is ambiguous, or has been changed), all the other main categories are problematic and have blurred boundaries. For instance, people of mixed race, as Nanton (1992) points out, are the fastest growing group among British ethnic and 'racial' minorities. Similarly, who is counted as an 'older' worker, or as someone with a particular sexual orientation, or as a disabled person is perhaps easy to resolve in the majority of cases, but not all.

Parekh (1992) also admits that preferential treatment policies in India, targeted at the 'scheduled castes', can be misused by unscrupulous individuals and groups. But for Parekh and for others who defend preferential treatment of the historically disadvantaged, this and the other problems mentioned above are essentially administrative difficulties; they may be serious, but they are questions of 'how to institute preferential treatment' rather than whether to do it.

Less easy to resolve is Parekh's initial point that proportionality is an important but not a *required* part of tough affirmative action. Parekh's argument is that, so long as policies of preferential treatment continued, the traditionally low status of minority groups would be raised and succeeding generations would be offered equal life chances and choices. This is why, for Parekh, it is crucially important that such programmes are not to be policies implemented by well-meaning government on behalf of marginalised minorities. The formerly disadvantaged should play a leading role in shaping such policies themselves.

Such hopes, in our view, are unrealistic. The lesson of history is that power and authority are closely associated with occupational position and access to elite education. If succeeding generations of minority groups choose not to enter the 'best' schools and universities or the corridors of power (except for the administration of preferential treatment programmes), they would always be prey to a re-establishment of traditional forms of discrimination and inequality. Sooner or later they would be manoeuvred by central authority into accepting cuts in, or abolition of, preferential treatment policies.

In our view, therefore, Parekh's position may be logical in theory but is not convincing when set against historical and political realities. The choice is a somewhat starker one: either maximalist policies with proportionality built into every occupation and educational route, or 'softer' affirmative action without strict proportionality in the form of quotas. The latter might, in effect, be little different from the principles of positive action described in the previous section – although, as we stated there, this is not to devalue positive action policies; in most countries they are untried. Proportionality 'targets' are relatively rare, let alone quotas.

In sum, the notion of proportionality at first seems to present an unanswerable case for righting wrongs. There are scarcely any women, or disabled people, or people from various minority ethnic groups in certain jobs or grades, so the goal is simple even if the means for attaining it are complicated. However, we have tried to show that the case for proportionality itself, irrespective of administrative problems, is not as clear-cut as it may first appear. 'Disproportionality' is often, *but not always*, a result of injustice, discrimination or inequality. Even those, such as Parekh, who are strongly wedded to maximalist ideas of equal opportunity do not suggest that proportionality should become an iron law governing recruitment to every occupation.

Apparently 'technical' or administrative problems of how to define proportions, or categories, seem to lift deeper problems to the surface. For example, there are ethical concerns about wrongly labelling individuals and about the justice or fairness of the 'correct' proportions to be achieved in various occupations. Above all, there is a concern – voiced for example by Glazer (1987) – that attempts to create proportionality revive and strengthen the very distinctions of gender, 'race', disability, etc., which equal opportunity policies have sought to weaken.

However, these criticisms do not always invalidate a maximalist equal proportions policy. Even Glazer is prepared to admit that one's conclusions about it should be related to the country or society under discussion. Preferential treatment of, and job reservations for, 'scheduled castes' in India are an example for which Glazer thinks 'an excellent case' can be made (1987: 200). South Africa, where extreme and entrenched racial inequality persists, presents another case for preferential treatment of black people and the urgent necessity of moves towards proportionality.

Merit, desert and fairness

Another criticism of policies aiming for proportionality is that they override considerations of merit. Implied in this criticism are a number of points: first, while merit (as shown by educational qualifications or work record) is never a perfect measure of ability it offers the fairest and most objective way of establishing who should be given a job or an educational place. All candidates' abilities and potential can be verified by reference to evidence, and qualifications provide a way of individually matching people to positions.

Secondly, individuals have devoted much time, effort and perhaps financial sacrifice towards becoming qualified. Public resources on a huge scale are also poured into education and training. To apparently devalue the importance of merit, as measured in qualifications, would seem to dishonour and overturn these previous understandings and commitments. It is commonly assumed that those who have the best qualifications *deserve* a job or educational place in any competitive situation. This appeals to a sense of justice and the wrongness of disregarding the rights of individuals with merit. Incidentally, it is often those who are from underrepresented groups, and who have attained higher education or professional employment, who are the most vehement in opposition to any suspicion of reverse discrimination in favour of 'their' group: for example, black people often say that they would prefer to persevere than feel they got their jobs because they are black.

Thirdly, from the employer's or educational institution's point of view, merit criteria seem to offer a way of selecting those individuals who will most efficiently work, or learn, or contribute most to the organisation. If less able candidates are chosen, or people who will struggle to perform their tasks, the organisation's efficiency will plummet. This is more an argument about consequences (i.e. inefficiency) than about the moral wrongness of departing from merit.

There is more to these criticisms but first, how do those who wish to defend tough affirmative action respond to the apparent disregard for merit? The debate about affirmative action has been heated, prolonged and complex, especially in the United States, so it is difficult to summarise. However, two main kinds of defence stand out.

First, affirmative action does not entail throwing merit out of the window. *Some* preference in selection might be mixed with *some* consideration of merit. Merit alone, however, does not constitute as fair a way of allocating employment and education as is often claimed. Other considerations such as individual need (for a job or education), recognition of past efforts, hard work or loyalty, and equality itself have to be combined with merit.

Secondly, merit itself may be re-thought. Has merit, as it has been defined traditionally, revealed 'true' merit and abilities? Are educational qualifications, for example, as objective and fair a way of identifying merit as is usually supposed?

Taking the first point, supporters of 'tough' affirmative action could argue that candidates for jobs or educational places need not be chosen solely on the grounds of their gender, racial identity, or whatever. There could be a bar to establish a required level of ability (or perhaps clear evidence of potential ability) which would prevent selection of individuals who were not up to the job or unlikely to stay the educational course. In practice, levels of ability and merit tend to cluster around a mean among any sizeable group of candidates. Therefore it is often a matter of exercising a preference for candidates who, though from disadvantaged or underrepresented backgrounds, are arguably not that different as individuals, in terms of ability and potential, from the candidates who would have been chosen had the preference policy not been operating.

In any case is there an overriding case for selecting the *most* able or meritorious candidates? Perhaps if a competent person from an underrepresented group were to be chosen instead of the very ablest candidate from an overrepresented group, that might be an acceptable trade-off between the interests of 'equal proportions' and merit criteria. Schaar (1967) captures the feeling that merit criteria might be taken too far in the search for those able to do a job or perform a task. He uses the analogy of a race in which an international athlete competes against an averagely competent group of older amateurs, some of whom are 40-year-olds and some are overweight. In that situation the international athlete will always win. But should the pace or standard set by a star always influence our judgements of the other competitors, some of whom, if not excellent, may be quite satisfactory?

According to Parekh, the highest merit does not by itself give rights to employment or education:

> The argument that [the better formally qualified candidate] has a *right* to the job and that his rejection is *unfair* rests on two fallacies. It views merit as the sole basis of desert, which it is not . . . it is an important source of claim, but not the only one. Secondly, the argument wrongly assumes that merit's claim to reward is morally self-evident and needs no justification. Whether or not to reward merit, how much, and what constitutes merit are social *decisions* and a matter of social *policy*. (1992: 275–6)

Picking up the first of Parekh's two points, Pitt (1992) suggests that for a variety of reasons, a selection board might decide not to make any appointment. As long as 'irrelevant' criteria of unsuitability were not used to reject the candidates (e.g. gender, race or religion), she concludes that not appointing anyone does not violate any 'rights' to a job or any kind of contract between employer and applicants. No employer can be *forced* to make an appointment.

Giving a different example, Pitt suggests that we would not think the selectors had done wrong, or violated the rights of the best candidate, if they gave the job to the 'next best' when, for instance, the best candidate has a secure well-paid job while 'the next best has been unemployed for some time' (1992: 297). In the latter case, need for a job combined with merit would have outweighed merit alone.

Another way of looking at the significance of merit is to consider the levels of life-saving skill and professional knowledge required in employment. Perhaps merit, as traditionally estimated by educational qualifications, is not all that important in many jobs, particularly the semi-skilled and unskilled. Therefore preferential treatment and tough affirmative action might work better in such occupations.

The problem with the idea that tough affirmative action can only be introduced in the unskilled and semi-skilled occupations is its social divisiveness. Basically, it would mean that affirmative action would be a policy for the working classes but not for the professional and middle classes. One of the main goals of preferential treatment, which is to bring about representative proportions of every major social group in *every* walk of life, would be lost. Invidious and problematic distinctions are made between, on the one hand, 'really important' or responsible work and, on the other, less important work which has less responsibility for human life. But in reality there are many white collar and professional jobs which carry little immediate responsibility for others' welfare, while many relatively low-paid occupations do (for example the ambulance service, firefighters, workers responsible for electricity and gas supplies).

So while there are undoubtedly a great many undemanding jobs with relatively little required in terms of responsibility, it is difficult to draw a firm line between these and other more demanding jobs with critically important skills. In fact the performance of every job (unless it is completely insignificant) will have *some* sort of impact on the organisation and its efficiency, and arguably merit is the most important selection criterion in every case.

Sher disagrees with the suggestion that consideration of merit can be reduced to that of a threshold level, with the implication that as long as candidates satisfy a basic competence requirement one could make preferential selection from underrepresented groups. He argues that this

> presupposes a very limited – I think unacceptably limited – vision of the aims of employment and education. It presupposes that the point of employing someone is merely to ensure that the job is adequately done and that the point of educating is merely that academic subjects be mastered in some fashion. However, in general, purposive activity aims not merely at achieving satisfactory results but at achieving the best results that prevailing conditions allow. (1988: 120)

But while Sher disagrees with the idea of putting proportionality before merit, he does however conclude that a limited use of preference in selection is justified. On grounds of taking into account the effects of past discrimination, Sher suggests 'we should, if possible, extend just enough preference to the less-well-qualified applicant to restore him to the competitive position that he would have occupied in the absence of wrongdoing' (1988: 125). Again, this is not far removed from the concepts of positive action considered earlier.

Thus there are a number of arguments against the idea of 'diluting' merit or combining it with other criteria in selection and appointments. The strongest arguments seem to be those which raise pragmatic questions about ability to learn or to do the job rather than abstract rights based on merit. Even these difficulties might be overcome if sufficient thought and resources are given to training or to other ways of improving skills and abilities in a particular organisation.

Greater problems would be experienced, however, if a whole country's policy were to be switched from the use of traditional merit criteria to other 'preferential' selection criteria. Though it could not be strictly defined as an affirmative action policy, for example, Tanzania's socialist experiment in educational selection proved to be a disaster (Cooksey, 1986). Designed to meet egalitarian goals by improving access to secondary and higher education among the children of poorer peasant families and from the poorer regions, Tanzanian education policy achieved exactly the opposite results. The dilution of merit criteria actually worked against able children from poorer backgrounds. By bringing in other criteria for selection to higher education such as evidence of community service or commitment to the governing party, children from the more influential and better-off families were often given an extra advantage.

However, there is a second set of arguments about merit. Rather than just considering merit in its traditionally accepted form and asking whether other criteria should be balanced against it, what about a reconsideration of the meaning of merit itself? Traditional merit criteria are a hoop for all candidates to jump through, but a hoop designed and held by the established and the well-educated. Thus one argument is that such merit criteria lend an air of objectivity to what are basically unfair competitions.

But while it is undeniably true, as Parekh says, that different societies decide to reward merit in different *ways* and to differing *degrees,* one wonders whether merit *itself* is as socially relative as Parekh suggests. It is a very difficult question to answer with any certainty because one is drawn back to the debates about how far aptitudes, abilities and intelligence are more or less fixed in childhood and youth (by a combination of genetic and environmental influences) and how far they are malleable and open to development at later stages (see pp. 48–51).

Can less able students or employees be selected for affirmative action reasons with the certainty that their potential can be developed, and that in the end they will perform as well as more able candidates? As far as there is doubt about this, Parekh's argument is weakened. It is significant that Parekh does not present any hard evidence to support his point, beyond the assertion that merit has been defined in a rather overintellectual way and that 'merit' ought to include a much wider range of social skills and abilities (1992: 273).

For example, Parekh makes the valuable point that intellectual ability and even technical competence or practical skills are not everything: being a good doctor means communicating well with patients and with others in the health service and being able to respond sensitively to a variety of human needs. Problems would surely arise, however, if communication skills and sensitivity began to rival other criteria such as practical competence in medical techniques or sufficient intelligence to understand and apply scientific principles? While it is possible to envisage ways to improve the social skills of most intelligent and able students, it is not so certain that the medical skills of the incompetent or struggling student can always be brought to an acceptable standard.

One way to resolve this is to argue that much depends on the field of education or the type of work in question. In fields such as business management and social work, human qualities (for example maturity, assertiveness, or ability to work effectively in a team) may be much more important than the abilities usually measured by educational qualifications. Even here, though, it is often forgotten that people in social work need to be intelligent and to think, as well as be empathetic, and the failure of industrial management to use theoretical knowledge or respect advanced training is often remarked upon, especially in Britain.

Finally, it must be made clear that two aspects of merit have been set aside in our discussion. The first is the example of membership of a minority group as a qualification for employment. Ability to speak a minority language, for example, constitutes merit, as may the insight gained from being a member of an underrepresented minority such as disabled people in employment.

Another point is that we have discussed merit mainly with regard to *selection* for work or educational places; being selected is the 'reward' for merit. However, it is possible to separate the question of rewards, and whether people deserve such rewards, from questions of selection according to qualifications or work performance. For example, an employer may decide that certain workers should be rewarded with higher salary increments for their loyalty or their length of service, irrespective of actual work performance or how well-qualified they are. Or an employee who has been ill or has experienced personal difficulties might be given special consideration. Most equal opportunity debates have been about how people are assigned, or achieve, the positions they do, and how far traditional conceptions of merit should be reconsidered to bring about a representative workforce. This latter topic of 'perks' and rewards, or special treatment for certain categories of employees, perhaps deserves fuller attention than it has yet received in equal opportunity research.

Compensation and redress

Whereas arguments about proportionality and merit look to the *future* consequences of affirmative action, compensation may be described as 'backward-looking' because it is concerned with the effects of historic injustices and disadvantages (Sher, 1983).

On the face of it there is a strong case for the compensation idea. Sociological evidence demonstrates that opportunity and advancement, together with their opposites, blocked opportunity and poverty, are transmitted from generation to generation. Each successive generation does not compete on a board swept clear of pieces from a previous game, but has to make do with whatever position it finds itself in. If inequalities are stacked against certain players or certain groups *and* if the advantages of the successful were acquired illegitimately or by cheating in the past, there is surely a case for giving the losing side or group some redress?

The case looks even stronger when we recall that past injustices may have taken place not all that long ago. It is true, for example, that the enslavement of African Americans formally ended in the mid-nineteenth century, but its legacy lives on and has been woven deeply into whites' and blacks' perceptions of each others' identity. Britain's colonial control of African and Asian countries ended even more recently. The effects of this relatively recent discrimination could be said to linger in the depressed skills, chances and ambitions of the younger generation.

There are, however, some serious problems both with the idea of compensation itself and with conceiving ways in which compensation could be worked into the process of allocating jobs or educational places. This does not mean that compensation is a completely invalid idea: far from it, because any policies which take account of the realities of historic patterns of discrimination, including positive action as well as tougher forms of affirmative action, are in some sense employing a notion of compensation. It is when particular aspects of the idea are examined that difficulties surface.

To begin with, there are problems in equating *individual* compensation with *group* compensation. With the former, the actual value of what has been lost or denied can usually be worked out; it may be defined legalistically and the beneficiary is often compensated according to a publicly accepted scale. For example, there may be set payments for impairments incurred as a result of injury at work. Pitt refers to the same idea when she gives the example of someone who has been discriminated against and denied a job, and who is later compensated for the discrimination by being offered the next available job: this is 'genuine' compensation in the sense that

> The reason for giving X the next job is not X's race or sex, but compensation, proved by the fact that X is entitled to the next job not only if there is a better white or male candidate, but also if there is a better candidate from X's own group. (1992: 284–5)

The case for compensation loses clarity, however, when wider categories of 'victims' of past injustice – and those who have supposedly gained from it – are involved. It is not clear, for example, that all women today have been equally affected by some generalised pattern of discrimination against women in the past. If they have, how much has each woman been affected and in what ways? How could any differences in effects be demonstrated? Similarly, it would be difficult to trace the specific effects of racism, colonial exploitation and slavery upon Asian and black people – at least in ways that could be used as a basis for compensation to whole groups or communities. This is not to deny the terrible legacy of these things, only to point to the clumsiness of the compensation idea.

Also those who are most likely to benefit from compensation (job-seekers, or those applying for higher education) are those who are probably least affected by the legacy of the past. The people who are the poorest and with the fewest skills will not be in a position to even begin to compete for a job or for higher education, while those who do have certain advantages (and belong to an underrepresented group) do benefit from any policy of compensation. This has led Sher (1983) and Parekh (1992) to argue that, if compensation is utilised as a principle of policy at all, the benefits would be better distributed in the form of money or services to all members of the affected groups than as jobs for those in a position to apply for them.

Others are even more critical of the compensation argument. Glazer (1987), for example, observes that the United States is largely an immigrant society and that all the main immigrant communities have experienced discrimination at one time or another. In his view, judging the differing amounts of compensation due to African Americans, Mexican Americans, Japanese, Italian and Irish Americans would be an impossible task.

The second main problem with a broad view of compensation is defining who will bear the cost, and why. It is not necessarily an easy task to show how people in 'dominant' or overrepresented categories (e.g. white males) are accountable for the exploitation and injustices visited upon disadvantaged and minority groups in the past. Most are not linked in any clearly demonstrable way with the past actions of exploitative or dominant groups. In the United States, for example, it would seem to be unfair to ask (white) Irish, Jewish or Italian Americans to forgo education and employment opportunities in order to compensate African Americans for slavery and its legacy; most of the forebears in these white minorities came to America after the abolition of slavery and were not involved in trying to perpetuate it. Similarly, would it be fair to ask present-day white working-class Britons to compensate for the actions and profits of eighteenth-century slave traders? In any case, the British government was the first to ban slave traffic across the Atlantic Ocean, and coastal African states were themselves heavily involved in capturing and selling people into slavery.

Besides these points about innocence and guilt, however, there is an argument that one may continue to benefit from the injustices of the past without being directly responsible for those wrongs or directly descended from the people who were. To use an individual and prosaic example, X may innocently buy something only to find it is stolen property. Despite the difficulties this may cause X, there is little argument about the justice of returning the property to its original owner.

Following the same principle, it could be argued that people in disadvantaged or underrepresented groups are owed restitution, or the restoration of opportunities which were unfairly taken from them. For example, historical enmities and conflicts between the two religious communities in Northern Ireland resulted in systematic discrimination against Catholics in certain industries. These historical patterns may continue to benefit Protestants whatever their feelings and whether or not they themselves discriminate against Catholics. Similarly, men may be sympathetic to policies which seek to equalise opportunities for women, but there is a case for saying that many of these men have benefited from historical trends and attitudes which have held women back in various spheres of employment.

It is this latter relatively 'guilt-free' approach to compensation which seems to find favour with a number of commentators. Perhaps it is because it seems to put as much emphasis on present-day institutional barriers to opportunity as it does on backward-looking justifications for compensation. As Pitt suggests, 'reverse discrimination' can then be seen as 'a counter-balancing measure, attempting to compensate for the inherent bias of the system' (1992: 286).

In sum, then, there are basically two approaches to compensation as a justification for tough affirmative action. The strength of the first, more legalistic approach is that it draws a parallel with 'genuine' compensation. For example, a business firm could be accused of systematic discrimination against a particular group of job applicants or employees over a given time period; a court could then decide what restitutive actions that firm would need to take in order to compensate those discriminated against. As we have seen, however, this approach may run into difficulties of proof and establishing who will be compensated. For instance, the business firm might be ordered to equalise, over a five-year period, the numbers of men and women employed in various grades. But in doing this the fruits of compensation might be given to other people than those who originally lost out.

The main flaw of the second approach to compensation is that it is also difficult to put into effect. It treats the disadvantaged or underrepresented as generalised categories, and all members of these categories as deserving of compensation for past injustices. Also, there is a danger of unthinking acceptance of the culpability of all men, for instance, or of the guilt of all members of a particular 'race'. This may lead to a generalised spreading of guilt which is not helpful in bringing about change, and which unfairly labels at least some men or at least some white people. On the other hand, some approaches to compensation can be interpreted as relatively guilt-free about discrimination in the past while recognising the realities of discrimination in the present. Compensation can then be usefully portrayed as one way of restoring justice and of replacing some of the opportunity lost in previous generations.

Utility

Appeals to 'utilitarian' justifications for affirmative action are rather different from the preceding arguments, which have been based on such principles as equality, rights, justice and redress. In its barest form a utilitarian argument is unprincipled: the justification of the policy is that it brings the greatest benefits to the greatest number, no matter how.

Perhaps this is an oversimplification because, as Jencks (1988) argues, there is a distinction between what he terms 'myopic utilitarianism' and 'enlightened utilitarianism' in his discussion of equal opportunity. The latter is the idea that the value of any equal opportunity policy must be judged by its benefits to society *in the long term.*

How do these ideas about utilitarianism relate to justifications of affirmative action? Pitt (1992) conveniently summarises the main justifications. First, affirmative action might help to reduce social tensions. This is an argument of expediency. From the time of Roosevelt's period of office in the United States, for instance, it could be argued that political and utilitarian motivations (that is, winning and maintaining black people's support for the Democrats) have played a significant role in encouraging the recruitment of black people to public service in employment-generating government programmes. Note, however, that this argument is not necessarily an example of 'myopic' utilitarianism or of 'knee-jerk' reactions to riots or disaffection among minorities, for if social discontent is eased the majority benefit in the long term, as well as the minority who gain employment.

The problem is that tough affirmative action, if it is seen as shading into reverse discrimination, might inflame public passions and increase conflict rather than reduce it. However, a pragmatic utilitarian would simply argue that this is a matter of calculation: it is not an argument against using policies for utilitarian ends *if* there is a chance they will work or good evidence to suggest they will.

A second argument for affirmative action on utilitarian grounds is that it will rapidly put into position 'role models' or examples of success. Within a short space of time people in both majority and minority groups are able to see for themselves that women, or disabled or older people for instance, are competently working in jobs which previously they had been considered unfit for. As a result those in underrepresented groups gain confidence and are able to raise their aspirations, while yet more gain a general sense of worth from identification with their 'role models'. At the same time people in majority groups are affected. They may begin to treat minority groups and women with more respect and to see their attainment of senior positions as 'natural'.

Again the flaw in this approach is that a utilitarian justification is an empirical question rather than one of principle. If people in the majority and the minority alike see affirmative action as a token policy which promotes only 'acceptable' black people, women or disabled people, the utilitarian gains from 'role models' and greater social integration may be cancelled out or backfire. As we have mentioned, it is frequently those of minority identity who have reached their positions the 'conventional' way who most strongly object to this idea.

Thirdly, there is a utilitarian argument that affirmative action policies will create diversity in organisations, a feature which may have general benefits (see Chapter 8) but which may be particularly helpful in those which provide face-to-face services to a diverse community. This is rather similar to the idea of minority identity being counted as part of a broad definition of merit, as we discussed above.

As with the preceding utilitarian arguments the test is workability rather than principle. For example, the presence of Asian practitioners and welfare workers is enormously helpful to service users, especially older Asian women (Blakemore and Boneham, 1994). On the other hand the expectation that Asian patients will invariably benefit from being registered with Asian doctors is often misplaced. Differences of religion, caste and language sometimes serve to create as much social distance between an Asian patient and the Asian doctor as between the Asian patient and a white doctor from the majority community. Conclusions about the value of this idea can therefore only be drawn, as with the other examples, in relation to the sensitivity with which it is translated into action.

Conclusion

Conclusions about the relative merits of arguments for and against equal opportunity policies are certainly difficult and probably impossible to make in the abstract. It is possible to weigh the merits of competing ideas about the nature and causes of inequality (including the role of genetic factors) and the desirability of taking one course of action rather than another to redress or reduce these inequalities. But in our view one could never reach a hard and fast conclusion that tough affirmative action or reverse discrimination could *never* be justified, for example, or that positive action is *always* ineffective.

For one thing, the distinctions we have made between three main categories or definitions of equal opportunity – prospect-regarding, positive action and strong affirmative action – are not always clear-cut. In 'real world' cases of recruitment to jobs or education, there are borderline examples of equal opportunity policy which could be seen as positive action or tough affirmative action. This is particularly the case when positive action shifts (perhaps without formal recognition) to strong preference for underrepresented categories of applicants and targets of equality almost become quotas. However, as Pitt suggests, 'positive action is not *committed* to the preference of a less-qualified candidate' (1992: 282) and this does remain an important distinction.

The main argument for evaluating equal opportunity policies on pragmatic grounds are, first, that patterns of inequality differ and that societies differ. It will be recalled, for example, that Glazer (1987) concludes tough affirmative action has exerted a baneful influence upon American public life, but that a reasonable case for this concept and its application can be made in relation to India and entrenched caste inequalities. Whether or not one agrees with Glazer's views, his fundamental argument, that these matters cannot be resolved in the absolute sense and only in relation to specific circumstances, seems to be a strong one.

To the differences between societies and nations, we might add the differences between different *forms* or bases of inequality: gender, 'race', disability, and so on. One concept of equal opportunity might be better suited to one form of inequality in a particular setting or organisation than another. For example, the seriously underrepresented status of one group in middle-ranking positions might indicate a strong case for affirmative action, at least for a limited period, whereas the less disadvantaged position of another category or minority might not appear to merit such action.

Thus we have shown that although there are important philosophical arguments to consider in relation to different concepts of equal opportunity, they cannot be applied as absolute principles. For example, it is difficult to demonstrate conclusively that anyone has an absolute right to an appointment or to an educational place on the basis of merit or qualifications. Leaving equal opportunity or affirmative action out of the picture, it is already clear that selection decisions are made on the basis of a range of criteria. Merit may be the most important, but other criteria of suitability or of need (for the job or educational place) are used. Often these criteria are applied unfairly, but as long as they continue to be used – and there are sometimes strong arguments for their retention – it would hardly be justifiable to exclude criteria of equal opportunity.

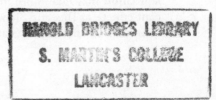

4
GENDER AND EQUAL OPPORTUNITIES

Introduction

The central question of this book is whether – or how far – equal opportunities policies have by themselves brought about change. In this chapter we begin to focus on the outcomes of equality policies, beginning with the role of men and women in the labour market.

One wide-ranging survey of equal opportunities legislation in Europe and North America (Sloane and Jain, 1989) concluded that, with some exceptions, changes in employment patterns among men and women and improvements in women's pay had begun to take place *before* legislation had been put in place.

In Chapter 2 we discussed improvements in women's educational levels, changing attitudes towards child care and the family, and changes in the nature of employment as important factors in accounting for increases in the proportion of women in paid work. According to Sloane and Jain, however, equal opportunities legislation appeared to follow emerging trends rather than bring them about.

There are three points to raise, though, about these conclusions. The first is that Sloane and Jain's survey was of the first appearance of equal opportunities and anti-discriminatory laws. Legislation may not have played a leading part in *initiating* the changes in women's pay and patterns of employment which began to be evident in the 1960s and 1970s. But equal opportunities legislation may take more than a decade to begin to have significant effects, as Dex and Shaw point out in their comparative study of women in the United States and the United Kingdom (1986).

Also, as women's participation in the paid labour force continues to rise, legislation has potential in performing a 'backstop' role: that is, establishing a basic standard of fairness and a framework in which to seek redress, despite the limitations of legal systems.

So while equal opportunities legislation may not have had a strongly causal role in bringing about change in the first place, this does not necessarily mean that such legislation is unimportant or may not play a role in affecting men's and women's employment conditions in the future.

A second point about Sloane and Jain's survey is that it is of the effects of equal opportunities and sex discrimination *legislation* rather than the whole field of equal opportunities policy. Legislation is a very important indicator of how seriously problems of inequality and discrimination are taken, but it is not the only indicator. There is a case for arguing that once legislation is in place, the climate for other kinds of change or policy improves (see Chapter 2). A third point, to put into perspective Sloane and Jain's rather sanguine conclusion, is that it is useful but rather generalised. Other studies, for example those discussed by Dex and Shaw (1986: 14–19), have shown mixed results. In some tests it has been found that equal opportunities legislation does not appear to have had an independent positive effect, mainly because it is difficult to disentangle the possible effects of legislation from other economic and social factors influencing men's and women's wages and employment. But other tests, for example in the United States, have revealed 'positive, though generally not very large, effects of these programmes on women's employment, earnings and occupational advancement' (Dex and Shaw, 1986: 17).

Thus it is worth keeping an open mind about the effects of equal opportunities legislation and policies. We will further examine the findings of various studies of outcomes below, but before looking at the evidence it is important to ask some more questions about *how* we should evaluate outcomes and *what* is being evaluated.

How should outcomes be evaluated?

Any evaluation of outcomes, as far as women and men are concerned, would be incomplete without an awareness of why women find it difficult to compete equally with men in the labour force.

An examination of these problems could be restricted to the sphere of paid work: for example, examining whether barriers to women's employment have been removed, or comparing the proportions of men and women on different pay scales. However, though such evaluations of outcomes are valuable they offer only a limited explanation of the inequalities women face. A more complete evaluation of the success or otherwise of equality legislation must also take into account the dual role of paid work and family responsibilities that many women have to balance. As Meehan and Whitting put it, 'Women's roles in the family affect their employment experiences, not only in terms of access to work in general, but also in terms of the type of work into which they are channelled and the pay that they receive' (1989: 283).

There is debate, though, about how strongly and in what ways family and paid work roles, and the values or belief-systems which underpin inequalities between men and women, create difficulties for women. There are broad differences, for example, between those who hold a liberal feminist perspective and those who have a radical feminist view. The former put the emphasis on the significance of removing institutional barriers so that women can enter existing institutions and organisations to compete with men on an equal footing. The latter suggest that a much more fundamental rethink of the nature of work is required. Not only has the respective contribution of men and women in paid work to be reconsidered, but also their roles in the domestic and family spheres. Rather than accepting existing social institutions and the conventional division between paid work and home as they are, a radical feminist perspective would seek policy outcomes which reduce the continued dominance of men in high-status or highly paid and powerful positions, and challenge their continued absence from many domestic responsibilities.

Going beyond this basic distinction between liberal and radical feminist perspectives, it is possible to find other ways of looking at equal opportunity in relation to gender. For example, Ruggie (1984) has usefully applied three perspectives on gender roles and employment to the British and Swedish contexts, adapting three models which were originally put forward by Kanter (1976).

The first, an *individual model*, focuses on the employment characteristics of individual women and on the policies or strategies that are required to change these characteristics. Thus a successful outcome would be one in which an increasing number of women employees gain employment, or promotion in their existing jobs, as a result of having received training, resocialisation or a positive change in their aspirations. Ruggie gives the example of assertiveness training for women, but any additional management training, or courses to increase women's technical and other skills, could be included in this model (see also Chapter 8).

The individual model is open to the criticism that it assumes existing institutions and working environments to be non-problematic. As Ruggie suggests, the model 'allows for change, but it places the burden of change wholly on women and their abilities to contend with the requirements of success' (1984: 89). A lot of weight is put upon the importance of socialisation in this model, as women tend to be socialised in ways that lead them to limit their own success: for example by choosing subjects in school which will steer them towards less well-rewarded 'feminised' occupations. Thus resocialisation, or training which addresses low esteem and shortfalls in women's previous education, can break the mould.

We must be careful not to reject the individual model entirely. While it emphasises change in women rather than in men or in established social institutions, the individual model recognises the need to provide second chance opportunities in training and employment. This is not to stereotype women but to provide some redress. As Ruggie herself concludes, the individual model, despite its flaws, 'aptly identifies some of the employment problems women encounter' (1984: 90).

However, the second model outlined by Kanter and Ruggie, a *role-related model*, is a perspective which claims to go further. It looks not so much at individual characteristics or needs for training as the dual roles of domestic responsibility and paid work which most employed women have. The main implication of this model is that it brings into the picture social policies and employment practices which may either help or hinder women to manage their dual role dilemmas. Thus outcomes could be measured in terms of the effectiveness of such provisions as nurseries for young children, after-school care of older children, possibilities for working on a 'flexitime' basis, all of which could enable women better to combine family responsibilities with paid work.

Again, as with the individual model, there are some conservative assumptions in the role-related model. Though it shifts attention away from women's individual capabilities and aspirations, it nevertheless assumes that women rather than men will largely be the object of policy: it is they who will be making the arrangements for nursery care, or for their working hours to coincide with child care responsibilities or school hours.

This is not to downplay the importance of nursery provision or any of the other measures mentioned above. In a country such as Sweden for example, a great deal has been achieved in terms of child care and parental leave from work. These are achievements which many in Britain, for example, would be glad of. However, it is noticeable in Sweden that though both mothers and fathers are entitled to parental benefits without any significant loss of income, only a fifth of Swedish fathers choose to take parental leave during the first 12 months of their children's lives; even those who stay at home do so for a much shorter average stay (41 days) than the mothers (Ministry of Labour, Sweden, n.d.: 17).

Gender equality and the outcomes of Swedish policies will be discussed in more detail below, but it is in Sweden and in other Scandinavian countries that probably the most has been done to recognise the limitations of both the individual and role-related models. A third, more radical feminist strategy based on a social structural model reached the top of the political agenda in Sweden in the 1980s.

A *social structural model*, unlike the first two, does not accept that the primary aim of policy is to make arrangements for women to change or adapt to the existing labour market. Rather, this model would support policies which will break down sex segregation in employment and challenge the social structures and values which underpin gender inequalities. In terms of outcomes, the social structural model would therefore lay more stress than the other two models on how successfully targets for a more equal representation of women and men had been achieved in the workforce, and in particular in certain 'key' occupations or industries which have been traditionally male-dominated. Maximalist policies of affirmative action (see Chapter 3) would be supported by this model, underlining the point that the main aim would be to revolutionise opportunity structures for women. Policies would concentrate on increasing *demand* for women workers rather than on apparent problems of labour *supply* affecting women (shortfalls in skill levels, needs for retraining, or lack of child care services).

Being an expression of radical feminist ideas, however, a social structural model involves consideration of policies outside the world of paid work. If the sources of gender inequality and sex discrimination are in the social structure itself, it follows that educational and other policies must aim to eliminate gender role stereotypes in the home, school and other social arenas.

Ruggie maintains, though, that adopting a social structural model does not necessarily imply rejection of the other strategies (1984: 93). The point is that, from a social structural perspective, these measures are not enough. Only when policies combine to address the respective roles of men and women in both the domestic and paid work spheres, and traditional values and assumptions about gender roles, will there be any progress towards social equality. Thus the social structural model presents the most demanding standards for evaluating the outcomes of equal opportunities policies yet, according to Ruggie, it outlines realisable goals. These are demonstrated in at least one country, Sweden, which she sees as 'approaching' the social structural model.

One wonders, however, whether this is an entirely accurate depiction of the Swedish case. Until a tougher or more maximalist approach was adopted in the 1992 Act Concerning Equality between Men and Women (see Ministry of Culture, Sweden, 1992), the bulk of Sweden's policies towards gender equality have been guided more by individual and role-related models or assumptions than a social structural feminist model.

Both Lawson (1990) and Persson (1990), for example, show how Swedish women's incorporation into the paid labour force was achieved through the operation of traditional social democratic institutions of trade unions and welfare state. These institutions have improved the supply side of employment among women by ensuring that they have plenty of opportunities for employment training and by providing perhaps the most generous and comprehensive state-supported system of child care in the world. To date however, these policies have not resulted in radical changes to gender divisions in paid employment or in domestic roles. In fact Persson argues that Swedish improvement of working and living conditions for women has had the opposite effect: it has weakened incentives to break down job segregation between men and women for reasons which we will explore in more detail below.

What should be evaluated?

So far we have suggested that considering the outcomes of equal opportunities policies is not simply a matter of working through a list of indicators of 'success' or 'failure'. The model of gender relations and inequalities which we have in mind will affect how we evaluate the outcomes and what we are looking for. The following headings summarise some key indicators of gender inequality in employment, and in the rest of the chapter we will examine evidence and outcomes under these headings, followed by concluding remarks about the effectiveness of gender-related equal opportunities policies in Britain and other countries:

- The proportions of women and men in full-time and part-time employment.
- The value, amount and take-up of child care, parental leave and maternity benefits.
- The degree or extent of occupational segregation between the sexes, and the impact of policies which aim to reduce it.
- The relative proportions of women and men in different levels of the job hierarchy (for example in management or supervisory positions).
- Wage or income levels among women and men, and the impact of equal pay and equal value legislation.

Women's and men's participation in the workforce

In the crudest sense employment opportunities have become more 'equal' between the sexes if we consider either the increasing proportion of women who are 'economically active' (that is, employed *or* unemployed and able to work) or the numbers of women in paid jobs compared to men.

In Britain the pace of change is quite remarkable. For example, between the end of 1992 and the beginning of 1994 British private sector companies created 97 000 new jobs for women and shed 93 000 jobs held by men (Chote, 1994). An Equal Opportunities Commission Survey (EOR, 1994b) forecast an increase of 600 000 in the number of women employed in the 1990s while employment among men will fall slightly. It is already the case that in certain parts of the United Kingdom, for example South Wales, the number of women outnumbers men in employment.

Across the European Union the economic activity rate of women has increased substantially over the past 20 years and it has been estimated that women are now filling well over half of all new jobs created (Commission of the EC, 1992: 126), though men still outnumber women in the labour force in the EU as a whole. Differences in the proportions of women who are economically active are considerable among the member states. As Table 4.1 shows, there is a range from almost two-thirds of Danish women being economically active in 1991 to only a third of Spanish women.

However as the EC Commission report (1992) points out, two of the countries with the lowest rates of economic activity among women, Spain and Greece, have increased faster than elsewhere. Both countries registered 25 per cent increases in activity rates among women from the beginning to the end of the 1980s, and these were substantial changes well above the European average. On the other hand, in Ireland and Italy (which also have relatively low rates of economic activity among women) increases have been slower than average.

As a result it is hard to find firm evidence that gaps between European countries in their rates of economic activity among

Table 4.1 Economic activity and gender in the European Community (1991) (percentages)

Country	Women	Men	Difference in activity rate
Denmark	62	75	13
United Kingdom	53	75	22
Portugal	51	74	23
Germany	49	73	24
France	48	66	18
Netherlands	45	72	27
Belgium	39	63	24
Irish Republic	37	73	36
Italy	37	68	31
Luxembourg	36	70	34
Greece	34	66	32
Spain	33	67	34

Note: Activity rate is defined here as the civilian labour force aged 16 and over as a percentage of the population aged 16 and over.
Source: Central Statistical Office, 1994a, adapted from Table 4.7, p. 48.

women are closing, despite the shared trend of a general increase. Convergence is a possibility, but the EC Commission report concluded that it is 'not yet clear whether the changes which have occurred presage . . . a general narrowing of the still substantial differences in participation rates between men and women in most Member States' (Commission of the EC, 1992: 128).

This variability is also shown by the proportions of women actually in paid employment (as distinct from the larger number defined as economically active and including the unemployed). For example, in 1980 two European countries with among the highest rates of employment of women were Sweden and Denmark; France and the United Kingdom occupied an intermediate position while among the low scorers in this respect were the Netherlands, Ireland, Spain and Greece (see Table 4.2).

By 1990 the employment rates of the 'low' scorers had matched those of the 'intermediate' scorers in 1980 – a striking change – while there was such a substantial rise in paid employment among Dutch women that the Netherlands rose from a 1980 'low' to a 1990 'intermediate' position. However, the rises between 1980 and 1990 in Sweden and Denmark were also so substantial that the 'high' and the 'low' group averages had *widened* slightly by 1990.

These illustrations are selective and focus on a few countries in Europe, so it is important to bear in mind the proportions of women in paid employment in other countries. For example,

Table 4.2   Paid employment among women in selected European countries, 1980 and 1990 (percentages)

	1980	1990
Sweden	65	83
Denmark	45	78
UK	36	64
France	34	56
(Neth)		53
Netherlands	24	
Ireland	21	37
Spain	20	42
Greece	21	41

Note: Percentages are of all 15–64-year-olds in the labour force (Sweden from 16 years; Ireland 1988; France 1989; UK 1988).
Source: Statistics Sweden (SCB) (1992). Adapted from table on page 36.

taking 1985 as a mid-point to compare with progress in the European countries listed in Table 4.2, it is interesting to note that Japan (40 per cent), Australia (38 per cent) and New Zealand (36 per cent) were all at that time nearer the lower end of the participation spectrum (Forbes, 1989: 23) though since 1985 there have also been considerable changes in these countries.

Also, rapid change continues so that rankings into 'high', 'low' or intermediate groups of countries soon become outdated. As the EC Commission report (1992) points out, the lower rates of workforce participation among women in southern Europe (and in some northern European countries such as Ireland and Belgium) are based on traditions which are rapidly eroding.

Many women in Japan, though, are still bound by such traditional expectations. They usually leave paid employment by the age of 30, irrespective of education levels. As Whitehill notes, an Equal Employment Opportunity law (1986) exists in Japan but it does not require employers to take on greater numbers of women. Even after completing university education women are 'on a different track to men' and are still widely regarded by them as '*shokuba no hana*, or office flowers' (1991: 71). Consequently women who do return to work after a spell of full-time child care do so in the knowledge that they will be steered into low-paid and less skilled employment. In Europe, on the other hand, the evidence reviewed by the EC Commission shows that the typical patterns of the past are already being much modified. Activity rates among younger generations of women in formerly low-participation countries (for example, Greece, Spain) are rising rapidly (1992: 128).

Part-time work

Along with availability of child care facilities, taxation policy and other influences, part-time work is highly significant in some countries in explaining why women take the employment they do, and what they achieve from it relative to men.

However, it is highly important not to generalise from the British case by assuming that part-time work is of growing significance everywhere. Britain and the Netherlands stand out as European countries in which part-time work among women is common (Commission of the EC, 1992: 142). Britain alone has a third of all European Community women working part-time, while the

Table 4.3   Part-time work among women and men in Europe (1991)

	Part-time work as % of all women/men in employment		% of part-time workers who are women
	Women	Men	
Netherlands	58	15	70
UK	44	6	86
Denmark	42	9	79
Germany	31	2	91
France	24	3	84
Belgium	23	2	87
Ireland	17	4	68
Luxembourg	15	2	81
Portugal	11	4	67
Greece	10	3	66
Italy	10	3	63
Europe 12	28	4	82
Sweden[a]	45	8	—

Sources: Eurostat (1992: 62–3); [a] Statistics Sweden (SCB) (1992: 38).

Netherlands, which accounts for only 4 per cent of the total Community workforce, has proportionately four times as many part-timers (men and women).

With the exception of France, where relatively high proportions of women are in paid employment *and* a substantial majority work full-time, countries which have a higher proportion of women in work also have larger proportions of part-time workers. On the other hand, countries which have had historically low proportions of women in paid employment, such as Spain, Italy and Greece, also have relatively few women in part-time jobs. And even though the proportions of women workers in the southern European countries are increasing, the role of part-time work, already small, has declined even further. As the EC Commission concludes, 'there is, therefore, little sign of any convergence in the relative importance of part-time working across the community' (1992: 143).

Contrasts are also evident between the United States and Britain, and these two cases point to some of the reasons for higher rates of part-time work in some countries as opposed to others. Dex and Shaw (1986: 25) found part-time work (less than 35 hours a week) was approximately half as frequent among American women compared to British women (working less than 30 hours a week) in a range of age groups.

Neither country has much publicly supported child care or nursery provision so it is not possible to say that American women work full-time far more often because they can depend on such subsidised facilities. In both countries women with children in paid work have to rely on family support a great deal. However, Dex and Shaw found that there are differences between the Americans and the British in the nature of family support available: for example, between a quarter and a third of British male partners/fathers provide some care for school-age children when the mother works, while the proportion of American male partners who do this is much lower (Dex and Shaw, 1986: 37).

American parents are more likely to depend on other relatives and, outside school hours, upon older children to look after younger children. As the divorce and separation rate has continued to climb in Britain, though, an increasing proportion of British women are also faced with the task of making complicated care arrangements for their children with grandparents, other relatives or friends. Themes in film and drama about 'home alone' children, and the wide publicity given to cases of very young children who have been left unattended while their mothers are at work, highlight a shared preoccupation on both sides of the Atlantic about child care and the roles of men and women at work and in the home.

In neither the United States nor Britain have public policies done much to erode the widespread assumption that it is the woman's role both to take responsibility for child care arrangements and to tailor her career or pattern of working hours to those arrangements. However, there are some major differences between the two countries in terms of taxation policy and Dex and Shaw conclude that, among other things, these affect both demand for and supply of part-time jobs, and account for the higher proportion of American women in full-time work.

First, tax relief on private child care expenses or private nursery care makes it financially worthwhile for many American women to return to work earlier after the birth of their first child and to work full-time, as compared with British women. In Britain, employers have been given certain tax advantages if they provide child care facilities, but this is not equivalent to giving a direct or first-hand incentive to the parent.

Second, American employers are liable to pay Social Security and unemployment insurance taxes for their employees up to a given ceiling, and according to Dex and Shaw this means that 'it is cheaper to hire one person whose earnings exceed the ceiling than to hire two part-time people. . .and pay both of them less than the ceiling' (1986: 13). In Britain, on the other hand, disincentives to employ part-time workers were traditionally not so evident. Before 1977, when employment protection was extended to part-time workers employed for 16 hours or more per week, British employers could avoid paying insurance contributions and fringe benefits to part-time workers, and this helped to establish an earlier British trend towards low-paid part-time work.

Even though British employers may now pay as much, or even more, in national insurance contributions for two part-time workers compared with one full-time, the part-time workers must be on an equivalent wage level to a full-time worker for this to be required. As Cohen and Borrill report (1993), a rising proportion of part-time jobs are at the lower end of pay scales. Evidently British employers still find it economic to hire part-time workers, though recent changes in the law (from 1995) may begin to affect employer attitudes.

Earlier, the Equal Opportunities Commission (EOC) had brought a case against the government on the grounds that lack of protection for part-timers discriminated against women. A Law Lords judgment in 1994 upheld the EOC's view; lack of protection for British part-time workers contravened European laws on equal treatment of men and women (see Chapter 2). As a result of government acceptance of this ruling, 'at least 750,000 part-time workers who have had their jobs for more than two years stand to benefit immediately' (Milne et al., 1994: 1). They will receive the same protection as full-timers from unfair dismissal and redundancy, though other issues such as holidays and sickness pay have still to be resolved.

It remains to be seen whether equality measures for part-timers will reduce the supply of jobs, though it seems likely that two factors will continue to keep the rate of part-time work relatively high in Britain: first, the underlying changes in employment patterns in a post-modern society discussed in Chapter 2 and secondly, the limited nature of recent (1995) plans for the expansion of British nursery and child care provision (based on a nursery places voucher scheme). Large numbers of British women will continue to search for paid work which can be reconciled with child care commitments.

By contrast, French women have experienced the gradual development of widespread subsidised child care facilities. These are often provided by municipalities or other local authorities, though nurseries, crèches and other facilities are also provided in the voluntary sector as well as by employers and by private organisations. One way or another, most French women can now count on the availability of child care for children over 18 months of age to the extent that they can return to full-time employment if they wish. As Table 4.3 showed, less than a quarter of employed women in France work part-time, about half the British rate.

Provision of child care in itself, however, does not necessarily result in the 'French' outcome of a relatively high rate of full-time paid employment among women. As the case of Sweden shows, an exceptionally comprehensive system of subsidised child care, combined with other important benefits such as paid parental leave, may be associated with a high proportion of *part*-time working among women. To understand this we must remember the importance of economic incentives to work either full-time or part-time, taxation and its impact on single parents or couples, as well as employment conditions for part-time workers.

In Sweden, almost all the increase in women's paid employment between the mid-1960s and the 1980s was in part-time work. The proportion of women in full-time work increased by only a few per cent (Gustafsson and Jacobsson, 1985). As Gustafsson and Jacobsson show, men's wages grew relatively slowly in real terms during this period whereas women's incomes from paid work increased appreciably faster. Thus whatever social or cultural factors were influencing women's decisions to take up paid work, the economic background was one which increasingly made it more profitable for women to do so. Indeed, the relatively high cost of living in Sweden, combined with high rates of direct tax, often make a dual income a necessity for families.

Separate taxation of each partner's/spouse's wage income, compulsory in Sweden from 1971 on, increased the incentive to Swedish women to enter paid employment. Gustafsson and Jacobsson point out that the 'average' couple may benefit more, under the Swedish tax rules, if both partners work full-time. However, much depends on other factors such as the number of children a couple has. When day care needs for children are worked out, together with the advantages of subsidised nurseries or other facilities, generous parental leave benefits from the state (see below) and flexible working arrangements by employers, the incentives to work part-time can easily outweigh full-time paid work. Most Swedish women work 'long' part-time (over 24 hours per week) and this means that their earnings are relatively high. By contrast, Dex and Shaw found that almost a third of British women work less than 20 hours a week, and they form a substantial group of low-paid workers.

Work–family policies: outcomes

As we have already seen, a nation's policies in relation to provision of child care have important effects on gender equality at work and the pattern of employment among women, though these effects vary, as the examples of France and Sweden show, and depend on economic and social factors in each country. The same may be said of benefits for parents who are in employment and wish to return to work after the birth of a child. These benefits cover a range: payments and reinstatement rights targeted at mothers (such as statutory maternity allowance in the United Kingdom), shared parental leave, as in Sweden, and other policies and measures such as paid leave to look after a sick child, or career break schemes run by employers. They are best seen as 'work–family' policies in that they bridge paid employment and the home and are specifically concerned with protecting people from loss of earnings or opportunities which may result from family or child care responsibilities. Child benefit and other forms of 'family' policy or support are not considered in detail here, though they form an important part of the background to employment opportunities.

Work–family benefits and policies vary in scale and scope from country to country and have a range of effects on employment among women and men. Nevertheless the example of Sweden seems to bear out the proposition that sizeable benefits from social insurance, coupled with widespread public provision of child day care, may serve to reinforce gender divisions in certain respects as well as reducing them in others. Swedish women have yet to take

Summary of parental benefits/work–family policies in selected European countries

Policy/benefits	Period covered	Amount
Sweden		
Paid parental leave: may be shared equally, taken in one or several blocks up to age of 8 for each child	18 months	90% of earnings
Pregnancy leave	50 days	90% of earnings
Parent's right to work a 6-hour day	Up to age of 12 of child	—
Father's leave after childbirth	10 days	90% of earnings
Leave to care for sick child, or for child if caregiver is ill	90 days per year	90% of earnings
Leave to visit child's school	2 days per year	90% of earnings
UK		
Maternity allowance/benefit	10 months, of which 11 weeks before childbirth	90% of earnings for 6 weeks only; 12 weeks at low flat rate; no compensation for remainder
Germany		
Maternity benefit	6 weeks before, 8 weeks after birth	100% of earnings
Parental leave allowance	18 months	Low fixed amount for 6 months; means-tested for remainder
France		
Maternity benefit	6 weeks before, 10 weeks after birth	84% of earnings
Parental leave/reinstatement rights	3 years	Leave without pay
Italy		
Maternity allowance (commerce and industry sector)	2 months before, 3 months after birth	80% of earnings
Parental leave allowance	6 months	30% of earnings

Sources: Statistics Sweden (SCB) (1992: 27); Rapoport and Moss (1990: 12–18).

up an increasing or equal role in terms of full-time paid employment.

However, it is important to consider the Swedish case in more detail and to be aware of the positive effects of Swedish policies. Their value is perhaps best appreciated by considering them in the European context. Comparisons underline how far European countries are from a standardised approach to parental benefits and, in particular, how little has been done in Britain, given that the United Kingdom is a 'medium spender' on social security and social protection as a whole (Eurostat, 1992: 82).

The summarised information on parental benefits shows only the bare bones of what can be expected in each country; not only may there be additional benefits not mentioned here (for example, in France there is a means-tested benefit for assisting single parents for a restricted period) but more importantly the framework of policy or legislation tells us nothing about outcomes or what use women and men make of the available benefits. For instance the Swedes have found that in practice parents tend to take less leave than they are entitled to (Rapoport and Moss, 1990: 13), though the benefit itself is popular and almost all families with children have made some use of it. However, it has also been found that fathers make much less use of parental leave than mothers even though there are equal rights to the entitlement and no significant financial disincentives.

Swedish policy stopped short of introducing a quota system to require parents to share parental leave. According to Rapoport and Moss, stress was to be put upon 'educational, counselling and other programmes to encourage men to take leave' (1990: 15). Though a previous centre-right government has recently been replaced by a social democrat-led administration, there is still doubt about whether even this policy will be given much priority. Thus the Swedish approach stopped short of a completely 'social structural' attempt to restructure gender roles in a fundamental way.

This is also illustrated by the implementation of the right of parents to work a 6-hour day. It is more often the mothers who take up this right and, according to evidence quoted by Rapoport and Moss, it has had the effect of sharply reducing the average time infants and young children spend in municipal nurseries. A benefit which is meant to be equally shared by mothers and fathers is having the effect of subtly confirming the mother's role as a carer at home.

Having said that, it would be wrong to dismiss the genuine changes in attitudes towards gender roles achieved by Swedish policies. Their advances are all the more evident in comparison with Britain, where shared parental leave has been absent from the national policy agenda.

Paternity leave became something of a public issue in 1994, when a European Union policy to phase it in was adopted (in 1994 only 4 of the 12 European member states provided paternity leave as a statutory right). However, as the United Kingdom has opted out of post-Maastricht social legislation in Europe, there is no legal right to paternity leave in Britain (EOR, 1994c: 14).

Paternity leave should not be confused with the broader concept of shared parental leave, which in its Swedish form carries connotations of shared child care and the possibility of parents deciding how to divide between them the time to be spent on looking after their children. Paternity leave may be 'strictly defined as a period of leave to be taken by a father at or near the time of childbirth', though 'some employers . . . include not only the father but any carer nominated by the mother' (EOR, 1994c: 14).

A majority of major British employers have some arrangements for paternity leave; some also operate career break schemes for mothers and provide child care facilities and other assistance to parent employees. But these schemes are often designed to retain women with 'management potential' or at least employees in whom training investment has been made. They are also built on the 'role-related' model and rarely assume that fathers will take up parental leave. Even if they do, however, British men tend not to make demands on the existing schemes; this suggests that, as in Sweden, any improvement in statutory rights to paternity leave will not be fully taken up or enthusiastically received by a majority of men. Phillips (1994) reports that

> employees of Shell, for example, can be visited at home by a childcare adviser employed by the company, who will help them make arrangements and, if necessary, monitor them too. However, although only 17 per cent of Shell employees are women, over 80 per cent of inquiries to the advice service come from women. (1994: 15)

Britain is far from alone in this respect, however. As Rapoport and Moss conclude, 'where parental leave exists, it is either unpaid or paid at a low flat-rate with no entitlement to take it part-time and little or no commitment to encouraging take-up by fathers' (1990: 18).

While work–family policies may subtly reinforce gender roles, though, they may in spite of that have positive outcomes in improving women's opportunities to return to work and of compensating them to some extent for absences as a result of childrearing. Evidence in Britain, for example, shows that retention rates of women employees improve markedly once career break schemes are introduced, and although it is too early to draw firm conclusions about the degree of 're-entry' difficulty women returners experience (for example, keeping up with new working practices, or not being considered for promotion), Rapoport and Moss found relatively few problems in a sample of UK companies operating career break schemes.

Occupational segregation

'Segregation' suggests complete separation, whereas the actual distribution of men and women in the workforce is one in which each gender tends to predominate in different sectors and subsectors. However, using the term loosely observers have found that segregation has been increasing since the 1970s in Britain, Sweden, Germany and in other industrial economies, though not in the United States (see for example Jonung, 1984). Occupational segregation by gender is mostly an outcome of:

- Underlying changes in the labour market, in particular the growth of the service sector.
- 'Push' factors (direct sex discrimination).
- 'Pull' factors (expectations of certain jobs by each gender; subtle reinforcement of sex-stereotyped career choices).

Increases in occupational segregation seem to be happening in some countries irrespective of attempts to reduce it, for example by trying to change boys' and girls' career aspirations while they are at school or by incentive schemes to employers which aim to encourage them to employ greater numbers of the underrepresented sex. In fact there is an argument, as we have already seen, that certain 'equality' policies may be adding to occupational segregation rather than reducing it.

Table 4.4   Employment sectors: the growth of services (percentages)

| | Total employment by sector | | | | | |
| | Services | | Industry | | Agriculture | |
	1958	1989	1958	1989	1958	1989
EC (12)	39	61	42	32	19	7
USA	58	71	34	26	8	3
Japan	40	51	27	34	33	15

Source: Commission of the EC, Eurostat 6-7/1991, adapted from table on p. 19.

Recent outcomes may be summarised as follows. First, most new jobs over the past 20 years have been created in the service sector as industry and agriculture have declined relatively. Japan is an interesting exception: there, both industry and service sectors have grown relative to agriculture (see Table 4.4).

Occupational segregation cannot be understood without reference to the profound change towards service employment because most service sector jobs have been taken by women; the number of women working in services in Europe, for example, 'has grown consistently at around twice the rate for men' (Commission of the EC, 1992: 136). As the Commission notes, this is not unconnected in many cases with the tendency to expect women to work for lower wages than men and in some countries to work part-time in the service sector. By 1990, in the EC as a whole, three-quarters of all women in paid employment worked in the service sector and only a fifth in industry, compared with just over half of all employed men in services and over two-fifths in industry.

Secondly, while women's employment is increasingly concentrated in the service sector, men's employment is more evenly distributed. As the Commission of the EC notes, 'most of the sectors which are the most important employers of women are also major employers of men' (1992: 139). This is why the term 'occupational segregation' can be misleading. To illustrate, the distribution of British men and women in the main labour market sectors is shown in Table 4.5.

There are, as the Commission also shows, some subsectors such as health services where women employees vastly outnumber men, but it must be remembered that in the service sector as a whole there are considerable numbers of male employees.

Table 4.5 Employees in the United Kingdom by gender and employment sector (percentages)

Sector	Women		Men	
	1981	1993	1981	1993
Manufacturing, energy, agriculture, etc.	21	14	43	32
Distribution, hotels and catering, etc.	24	24	15	19
Banking, finance, insurance, etc.	9	13	7	12
Public administration and other services	41	45	18	21
Other (construction, transport, communication)	5	4	17	16
Total	100	100	100	100

Notes: Percentages have been rounded and are of all employees in employment. 'Employment sector' refers to the authors' own groupings of the Standard Industrial Classification categories cited in source.
Source: Central Statistical Office (1994b: 72–3), adapted from Table 5.7.

Thirdly, many of the new jobs entered by women in the 1970s and 1980s were in particular occupations *within* the service sector. This was particularly evident in Sweden, where public sector employment continued to grow significantly during the period and provided jobs in education (including nursery and pre-school education), health and social services. While these trends are particularly marked in Sweden, however, they are also evident in other industrial economies. In addition to concentration in public sector occupations, we also find that women are concentrated in certain private sector service industries such as retailing. In six EC states (the United Kingdom, Denmark, Germany, France, Spain and Belgium), over half of all employed women in 1990 were to be found in just 6 out of 58 subsectors of the labour market: in retailing; health services; education; public administration; social and cultural services; and in banking, finance and insurance (Commission of the EC, 1992: 139).

The above outcomes indicate that in most industrial countries a sharp division of labour between women and men persists in the labour market as well as in the way domestic and paid work are shared. It may be called horizontal segregation in that it may not in itself indicate inequality, or vertical segregation. However, as we point out below, horizontal segregation does have implications for pay differentials between women and men.

Thus a key theory to explain occupational segregation is that it is one way in which discrimination against women can be perpetuated once principles of equal pay for equal work have been established in law (Persson, 1990: 243). The more feminised occupations tend to attract lower wages, on average, than the more masculinised occupations to which entry is more difficult for women, for a variety of reasons.

This hypothesis can be challenged by the example of Sweden, though this is not to say that it cannot provide some explanation for occupational segregation in other countries. In Sweden, however, pay differentials between men and women have been progressively narrowed so that they are now among the smallest in the industrial world (see below). An alternative hypothesis therefore is that occupational segregation is strengthened because 'the economic incentives for Swedish women to make unconventional occupational choices and overcome. . .the difficulties of working in male-dominated occupations are weak' (Persson, 1990: 243).

This latter explanation can only be taken so far, even in Sweden, because although pay differentials between men and women have been reduced, they still exist and may begin to widen again in the future. However, there may be some truth in the theory that, as women tend to be socialised to expect to work in feminised occupations (such as those involving care work), greater wage equality between men and women will tend to relatively strengthen, not weaken, the influence of such social expectations and gender roles. Women are more prepared to work for slightly lower pay in a feminised occupation.

As we have seen, the growth of the service sector over the past 20 years has meant that increasing numbers of women could enter the labour market without directly competing with men for jobs. As the Commission of the EC (1992) points out in relation to Europe, and as Table 4.5 shows in relation to Britain, both men and women have lost work in industry and agriculture in roughly equal proportions. Women have not been *replacing* men in industry, at least not in any great numbers.

This has important policy lessons, because it has been found in Sweden that measures to encourage a more representative gender balance in certain occupations meet with varying success. Ruggie

(1984) reports on pilot schemes which added on jobs by subsidising private sector employers who were prepared to employ more women in 'non-traditional' areas of work. These met with more success than other schemes which appeared to threaten 'male' jobs. However, if as a result of economic retrenchment there are restrictions on such subsidies it will prove to be increasingly difficult to improve equal opportunities in the former, 'easier' way. Only tough or maximalist policies are likely to make much difference to a strengthening trend towards occupational segregation, but these are the more politically sensitive and socially questioned policies.

The glass ceiling and the stone floor

These images illustrate how on the one hand women experience 'invisible' forms of discrimination when they approach the higher levels of management and the professions, and on the other how a larger group of women are left on the low-wage employment floor with little prospect of lifting themselves above it.

In order to give a sense of how many women and men are in higher, lower and intermediate positions in the British employment market, Table 4.6 compares the situation in 1975 (when sex equality legislation was introduced or implemented) with more recent times. Table 4.7 shows how longer-term changes have occurred in women's positions in the British labour market. For example, Halsey (1988) points out how the proportion of women in managerial, supervisory and professional jobs rose in the late twentieth century, though there is still marked under-representation. Also, while the proportion of women in manual work remained remarkably constant between 1911 and 1981, the proportions in clerical and sales work boomed as these occupations became feminised.

The glass ceiling and stone floor illustrate a fundamental dilemma of equal opportunities policy: if policies are directed to one group, do they inevitably lead to the neglect of the other? Can equal opportunities policies benefit both 'upper' and 'lower' social class groups of women? This dilemma is well expressed by Coyle, who points out in a review of equal opportunities policies in local government that

Table 4.6 Occupational positions of women and men in Great Britain, 1975 and 1991 (percentages)

Socio-economic group[1]	1975		1991	
	Women	Men	Women	Men
Professional	1	5	1	7
Employers and managers	4	15	9	19
Intermediate; junior non-manual	46	17	48	17
Skilled manual, etc.	9	41	9	38
Semi-skilled manual, etc.	31	17	22	14
Unskilled manual	9	5	11	5
Total	100	100	100	100

Note: [1] The socio-economic group is based on the informant's own job (or last job if not in employment). Those who are in the Armed Forces or who have never worked are excluded.
Source: OPCS (1993) General Household Survey, adapted from Table 5.6, p. 91.

Table 4.7 Women workers in major occupational groups in Great Britain, 1911–81 (percentages)

Occupational group	1911	1931	1961	1981
Managers	20	13	16	21
Higher professionals	6	8	10	13
Lower professionals and technicians	63	59	51	55
Forepersons and inspectors	4	9	10	24
Clerical and related	21	46	65	78
Sales employees	35	29	55	78
All non-manual	30	36	45	43
All manual workers	31	29	26	29

Source: Halsey (1988: 166, adapted from Table 4.2).
Reproduced with permission of Macmillan Ltd.

Women are not an homogeneous group; their interests and needs are not the same. The concerns of manual women workers are the exploitation of low pay and part-time working, and they cannot always share the concerns of women in higher grades, who are seemingly better off. Black and white women may both be disadvantaged but the experience of disadvantage is different . . . (1989: 47)

While it is often suggested that the impact of equal opportunities policies is greater upon women in the higher grades or in managerial positions, the example of Sweden is interesting in that it appears to show the opposite. Sweden's traditional emphasis on improving conditions for the mass of working women and encouraging gender equality has resulted, as Persson concludes, in a broad-based positive outcome for women as a whole. However, there appears to be a 'basic contradiction between a positive equal status *mass* outcome and a positive equal status *elite* outcome' (1990: 243).

A system which creates a positive outcome for the majority must be one in which there are narrowing wage differentials between higher and lower job positions. At the same time there must be relatively high taxes and social insurance contributions to pay for the facilities which bring this greater equality. These things act as disincentives against career striving and, Persson points out, often make the cost of pursuing a career to a higher level greater. In the United States, by contrast, Dex and Shaw's review of the effects of equal opportunities legislation and policy shows that 'the largest impact has probably been on opening up more managerial and professional jobs for women' (1986: 19).

The contrast between equality outcomes in Sweden and the United States illustrates the significance of underlying social values and the broad political and legislative framework in which equal opportunities policies exist. In the United States it would have been impossible to have achieved the narrowing of wage differentials which were engineered in Sweden during its heyday of social democracy, because the United States has many non-unionised workers and no equivalent corporatist or centralised machinery for wage agreements.

However, the United States does have one of the world's toughest sets of laws on gender equality in terms of recruitment, training and promotion. As a result of anti-discrimination laws combining with a more individualistic success ethos than exists in Sweden and other parts of Europe, it is perhaps less surprising that American managerial and professional women have gained more from equality policies than their lower-paid or working-class counterparts.

For example, Dex and Shaw cite research which examined the effects of federal contract compliance programmes: the equality targets and requirements which have to be met by firms which obtain contracts with the federal government. In one study, firms with and without federal contracts were compared, thus isolating the effects of one particular equality measure (though all firms would have been subject to other equality legislation such as Title VII (see Chapter 2)). It was found that women in firms with federal contracts had a significantly greater increase in upward occupational status than those in firms without contracts. However, there were no changes in outcome among manual or 'blue-collar' women workers.

Dex and Shaw mention other studies which confirm that other affirmative action policies in the United States tend to have the same differential effects on women workers as federal contract compliance. For example, one company survey found that most 'improved' equality procedures for recruitment and promotion were targeted at women destined for managerial positions.

Despite these findings not all the effects of US equal opportunities policies are effective only among higher ranks of women employees. Dex and Shaw also mention the wider effects of American equal opportunities legislation on the employment 'climate' and on general attitudes: for example in relation to training, especially for younger women workers, and a growing attitude among American women that they have the right and ability to enter non-traditional areas of work. It will be recalled that the United States is something of an exception in not experiencing increases in occupational segregation.

Thus American gender equality policies may not have resulted in an overwhelming rise in opportunities. Dex and Shaw, among others, are cautious about outcomes for women in the United States. However, even equality strategies aimed at managerial levels could conceivably act as a model for developing equal opportunities programmes lower down the occupational ladder, as well as being something of a gain for managerial American women.

Comparison between the United States and Britain underlines this point. British women in managerial, technical and professional occupations are not doing as well as is often claimed in popular media reports or as perceived in the public imagination. Perhaps this is because women's increasing access to managerial and professional jobs in the 1980s has been confused with equalisation with men.

A study by Gregg and Machin of top executives and managers shows 'no evidence that the glass ceiling is cracking in corporate Britain' (1993: 18). Using the British Institute of Management salary survey from 1989 to 1992, Gregg and Machin analysed promotion and pay differences among 29 000 men and women in over 500 firms. They discovered that in this large sample, only 8 per cent of senior executives were women. Although women are better represented at lower and middle levels of management, it would be a mistake to assume that in time greater numbers will be promoted to the senior or top positions. Following their sample through time showed that women in middle and lower management levels are leapfrogged by men, and that this seems to occur even when the effects of men's and women's ages and type of firm are controlled for.

Even when women do reach senior positions they are paid between 6 to 8 per cent less than their male counterparts (Gregg and Machin, 1993: 18). This pay differential is an example of direct discrimination in that it reflects the gap between men and women who are in similar positions. On average, according to Gregg and Machin, women executives are paid 30 per cent less than men in executive positions – but the 6 to 8 per cent gap remains after the effects of job function and type of firm are removed.

These findings are a reflection of what has been happening in the private sector and at the top levels of 'corporate Britain'. It would be wrong to generalise from this and to assume that exactly similar trends are occurring in other employment sectors. For example, women's advances into the civil service, teaching and other professions were strong in the 1980s (Chote, 1994).

However, there are also other points to remember about these gains in opportunities: first, according to Chote, women moved into civil service and teaching jobs at a time when middle-class men were moving into comparable jobs that were better paid. Thus there was an 'escalator' effect and, while middle-class women moved up as well as men, their relative positions did not change much. The second point to remember is that women may have advanced in jobs in which they can apply their individual expertise as practitioners (for example in law, medicine, social work), but much less so in the management of their professions. In this there is a parallel with the private sector: women are still greatly underrepresented in the highest positions which strategically determine employment policy or the control of resources.

Women are also underrepresented in a considerable number of middle management positions. For example, in education it is still the case that women comprise the bulk of the profession (four-fifths) but hold fewer than half the headships of schools and two-thirds of deputy positions (Miekle and Redwood, 1994).

A similar pattern has emerged in another public sector institution in which women predominate numerically, the National Health Service. Summarising the evidence on inequality in management and supervisory positions in the NHS, Harding shows that it is mainly sex discrimination rather than discrepancies in either skill levels or qualifications which accounts for the imposition of 'a male career structure upon a female workforce' (1989: 51). As in education, there is little evidence of direct or overt discrimination in the sense that women are openly directed into lower-status career paths. However, women are disadvantaged in the NHS as a result of the ways in which full-time working is valued in comparison to part-time, the assumption that pregnancy is a major cause of wastage of women scientific workers (when it is not) and the lack of any specific policies to challenge existing recruitment and promotion practices.

Wages and equal pay

Our discussion has focused on outcomes as far as the occupational positions of women and men are concerned. However, pay inequalities, and the impact of equality policies on pay, are no less important and add to the picture of vertical inequalities.

As so many of the jobs created in recent years have been part-time and for low pay, especially in Britain, the dismantling of minimum wage protection is highly significant for equal opportunities. Wages councils (bodies originally created to set minimum hourly rates) had never fully succeeded in eradicating low pay or guaranteeing the use of bargaining mechanisms between employees and employers which would have improved wages (Glucklich, 1984). However, their abolition was regretted by the Equal Opportunities Commission because a minimum wage policy represented one way of maintaining some pay equality between men and women (Cohen and Borrill, 1993).

Table 4.8   Women's wages as a percentage of men's (hourly wages of manufacturing workers)

	1970	1980	1990
Increased gender gap in earnings in the 1980s			
Denmark	74	86	85
Ireland	56	69	68
Netherlands	72	80	75
UK	58	69	68
Sweden	80	90	89
Narrowed gender gap in earnings in the 1980s			
Belgium	68	70	76
West Germany	70	73	73
Greece	68	68	76

Source: Statistics Sweden (SCB) (1992: 47).

Erosion of the value of wages among the low-paid shows that we cannot assume gradual progress in women's relative earnings. In fact the improvements for women as a whole that were evident in the 1970s and the early 1980s have not been sustained in Britain and certain other European countries, if one takes earnings in manufacturing industry as a guide (see Table 4.8). Manufacturing employs only a relatively small proportion of women workers but, in a Europe-wide survey of other employment sectors, the Commission of the EC concluded that there is 'no uniform tendency for the pay gap between men and women to close over the recent past' (1992: 153).

In the sector most important for women, services, there are serious shortcomings in the data available, and it is difficult to make comparisons between women and men in public sector services. However, in private sector services (for example retail distribution, banking and insurance) there were two discernible patterns: one is a tendency for Britain to have the largest pay gap between men and women when compared with other European countries. In retailing, for example, British women earned 60 per cent of men's wages, compared with an average of between 65 and 70 per cent in other European countries and 80 per cent in Greece. Taking all non-manual work categories, Britain again had the largest pay gap at less than 60 per cent of men's earnings (Commission of the EC, 1992: 151).

Pay disparities tend to be higher in non-manual work than in manual employment, and it is true to say that these disparities have narrowed slightly in Europe recently, but these trends have not been strong enough to make a significant difference to gender inequality in pay as a whole.

Why has the gender gap in pay not continued to narrow, at least in some countries such as Britain, and why have equality policies not had the success that some once hoped for? Answers to these questions depend partly on the type of work or sector of employment in question, but it is possible to pick out some important and wide-ranging reasons:

(1) *Occupational segregation.* The Commission of the EC suggests that, where women's relative wages *have* improved, this may reflect switches of significant numbers from one set of occupations to other better-paid areas of work as much as any effect of equal opportunities policy or incomes policy. Earnings tend to stagnate in some industries (for example clothing and footwear) but rise in others. However, as we have already seen, there is a continuing tendency for women to be concentrated in jobs where their skills are undervalued. Occupational segregation tends to confirm traditional assumptions about the higher value of skills used in employment where men predominate, whereas traditionally 'female' skills are given a lower economic value (whether they are demonstrated by men or women).

Sweden is an interesting exception because, for a time, increasing occupational segregation was accompanied by a narrowing wage differential between women and men. Gustafsson and Jacobsson (1985) suggest that Sweden's 'solidaristic' wage policies help to account for this but, now that the former centralised style of making national wage agreements has been abandoned, Swedish women are exposed to a greater risk of widening pay disparities. At the same time, threatened reductions in welfare spending have begun to erode both the number of public sector jobs upon which so many Swedish women have depended, and the pay and conditions attached to such jobs.

(2) *The occupational hierarchy.* There have been significant changes in the employment market in the twentieth century and some gains for women in terms of their position in the labour force: an increasing number have risen to managerial positions,

for example (see Table 4.6). As we have seen, however, women are still subject to forms of discrimination which result in two kinds of outcome: either they are 'passed over' for promotion and experience greater barriers than men in their careers, thus depressing their pay relative to men, or even if they reach similar positions their pay may be set at a lower level than for their male counterparts.

(3) *The 'failure' of equal pay and equal value legislation.* The word 'failure' is used advisedly because, as we suggested earlier, the impact of equality legislation on pay is a matter of debate. Though commentators such as Sloane and Jain (1989) argued that earlier rises in women's pay occurred for other reasons than equality legislation, and usually predated such legislation, others (for example Dex and Shaw, 1986) suggest inconclusive results in Britain and moderate positive gains to women's earnings in the United States as a result of equal pay laws.

Glucklich maintained that although the Equal Pay Act and Sex Discrimination Act had not achieved pay equality in Britain, 'it does appear to have had some impact'. Quoting a rise in women's hourly average earnings from 63 per cent (1970) to 75 per cent (1977), an improvement that was later eroded somewhat, she adds that this 'considerable' and 'sometimes dramatic narrowing of differentials' can be considered 'to be greater than could be attributed solely to the pay policy which was in operation at the time' (1984: 108). Also, the law is not static: laws which have a protective effect on women's wages (such as minimum wage legislation in Britain) may be amended or withdrawn, while others – for example European laws – may be toughened.

Having said this, it is possible to identify some major flaws in earlier legislation on equal pay and consequently some of the causes of disappointing outcomes. For example, taking Britain's Equal Pay Act (1970, implemented from 1975) and the earlier (1963) Equal Pay Act in the United States, it is not surprising that they had a limited impact. Neither dealt satisfactorily with industries or occupations which were staffed predominantly by women and in which there were too few men to base comparisons upon. And in both cases it was possible for employers to evade legislation by re-grading or reclassifying work so that women found themselves more often in lower-paid positions than men. Thus there is evidence that employers' reactions to equal pay legislation quickened the rate of job segregation between women and men.

In Britain, this process was achieved in the face of mere token resistance from trade unions, according to Glucklich (1984), and a failure of political will on the part of government to make pay equality a central issue. In Sweden, by contrast, there had long been cross-party consensus on the need to make progress towards equal pay a priority.

Following the first phase of equal pay legislation in Britain and the United States, the legal context has changed in both countries. In the United States the debate has now shifted towards 'comparable worth' and in some respects the laws governing equal treatment and equal pay have been strengthened.

In Britain, the earlier legislation on equal pay was found not to fulfil the requirements of European law in the form of the 1975 Equal Pay Directive (for a fuller discussion and reminder of the issues, see Chapter 2). The European Court of Justice ruled that Britain's Equal Pay Act was inadequate because it was based on the narrow notion that the only permissible comparisons were between men and women performing the same jobs. As a result, the British government was compelled to change the law and to recognise the principle of equal value: from 1984, when the amended Pay Act was introduced, it was possible to make a case that one should be paid an equivalent wage (and other benefits such as pension contributions) to others performing work 'to which equal value is attributed'.

In practice, the outcomes of the amended British legislation have also been disappointing. A number of reasons have been identified for this. Some reflect earlier problems with the first Equal Pay Act; others present more recent difficulties:

■ Pressures on those making pay equality claims to withdraw. These may be exerted not only by employers, who may resort either to victimisation or to making token pay rises, but also by work-mates or colleagues who may fear redundancy or plant closure, or who wish to retain existing pay differentials. For instance, Maxwell (1989) documents the intense pressure put upon data processing clerks by their colleagues, friends and neighbours in an economically depressed part of Northern Ireland when this small group lodged a pay equality case.

■ The time taken to review and adjudicate upon equal pay cases. This is to some extent unavoidable, as the work of independent experts (who are required under the revised British law to assess pay equality claims) must be thorough. However, an independent expert's report may not appear for 12 months or more from the date an industrial tribunal commissions it. To this time must be added lengthy judicial processes. A number of commentators have suggested that British law has been deliberately designed to create ambiguity and increase possibilities for appeal and delay by employers. Writing *five years* after the introduction of equal value legislation, Maxwell for example noted that in Northern Ireland '*no single case* has been *finally* resolved by the judicial process' (1989: 297).

■ 'Class actions' are not permissible. Unlike the American case, the revised British legislation on equal pay did not formally permit tribunals or courts to hear cases put forward by groups of employees. In practice, individual claims are highly significant to whole categories of employees but they can only be dealt with *as* individual cases. This is limiting because it prevents a tribunal or court from considering a a pattern of discrimination in one workplace, or comparing anomalies between a wider range of individuals.

■ The legislation may still be inadequate for workers in small firms, or for those who work at home or on a part-time or casual basis. Though recognition of equal value for comparable work was a step forward in Britain, comparisons may still only be made with men who work for the same employer (though comparisons may be made with other branches of the same company as long as conditions of work are similar). Thus there are still problems for some women in making legally acceptable comparisons. If they work in small firms where the workforce is predominantly female, there will be a lack of male comparators.

Conclusion

Despite the mixed fortunes of the movement towards equality between women and men at work, it would be wrong to be too pessimistic about the outcomes of equality policies and legislation. Sharp inequalities remain, but there have been at least some noticeable gains: for example, some of the more blatant forms of sex discrimination and gender stereotyping have been eliminated or at least reduced as a result of the Sex Discrimination Act in Britain and similar anti-discriminatory laws elsewhere.

Developments in European law have perhaps done more than anything else in Britain to create a climate in which women's equality is taken more seriously than it was before. Whether grudgingly or not, employers and opinion-formers in Britain have been forced to admit that certain traditional attitudes have to change. And though legal strategies have limitations, European law can give a positive status and a sense of approval to the idea that it is right to try to increase equality between men and women. As Maxwell (1989) notes, judicial delay in Britain on equality issues increases the extent to which claimants seek justice from European law and the European Court of Justice.

European laws and Equal Treatment Directives now cover a wide area of employment-related concerns such as the rights of part-time workers who are covered by laws to safeguard equal hourly rates of pay and comparable pension schemes. More generally, European laws have extended rights to equal treatment in training and education, promotion, social security and retirement ages.

Meehan suggests that gender equality was given 'pride of place' in the phase of social policy development which took place in the European Community during the 1970s and up to the mid-1980s (1993: 108). She concludes that in this process of development, Community law on gender equality was extended well beyond the rather narrow areas some member states wished for and (like Britain and Denmark on notable occasions) were eventually required to accept. In this respect European equality policy may have acquired a momentum of its own. Also, European influences are greater than laws alone, and include other institutions such as the European Childcare Network whose aim is to further gender equality.

Having said this, two major shortfalls in the achievements of equal opportunity policy stand out. The first concerns the continued and widespread prevalence of sexual harassment in the workplace and in educational institutions (see Chapter 1). Perhaps objective levels of harassment are no worse than they were; possibly some of the concern about this deep-seated form of discrimination reflects growing public recognition of behaviour which previously was completely discounted or denied by men. Whatever the history of the problem, however, there is little sign that present-day policies have yet achieved much beyond identifying it, though models of effective anti-harassment policy are being developed by some employers (Collier, 1995).

Sexual harassment remains a particularly marked problem in male-dominated work environments such as police forces. As Collier points out (1995: 35), it is a form of discrimination which uses expressions of power and sexuality to attempt to reinforce men's control over the workplace and either to severely limit women's opportunities at work or to make conditions so intolerable that they are forced to leave. However, she also draws attention to research on work environments in which men may not be in a majority and where the atmosphere is informal and apparently friendly, but in which there is nevertheless continual sexual banter and other forms of harassment; these kinds of discrimination also continue to enforce a sexual division of labour and make it difficult for women to establish themselves as equals or develop their careers (1995: 36).

We have also noted in this chapter how in only one country, Sweden, have equality policies been developed partly with a philosophy of 'social structural' change as well as 'individualistic' and 'role-related' views. Even here, most of the positive outcomes for Swedish women have been based on 'role-related' policies – better child care provision, maternity benefits and parental leave, improvements in pay and conditions for part-time work – rather than on tougher policies aiming to reverse a situation in which men continue to dominate in higher-status occupations and women continue with the major share of domestic or family responsibilities. It remains to be seen how effective the most recent (1991) Swedish Act on Equality between Men and Women will be, for example in reaching its specified targets of reducing segregation in Sweden's highly divided labour force. However, two broad changes – Sweden's accession to the European Union and economic and employment restructuring – are likely to water down Sweden's distinctive approach to gender equality.

As far as the European Union is concerned, all the advances mentioned above have been in 'role-related' policies: that is, in measures or provisions which are designed to ease women's entry to the workforce but not to undermine or challenge traditional assumptions about their family roles.

A European Directive on the rights of pregnant women is a good example of how a measure can have some positive outcomes yet illustrate the limitations of 'role-related' equality policies. This directive was much discussed in Britain in 1994, when an industrial tribunal in Leeds awarded Mrs Nichola Cannock £172,912 in compensation for her unlawful dismissal by the Royal Air Force in 1984 on the grounds that she had become pregnant (see page 37). Until August 1993, a ceiling of £11,000 compensation had been set. However, following a ruling by the European Court of Justice on another case at that time, the compensation ceiling in Britain was judged to be unlawful. As a result, a number of women subsequently received compensation at amounts averaging £54,000, though Mrs Cannock's set the record at the beginning of 1994 (EOR, 1994d: 2).

Although conservative opinion was much against the rulings of tribunals in Mrs Cannock's and other similar cases, this example illustrates the effectiveness of the law and perhaps counterbalances some of the arguments mentioned above about its weaknesses or limitations. As some observers pointed out at the time, the Ministry of Defence had no excuse for not knowing about the European Equal Treatment Directive (76/207) which came into force in 1978; attempts to dress up the case as a sudden and arbitrary application of a new European ruling were wholly unjustified.

The impact of these rulings and the substantial compensation involved will therefore be to make any employer think very seriously before dismissing a woman employee on grounds of pregnancy. At the same time it is noticeable that the law on fair treatment of pregnant employees, highly necessary as it is in view of prejudiced attitudes, is a 'role-related' measure which is protective of women's 'special' needs and motherhood role. As Meehan points out, it is significant that men cannot claim the same rights under European law. For example, the ECJ upheld a German court's ruling that an unmarried man who looked after his child from the earliest stage could not claim the same rights to work leave or to 'maternity' benefits and allowances which are granted to mothers (Meehan, 1993: 114).

We have referred in this chapter to a dramatic change in the gender balance of employment: to the march of enormous numbers of women into paid employment, to the fact that a large and increasing proportion of new jobs are taken by women rather than by men, and at the same time we have drawn attention to the feminisation of low-paid and semi-skilled work. A leading question for the future is how men who would have been in traditionally 'working'-class communities will react to these profound changes in the labour market. Will an increasing proportion of men make a bid for jobs in occupations seen as 'women's work' and in the low-paid or part-time sector? Reports from the Equal Opportunities Commission suggest that they are doing so in increasing numbers but that they are running up against employer prejudice against male workers, as evidenced by a growing number of sex discrimination cases being brought by men against employers. In such sub-sectors as retailing, distribution and packing, the hotel industry and the garment industry there is often employer discrimination against men. Custom and practice, together with the attitude that men do not have the necessary 'innate' skills (for example, dexterity), account for this unwillingness to hire men in industries where women have predominated.

Finally, the purposes of equality policies and legislation will not only be challenged by fundamental changes in patterns of work. Their aims will also be questioned by the pressure being put upon traditional domestic roles by the restructuring of employment. If women are becoming the main or sole breadwinners of many households this makes the 'Swedish' goal of shared parental responsibilities and shared rights to parental or other family benefits even more relevant than in an age when almost all men were in full-time permanent employment. Family research seems to indicate that only a proportion of unemployed men are willing to take on an equal or greater share of child care and other household work. Therefore a 'role-related' model of equality policy in the future will perhaps have to address the question of how to re-socialise men for domestic work rather than women for paid work.

5
'RACE' AND EQUAL
OPPORTUNITIES

Introduction

The study of inequalities between 'racial' and ethnic groups, and of the impact of equality policies on those inequalities, raises thorny questions about what 'racial' and ethnic groups are. There are also extremely important questions about how 'racial' discrimination can be defined and how it manifests itself at work. In the first part of this chapter we will therefore discuss concepts of 'race' and ethnicity relevant to equal opportunities.

The first and perhaps most important point to establish is that 'racial' and ethnic differences are socially constructed. That is, there are no hard-and-fast or scientifically objective distinctions between one 'racial' or ethnic group and another. Racial and ethnic distinctions are often of profound social and political significance and the evidence of increasing ethnic tension and conflict around the world confirms this. However, actual 'racial' differences between human beings are superficial; the significance of 'racial' and ethnic identity lies in the stereotyped images of one another that we have created or have learned from our traditions.

Differences between countries in the ways minority groups are defined and treated are particularly illustrative of the somewhat arbitrary and often politicised nature of 'racial' and ethnic categories. American and British census definitions of 'racial' and ethnic groups (see below), for instance, clearly demonstrate how categories are socially constructed and how they change over time (though from this point the constructed nature of 'race' will be assumed and we will no longer use inverted commas).

Categories raise further questions and moral dilemmas for equal opportunity policies. For example can, and should, clearer categories be created so that we may more accurately determine how many white and black people there are in different kinds of employment, or how many are unemployed? Or do efforts to categorise racial groups have the unintended effect of exacerbating racial tensions and racial discrimination?

In the second part we will examine in more detail the concepts of direct and indirect discrimination introduced at the beginning of the book and referred to with regard to gender (Chapter 4) and other aspects of inequality. We will focus on the legal framework in Britain at this point, with occasional references to the way racial discrimination is interpreted in other countries such as the United States. In this section we will therefore consider how interpretations of discrimination have developed, and we will review the outcomes of the British way of dealing with discrimination for black and white people in employment.

Following on from this, the third section concludes with a review of the position and outlook for black and minority people in the labour market, chiefly in Britain but also with reference to other countries. Of particular concern are continuing patterns of occupational segregation and exclusion, the position of black and other minority groups on the occupational ladder, inequalities in earnings and economic status, and day-to-day discrimination and harassment in the workplace.

Race and ethnicity – problematic categories?

The 1976 Race Relations Act in Britain defines discrimination on *racial grounds* as meaning any of the following: race, colour, ethnic or national origins, and nationality or citizenship. As can be seen, 'racial grounds' are something of a catch-all category. In order to comply with the Act, it is therefore important to be aware of its definition.

Note, however, that religious discrimination is not made unlawful under the Race Relations Act. Only in one part of the United Kingdom, Northern Ireland, is religious discrimination specifically outlawed under a Fair Employment Act (see Chapter 3). It should be made unlawful throughout the United Kingdom, the CRE argues (1991: 24), because it is at present within the law to incite hatred against a religious community and to discriminate against a person because of their religion, unless affiliation to a religion happens to be recognised as membership of an ethnic group (as is the case, for instance, with the Jewish and Sikh communities).

None the less, with the exception of religious groups, it can be accepted that British legal definitions of what counts as a racial category are wide-ranging. In practice, however, attention is usually focused on the groups more visibly identified as racial and ethnic groups, for instance people in Asian, African and Afro-Caribbean communities, than on European and other white minority groups such as Polish, Greek or Irish people.

This may not always be justified. It is not necessarily the case that white minority employees or users of services experience only minimal levels of discrimination. Prejudiced attitudes towards and discrimination against Irish workers in Britain, for instance, have a long history (Jackson, 1963).

However, it is the more visibly 'black' minorities which suffer the higher levels of discrimination, and we examine the evidence for this below. For the purposes of monitoring outcomes in a workforce, any racial or ethnic categories that are used must be able to both identify the basic black–white distinction and be sensitive to other ethnic or cultural differences. This is not to argue that simple and clearly defined monitoring exercises cannot be carried out: they can, and have been (for instance see Coussey and Jackson (1991) for practical guidance). But the key to success in such exercises lies in the reliability of the categories used and in the ability to compare results with the wider picture.

In Britain the Population Census now provides an important part of this picture. From 1991, when an 'ethnic' question was introduced for the first time, information has been gathered on respondents' *self-identified* ethnic identity (from a list presented on the doorstep to each householder). The results can be compared with evidence from other census questions on birthplace and nationality.

Before an ethnic question was included in the Population Census observers of race relations were largely reliant on the Labour Force Survey, an annual survey of a representative cross-section of people living at private addresses in the United

Table 5.1 'Official' definitions of race and ethnicity

Population Census (UK)	LFS (UK) 1984–91	LFS (UK) 1992
Black – Caribbean	Black Caribbean	Black Caribbean
Black – African	African (inc. African Asian)	Black African
Black – Other		Black – other
Bangladeshi	Bangladeshi	
Indian	Indian	Indian
Pakistani	Pakistani	Pakistani
Chinese	Chinese	Chinese
White	White	White
Other	Mixed and other	Other (non-mixed) Other (mixed) Black – mixed

Source: Employment Gazette, 1994a: 148.

Kingdom. It is carried out by the OPCS's Social Survey Division for the Employment Department. The ethnic or racial categories used in both the Census (1991) and the Labour Force Survey before and after 1992 are compared below. In 1993, the LFS showed that 5.8 per cent of the working-age population in private households in Britain were in the minority groups identified in Table 5.1 (*Employment Gazette*, 1994a: 147).

As can be seen there is considerable overlap between the official categories shown in Table 5.1. The Labour Force Survey included an additional 'Arab' category, not carried over into the Census, and a category which specifically mentions a mixed-race or mixed-descent background. As a result of a rapid rise of interracial marriages and partnerships, young people of mixed race now represent the fastest-growing 'community' or subgroup of all British minority groups (Nanton, 1992). Yet there is no summary in the *census* of how many people of mixed race there are in Britain. As people of mixed race often experience similar levels of racial discrimination or disadvantage to those identified as black and Asian, this is a significant omission.

The 'Black Other' category offers one way of estimating numbers of people of mixed race. This is a predominantly youthful group, according to the 1991 Census, suggesting that many younger mixed-race people do seem to have identified with it, though precisely how many people in this category are of mixed race is not clear.

Another shortcoming of the 'ethnic' categories used in both census and Labour Force Survey are that the 'White' group has not been subdivided into ethnic or national categories such as Cypriot or Irish; nor do the 'national' categories of 'Indians', 'Pakistanis' and 'Bangladeshis' reveal *ethnic* differences, such as those which exist between Punjabis and Gujaratis of Indian ancestry.

Explicit official recognition of race and ethnicity is much more apparent in 'immigrant' societies such as Australia and the United States, where ethnic groups form a relatively respected element in the political structure. In such plural societies, ethnicity can become an 'organising principle' of politics (Glazer and Moynihan, 1975). It is therefore quite significant that the United Kingdom, often seen as rather inexplicit in its approach to questions of race relations (Kirp, 1979), has eventually – and not without a false start in the 1981 census – moved towards acceptance of an official recognition of 'ethnicity' in the census of 1991.

In the rest of Europe though, inexplicitness and reluctance to officially categorise race are prevalent. In Germany distinctions based on country of origin and proficiency in the German language assume great importance. For instance, proficiency in German has been used since 1978 to determine whether an adult migrant can qualify for 'safer' residence status (*Aufenthaltsberechtigung*). The applicant must also satisfy other conditions, such as an employment contract, proof of adequate housing, and eight years' residence in Germany. All these conditions, including language proficiency, are judged by local police authorities whose testing methods leave much to be desired.

France presents another example of a country in which minority communities face an uncertain future. In recent elections leading politicians have encouraged anti-immigrant and racist feeling and, in order to satisfy right-wing demands for action, the so-called Pasqua laws (named after an Interior Minister, Charles Pasqua) were introduced in 1994.

The new laws, combined with other regulations which restrict the citizenship rights of children born in France of foreign parents, have thrown a great deal of power into the hands of police authorities. There are reports of frequent police checks, police intimidation and brutality towards black and north African people in France (Steele, 1995: 10).

As Steele adds, 'The irony is that the clamp-down came although immigrants have been integrating relatively smoothly' (1995: 10). For instance, over half of Algerian men marry French women and a quarter of Algerian-born women marry French men. These are rates comparable with black–white intermarriage in Britain. However, there is at least one strand of French politics which wishes to reimpose a 'guest worker' identity upon settled and integrating minority communities.

In a survey of older migrant workers in 13 European countries, EURAG (1987) found that tough attitudes towards residence rights and eligibility for citizenship were not restricted to Germany and France. In other west European countries a migrant who returns to the old country can find that insurance and pensions benefits are lost, even though s/he may have contributed for years to insurance schemes in the country of employment. In EURAG's report, a strong case is made for changing national policies to allow settled foreign workers to move freely between their home and host countries, and to be able to transfer at least some pension rights to their old countries.

The injustices experienced by migrant workers in European countries raise questions about the way richer western European countries will respond to a potentially much greater and more recent change: the break-up of the Soviet Union and the liberalisation of laws concerning out-migration from Russia and eastern and central European countries. Huhne (1993) believes that without large-scale investment in the eastern economies, migration to the richer west will be impossible to prevent for two main reasons. First, there are millions of eastern Europeans who have citizenship and therefore residence rights in the west: for instance, there are 3 million ethnic Germans living in Poland, Rumania and Russia. Secondly, the experience of the United States and Mexico demonstrates that it is impossible to prevent large-scale illegal immigration across a long land frontier.

However, Marshall (1995) questions fears in western Europe about large-scale migrations from eastern European countries, citing the examples of falling out-migration from Rumania and much lower than expected out-migration from Russia. Fears about large-scale migration to Britain are particularly misplaced. As Marshall points out, 'more Britons left home to live elsewhere in Europe in the last two decades than any other EU nationality, according to . . . the Council of Europe'. Britain is a net exporter of people, and has a lower proportion of foreign-born residents in comparison with Austria, Belgium, Denmark, France, Germany, Luxembourg, the Netherlands, Norway, Sweden and Switzerland.

Changing interpretations of discrimination

Not only do definitions of racial groups change in meaning and significance. What counts as discrimination also evolves. This is shown most clearly in the arrival of the idea of indirect or institutional discrimination in the early 1970s, as discussed in Chapter 1.

However, pinning down exactly what indirect discrimination means in practice can prove to be difficult. One of the main outcomes of the application of race equality legislation, at least in the United Kingdom, has been relative underuse of charges of indirect discrimination against employers. As McCrudden et al. conclude, 'the vast majority of cases heard by industrial tribunals were concerned only with direct discrimination, hence the tribunals were articulating concepts only in that area' (1991: 271).

Before examining the reasons for this, we should note however that the scope of the law and concepts of *direct* discrimination have evolved considerably since the earlier Race Relations Acts of 1965 and 1968. The 1965 Act prohibited direct discrimination in certain areas of life – notably in places of 'public resort' where whites-only admittance policies had previously been legal. Discrimination in employment and housing were not included at all until the second Race Relations Act (1968) was introduced.

In retrospect, the anti-discriminatory legislation and race relations policies of the 1960s were extremely tentative (Gregory, 1987; Jenkins and Solomos, 1989). For instance, despite some pressure to make direct discrimination a criminal offence, this option was ruled out in the framing of the legislation. Only incitement to racial hatred was to be thus categorised, and is still subject to the stronger sanctions of criminal law (from 1986, this offence has been subsumed under the Public Order Act).

The 1965 and 1968 Acts put the emphasis on conciliation rather than litigation. Individuals who sought to define cases of unfair treatment or discrimination in racial terms could not take their cases directly to the county courts: this was to be the responsibility of the Race Relations Board. A two-tier system of resolving discrimination cases was introduced. Local conciliation committees (put in place by the Race Relations Board) provided the first opportunity for those who felt that they had been discriminated against to have their cases heard. A case not settled at this stage could be referred to the Race Relations Board, which would then make its own judgement as to whether there were sufficient grounds for seeking a court injunction to require racial discrimination to cease.

What was supposed to be a progressive approach to race relations, seeking to take the heat out of disputes and to further mutual understanding, became a set of obstructions to justice for those oppressed by racial discrimination. Compared with the Equal Employment Opportunities Commission (EEOC) in the United States, for instance, the Race Relations Board had relatively few powers. By 1972 in the United States, on the other hand, the EEOC

> was permitted to initiate civil action where conciliation failed and also where it had 'reasonable cause' to believe there existed a 'pattern and practice of discrimination'. The mere existence of these powers had a most persuasive effect on the majority of employers, who preferred to draw up affirmative action programmes as part of a negotiated settlement, rather than risk a court judgement against them . . . a finding of discrimination would almost certainly involve the payment of considerable sums of money to the victims, including substantial pay arrears. (Gregory, 1987: 49)

Compared with this the Race Relations Board had no powers to 'summon witnesses, subpoena documents, require answers to questions or issue orders' (McCrudden et al., 1991: 9). Not surprisingly, the number of cases of alleged racial discrimination handled by the Race Relations Board was tiny: about 150 a year in the early 1970s. In comparison, the instances of racism reported in recruitment alone (for example Daniel, 1968) numbered many thousands.

But not only was it difficult for victims of racial discrimination to establish a case in the first place. Even when brought to the highest level, not much could be done in terms of sanctioning employers, improving practice in the workplace or bringing redress to those who had been wronged.

However, the first two Race Relations Acts did bring some positive outcomes in the employment field. Despite its shortcomings the legislation established in the public mind that direct racial discrimination was considered unacceptable by the authorities. The cruder signs of direct discrimination were challenged even though deeper and more pervasive effects of racism continued to be felt.

Thus the 1965 and 1968 Acts can also be seen as a necessary if hesitant first step. They were introduced in the teeth of considerable opposition and against the prevailing opinion that having any anti-discrimination law would only exacerbate racial conflict. Those who later pressured for a wider concept of discrimination and more effective policies were able to point to the fact that the world had hardly been turned upside down by the cautious race relations legislation of the 1960s.

The 1976 Race Relations Act reaffirmed the importance of countering direct discrimination and, as outlined in Chapter 1, included the concept of indirect racial discrimination for the first time. As far as direct discrimination is concerned, case-law and experience of implementation of the Act have established that the motives of a person who discriminates are irrelevant. The more important test is whether a person directly discriminates against someone else because of their race, nationality, religion or ethnicity. If they have done this as a result of pressure from colleagues, or because they believe that customers or outsiders will not readily accept the appointment of someone who is black or of minority status, their discriminatory actions result in an outcome which is the same as if the action were based on personal prejudice. But although this principle has now been defined in law, the CRE still seeks further clarification. The Commission suggests that the Act should additionally clarify that direct discrimination does not necessarily involve a racial motive, 'either by direct statement or by use of illustration as to what is meant by "on racial grounds" ' (1991: 22).

While there will continue to be legal disputes and differences in the interpretation of how direct discrimination can be proved, Lustgarten concludes that *in principle* direct discrimination does not raise any 'novel issues for the function of legal adjudication. Facts must be found – inferred – about specific past events involving a limited number of individuals' and 'The formal burden of proof is not an insuperable obstacle' (1989: 17). The 'real problem' in establishing whether direct discrimination has occurred, he adds, lies in the mechanisms for implementing equal opportunities legislation (such as the industrial tribunal system) and in society's reluctance to counter direct racism.

Establishing indirect discrimination has proved to be more difficult because no particular events, instances or individuals need be involved – the whole point is to establish whether a *pattern* of injustice exists, as evidenced for example by underrepresentation of certain minority groups in the workforce. It is quite possible for discriminated-against groups to be unaware of the pattern of injustice which affects them, and in the absence of 'plaintiffs' or complainants and 'defendants' – at least in the traditional sense – British legal principles, and the understandings upon which industrial tribunals work, have been ill-matched to the task of uncovering indirect discrimination.

The 1976 Race Relations Act introduced a number of new mechanisms and requirements which at first were hoped would establish a significant departure from the earlier legislation and begin to make a major impact on the persistent inequalities between white and black people in Britain. The 1976 Act first suspended the Race Relations Board, the Community Relations Council and the work of the local conciliation committees, and replaced these with a new national body, the Commission for Racial Equality (CRE). Like the Equal Opportunities Commission, a parallel body set up under very similar legislation to deal with gender discrimination (see Chapter 4), the CRE was empowered to:

- Conduct formal investigations of organisations or employers where there appears to be a case for examining whether racially discriminatory practices are occurring.
- Serve non-discrimination notices upon organisations in which there is found to be racial discrimination.
- Advise and assist victims of racial discrimination, and help them to decide how to take their cases further, for example to an industrial tribunal.

- Grant assistance to a number of complainants such as legal representation or finding other ways to settle a dispute (the terms of the Act restrict aid to people with the stronger cases, to those who are unable to pursue their cases unaided, and to cases which may create precedents or raise questions of principle).
- Promote a wider understanding of both racial discrimination and equal opportunities through educational and research work.
- And as part of the above role, it was empowered to issue codes of practice which would stress the value and importance of adopting equal opportunities policies. The need for positive action in such areas as monitoring the ethnic composition of the workforce or recruitment was to be emphasised as much as the need to stop racial discrimination.

Secondly, whereas under previous legislation individuals were discouraged from taking race discrimination cases directly to the courts, the 1976 Act introduced the freedom for complainants to do this. In other words, a dispute categorised as a race discrimination case no longer had to be channelled through a regulatory body such as the old Race Relations Board or the new CRE.

However, in Britain 'class actions' cannot be brought against employers or organisations in the way that they can in the United States. As Lustgarten (1989: 18) reminds us, the courts can permit representative actions and individual cases do create precedents or have implications for future interpretation of equality laws. But in Lustgarten's words, there are 'tight limits' to the consequences of a judgment against an employer. A judgment in favour of someone who has suffered racial discrimination may bring the individual compensation, but employers do not face the prospect of having to compensate other employees who have experienced similar mistreatment, as they usually would in the United States.

Thirdly, the 1976 Act did mark a breakthrough, though, in terms of recognising indirect discrimination as well as direct. Direct discrimination refers to the way in which people are treated differently and unfairly because of their racial, ethnic, national or religious identity (see Chapter 1).

Indirect discrimination, on the other hand, refers to a pattern of inequality which can persist even when people are treated equally, or in the same way. Thus under the revised law, a court or industrial tribunal can infer that racial discrimination is taking place even when directly discriminatory acts or differences in treatment are not obvious. Selection criteria for applicants to jobs, for instance, can be applied 'equally' and uniformly, but have been found in some cases to be biased against black or minority applicants. Where there is indirect discrimination, then, an organisation's culture, rules and procedures make it more difficult for people in certain racial categories to get a job, be promoted or obtain training than people in 'accepted' categories.

Outcomes of the 1976 Race Relations Act

Discrimination cases in industrial tribunals, which handle far more racial discrimination problems than the courts, offer one way of assessing the impact of the 1976 legislation. Tribunals were developed in the 1960s and 1970s as part of a strategy to improve industrial relations and to offer a quick and accessible way of resolving disputes between employers and employees, mainly in areas such as complaints over unfair dismissal.

An industrial tribunal consists of a legally qualified chairperson, an employer's representative and an employee's representative, each of which is drawn from a panel. The 1976 Race Relations Act required industrial tribunals to arbitrate where individuals wished to complain about racial discrimination. It also became possible (but not a requirement) for employees to obtain a hearing from ACAS (the Advisory, Conciliation and Arbitration Service) before taking a case to an industrial tribunal.

In crude terms, the number of cases dealt with shows that the legislation seems to have at least a few more teeth than the preceding laws of the 1960s, when only a hundred or so cases each year were processed by the Race Relations Board: between 1992–3 and 1993–4, the total of completed race discrimination cases dealt with by industrial tribunals rose from 1070 to 1304 – a 20 per cent increase (EOR, 1995: 37; see Table 5.2).

As can be seen, a substantial majority of race discrimination cases are either withdrawn or settled. Only a minority get as far as a tribunal hearing, although as shown in Table 5.2 the proportion of tribunal cases went up in 1993–4. Of these almost a third of

Table 5.2   Outcome of racial discrimination cases

	1992–3	1993–4
Total tribunal cases	391	571
of which:		
Successful	69	151
Dismissed	276	369
Disposed of otherwise	46	51
ACAS conciliated settlements	228	272
Cases withdrawn	451	461
Total cases	1070	1304

Source: Adapted from EOR, 1995: 37.
Reproduced in adapted form with permission of *Equal Opportunities Review.*

applicants were successful. Again, this was a slight increase over the previous year. Where applicants to industrial tribunals were successful in establishing that racial discrimination had occurred, compensation was awarded in almost four-fifths of cases. The amounts awarded are relatively small: the median award in 1993–4 was £3,500, although the upper limit on compensation for race discrimination has now been removed as it was for sex discrimination cases from November 1993 (see Chapter 4).

However, neither the industrial tribunal nor the ACAS systems are moribund as far as their use in race discrimination cases is concerned. The increase in cases from 1992–3 to 1993–4 was not atypical, and follows a longer period of gradual increase from the introduction of the 1976 Race Relations Act. As McCrudden et al. conclude, 'The system has proved far more popular with ethnic minorities than the comparable system has with women' (1991: 154–5).

To see a case through, an applicant must have considerable resources and strengths beyond the merits of his or her case: dogged determination, willingness to make some financial sacrifices before any compensation can be awarded, and courage to face possible victimisation or intimidation at the workplace even if the outcome is successful. The size of compensation awards and the complex nature of the appeal process ensure that only those who are willing to take a relatively selfless stand and to make a case on principle have a reasonable chance of bringing a case to completion.

What particular flaws or obstacles continue to stand out in the system for obtaining racial justice? First, the CRE is limited by its budget and by its brief in the number of individuals it can help in their cases with ACAS, at tribunal hearings or in court. People who receive backing from the CRE have a much better chance of a successful outcome than others. This is partly because the CRE must select the stronger cases, but the CRE's experience and moral support can make the difference.

Secondly, industrial tribunals, which were modelled on the idea of 'people's courts' and were intended to provide ready access to hearings in relatively informal settings, still have a long way to go before they can be said to have avoided all the drawbacks of the formal legal process. Admittedly three-quarters of race discrimination cases heard by tribunals are completed within six months of starting (McCrudden et al., 1991: 155), so the aim of providing access to hearings relatively promptly has been met to a degree. The main problems lie elsewhere: for instance, the lack of experience of tribunals with race relations or race discrimination questions, compared with the general run of unfair dismissal complaints without a racial component.

There are other shortcomings: the lack of interest by tribunals in following up the decisions they have made or in finding out whether applicants have been paid compensation when it is due (Gregory, 1987: 81); and the reluctance of tribunals to 'draw inferences from complainants' claims' (Lustgarten, 1989: 17). Tribunals have tended to retain a semi-adversarial, legalistic approach to investigating cases. Also tribunals tend to err on the side of accepting employers' or defendants' explanations at face value; they are reluctant to make deeper interpretations of situations in which racial discrimination could be occurring and this is tied up with the conservative reluctance of tribunals to discuss indirect discrimination.

Thirdly, the results of formal investigations by the CRE have been rather disappointing. The CRE was permitted under the 1976 Act to initiate investigations of particular businesses or employers without prior complaints about racial discrimination. Victims of racial discrimination are not necessarily aware of the ways in which they are being adversely affected, especially if racism is institutionalised and relatively subtle. The CRE's investigatory role was to overcome this problem and to demonstrate to discriminatory employers how their practices disadvantage black and minority employees.

The rather modest resources of the CRE, when pitted against the considerable financial, legal and political resources of big companies, resulted in a series of protracted and unequal struggles. The CRE soon became bogged down in formal investigations which proved to be rather pointless and counterproductive. Part of the problem lay in a 'serious lack of skills' in the CRE (McCrudden et al., 1991: 113) both in mounting an effective organisational strategy for investigatory work and on the technical side of gathering data on discrimination. In 1983 the CRE went through a fundamental management shake-up to try to deal with these shortcomings, but since then has been through several management crises when it has seemed quite likely that the Commission would be closed down by the government of the day.

The CRE's relative lack of success with its investigations strategy is illustrated by two landmark decisions by the House of Lords in 1982 and 1984. These rulings, in two separate legal cases, upheld challenges to the CRE's procedures when initiating investigations into particular organisations. The first questioned the grounds upon which the CRE formed a 'belief' that racial discrimination was occurring and introduced limitations on the CRE's terms of reference, or how far an investigation could go. The second case also tightened the requirements the CRE had to satisfy before conducting a formal investigation. The House of Lords ruled that the CRE could not mount an investigation of an organisation unless evidence or examples of unlawful discrimination could be produced beforehand; the CRE could no longer begin an investigation because it *suspected* racial discrimination but did not yet have evidence of individual cases.

However, this is not to say that no gains have been made from the policy of having a regulatory body such as the CRE with powers to launch investigations of discrimination. In addition to investigating specified organisations or companies, the CRE has powers to look into a general area of employment or industry. These surveys have undoubtedly added to public knowledge about the degree and nature of racial discrimination in Britain.

Despite unequal odds and strong opposition from some employers, formal investigations have brought some success in persuading others to revise their recruitment and personnel management practices. This is especially the case where public sector organisations or private sector companies have a high profile and where it is important that they retain a positive public image: the possibility of an investigation for suspected racial discrimination can be enough of an embarrassment to prompt change.

But most commentators on the progress of British race equality policy agree that the CRE simply does not have sanctions which are strong enough to push the less willing employers into better practice. For instance, the CRE is empowered to serve a non-discrimination notice following a formal investigation into an organisation which reveals that racial discrimination is occurring. The county court, if it accepts the non-discrimination notice, then has the responsibility of serving an order on the employer or organisation to stop discriminating in the ways identified. Even if matters reach this stage, however, non-compliance may only result in a relatively small fine being levied. Continued non-compliance can only be tackled by appeals to higher courts and lengthy legal proceedings. Not surprisingly, given these obstacles, policy within the CRE has shifted continually between an emphasis on investigatory or regulatory work, on the one hand, and educational, advisory and research work on the other. Here again, the latter functions have brought some gains in terms of publicising the nature and extent of racism, together with the dissemination of codes of practice and encouragement of procedures such as racial monitoring by employers. However, uncertainties about the CRE's role, and how far it should be a regulatory agency as opposed to a 'public awareness' body, have dogged its history and weakened its impact in the employment field.

Employment outcomes: black and white people at work

The thirty or more years in which Britain has officially had a race relations policy have witnessed both continuity and some very significant changes in the employment position of black and minority community people. In broad terms, continuities are evident in the discrimination which many black and Asian people experience in their daily lives and which has not abated; indeed, there are signs of increased racial tensions and racial harassment in the workplace and elsewhere (*Guardian*, 1994: 19). If comparisons are made between black people as a whole and white people as a whole, significant inequalities have persisted in terms of position on the occupational ladder, job segregation, earnings levels and rates of unemployment.

However, as mentioned in Chapter 2, there have also been marked changes among black and Asian communities' position in the employment market, both in relation to each other and in relation to the white majority (see Jones, 1993). These patterns of differentiation and change are complex and it would be pointless to ascribe them to a single cause. Employment prospects in each minority community are the product of a range of factors: the history of the minority's relationship with the majority, employer perceptions of employees from that minority, the economic and cultural resources of the minority community, and geographical or local labour market influences on demand for employees from each community.

At first sight, equality policies and laws seem the least likely explanation for growing differentiation between the various minorities. If they were having any impact, then surely they would be creating more equality between the minority communities?

However, this need not be so, for two simple reasons. First, equal opportunities policies are aimed at people in work or who are perceived as having a reasonable chance of obtaining it. Minority communities in which long-term unemployment is at a very high level will hardly be influenced by such policies, whereas minorities in which unemployment is average or below average will receive more attention.

Secondly, it is likely that differing minority attitudes towards equality policies and the differing economic roles of each minority community will play a part in affecting how frequently black and Asian people claim their rights under equality legislation or whether they are likely to be exposed to an active equal opportunities policy. A much higher proportion of Afro-Caribbean than Asian workers, for example, are employed in public sector organisations, which by and large have more active policies than private sector employers.

Thus 'equality' policies are likely to have disproportionate effects, perhaps contributing to growing inequalities among minority communities even if they are having some impact in reducing inequalities between some minorities and the majority.

Outcomes do not have to show narrowing gaps between all communities before we may conclude that equality policies are having some effect.

But what are the main outcomes in recent years? First, in terms of *occupational distribution*, it is clear that no employment ghettos exist in the United Kingdom. That is, no minority community has an overwhelming proportion of its employed members working in a single branch of industry or a restricted group of occupations; there is at least some representation in all the major kinds of employment.

However, as with gender segregation, overrepresentation in some areas and underrepresentation in others suggest strong connections between racial or ethnic identity and certain inequalities in the labour market. For instance, the proportion of black men in banking, financial and business services is almost a quarter less than the percentage of white men (see Table 5.3), although black women are only slightly underrepresented. A much higher proportion of women of Indian ancestry work in manufacturing (21 per cent) than women as a whole (13 per cent), and this illustrates a concentration of women in this ethnic group in relatively low-paid manual jobs in textile, assembly and distribution industries (see Table 5.3).

The percentages of all minority group men employed in services (71) and in distribution, hotels and catering (29) are far higher than the equivalent proportions of white men in the same fields (see Table 5.3). Service employment is more often feminised (see Chapter 4) and workers in this sector are more likely to be on lower than average rates of pay. The table reveals that the proportion of black women in service employment – and particularly 'other services', which include the health service – is even higher (91 per cent) than among white women (83 per cent). Interestingly, Indian, Pakistani and Bangladeshi women in work are somewhat underrepresented in service industries.

Secondly, position on the *occupational ladder* or the social class position of minority workers confirms the picture of diversity and emerging differences, although gender differences are also highly important and what holds for black and Asian men does not necessarily apply to employed women in the same communities. For instance, slightly more black and Asian men (56 per cent) than white men (52 per cent) are in non-manual occupations, but the

Table 5.3   Employees and self-employed by industry, gender and race/ethnic origin, Great Britain (1993) (percentages)

Industry	Race/ethnic groups					
	Black	Indian	Pakis- tani/ Bang- ladeshi	Mixed/ other	All min- orities	White
Men						
Manufacturing	24	28	28	14	24	28
Construction	9	—	—	—	4	11
Services	66	68	69	83	71	56
of which:						
Distribution, hotels and catering	18	29	40	32	29	17
Transport and communication	14	11	12	—	11	9
Banking, financial and business	8	10	—	20	11	11
Other services	26	17	—	24	19	19
N ('000s)	140	220	100	130	580	12,750
Women						
Manufacturing	—	21	—	—	13	13
Construction	—	—	—	—	2	2
Services	91	77	79	90	85	83
of which:						
Distribution, hotels and catering	16	33	—	26	26	23
Transport and communication	—	—	—	—	5	3
Banking, financial and business	12	10	—	16	12	13
Other services	58	29	39	44	43	44
N ('000s)	140	160	30	90	430	10,530

Note: Where cells are blank (—) there are less than 10,000 in the category and estimates were not shown.
Source: Adapted from Table 4, _Employment Gazette_ (1994a): 152.
Crown copyright is reproduced with the permission of the Controller of HMSO.

proportion of employed black and Asian women in non-manual occupations – about two-thirds – is greater still, although only on a level with the two-thirds of white women in skilled non-manual, intermediate and professional occupations (_Employment Gazette_, 1994a: 153).

It is only in recent years that the proportions of minority group men and women in non-manual employment have overtaken the proportions of white people similarly employed. According to the Labour Force Survey, in 1984–6 51 per cent of black and Asian employed people were in non-manual occupations compared with 54 per cent of whites. By 1993 the proportions had risen to 61 per cent and 59 per cent respectively (*Employment Gazette*, 1994a: 153).

This pattern has considerable significance because equality policies are likely to have had more 'bite' in non-manual than in manual occupations. While it does not prove that equal opportunities policies have been a decisive influence, it is conceivable that they have helped to bring about a greater representation of black and Asian workers in non-manual occupations.

However, there are two main reasons to be cautious about the impact of equality policies. The first is that no one in the United Kingdom is clear about longer-term trends in *earnings differentials* between Asian, black and white workers. Though the Labour Force Survey in Britain began to collect data on earnings among different racial and ethnic groups from 1991, there is a paucity of information from the recent past (Jones, 1993: 78). Jones mentions an earlier Policy Studies Institute survey (Brown, 1984) and a number of other national and local surveys in the 1970s and 1980s which indicate that on the whole men in minority groups tend to earn between 15 and 20 per cent less than white men, and that a significant part of this difference remains even when occupation and job level are controlled for. In other words, there was clear evidence of racial inequality in earnings even though not all of this can be attributed to outright discrimination.

This confirms evidence from other countries such as the United States, where again a significant amount of the wage inequality between black men and the majority has been attributed to discrimination (Jones, 1993: 78). But as in Britain, the American evidence is rather mixed. For instance, Sloane and Jain (1989: 9) point to substantial improvements in black people's earnings in the United States during the 1970s and 1980s, although paradoxically part of this is explained by rising unemployment among black men (withdrawal of less skilled men from the labour market means that average earnings are boosted by other black people in employment).

As Sloane and Jain conclude, conflicting evidence about earnings differentials between black and white employees suggest that results are 'sensitive to the data sets used, coverage of workers and the estimating model used' (1989: 9). Jones adds, as far as Britain is concerned, that 'what is remarkable is the lack of significant up-to-date research on the subject' (1993: 78). Therefore it is simply too soon to be able to make any firm judgements about the poss-ible impact of equal opportunities policies on the relative pay of black and white people. Even though it is possible to point to present-day inequalities in pay, evidence about longer-term pay trends is needed.

A second reason to be cautious about the impact of equality policies on racial inequalities is that, as with gender differences, a rise in non-manual employees does not in itself indicate a lessening of discrimination. A rising number of black and Asian employees may be making it to managerial and professional posi-tions, but the evidence of race discrimination cases and of studies of local labour markets suggests that they have often achieved these positions against considerable odds: having to attend two or three times the number of interviews, or make many more job applications than their white counterparts, for example.

Also, macro-level evidence of proportions of black and white people in manual and non-manual occupations, or in supervisory, managerial and professional jobs does not tell us about patterns of promotion, reward or discrimination within particular industries or areas of employment.

An illuminating comparison can be made with the United States, where there is relative underrepresentation of East Asian (Korean, Chinese and Japanese American) men and women in the boardrooms of large-scale business firms and the management structures of such corporate enterprises. This is surprising given that East Asians have been portrayed in America as 'model minor-ities' with high levels of education, strong commitment to the American work ethic and values of individualism and enterprise. However, a degree of cultural discrimination still operates against Korean, Chinese and Japanese Americans. If they are in the cor-porate world, they are more likely to be steered away from the boardroom and core management, and towards more specialised areas such as research and development.

In Britain, gains in higher educational attainment among some Asian communities, notably among Indian and 'East African' Asian groups and among some members (particularly women) of the Afro-Caribbean community (Jones, 1993), suggest that increasing proportions will be eligible for managerial and professional jobs. However, as in the United States with regard to East Asian graduates, there is a strong UK trend for higher-qualified Asians to enter professional areas of employment (law, medicine, pharmacy, etc.) than management positions in large-scale companies or organisations. Though more research is needed on this, there is a strong possibility that a significant proportion of minority graduates either expect or experience discrimination if they were to enter the corporate business world; independent practice as a doctor or lawyer, on the other hand, offers a route to professional status and income through which the individual is more likely to succeed on his or her own merits.

If this is the case there are serious implications for equal opportunities policies in the world of large-scale organisations, and especially in the private sector companies which appear to have a long way to go in encouraging the recruitment of black and Asian employees into higher management.

Conclusion

As we saw in Chapter 2, the world of employment has been changing in radical ways over the past two decades. The rise of mass unemployment and the permanent disappearance of many skilled and semi-skilled 'male' jobs in manufacturing, together with restructuring and re-location of other kinds of employment, are profound changes which muddy the waters and make it difficult to see what the impact of any policies on employment have been, let alone equal opportunities policies. Relative earnings between racial/ethnic groups, for instance, are likely to be affected by the state of the economy at least as much as equal opportunities policies (Sloane and Jain, 1989: 10).

Comparative and international evidence reviewed by the same authors suggests, however, that affirmative action and equal opportunities policies can have a decisive effect on at least some dimensions of racial inequality when they are enforced aggressively. The British approach to racial equality, however, is far from aggressive. Though some British employers – notably some local authorities, the Civil Service and some private sector companies (see Chapter

8) – have taken stronger initiatives and developed positive action programmes, the legal framework encourages a cautious approach. Neither the penalties a racially discriminatory employer faces nor the compensation awarded to the few who see a race discrimination case to its conclusion are sufficient to effect much *structural* change in employment (for example, in making permanent improvements to recruitment policies, monitoring promotion and redundancy procedures, and so on).

Despite these limitations the number of race discrimination cases brought to tribunals, arbitration or to courts continues to rise, and the proportion of these which were successful for applicants is also rising. Racial discrimination has been a marked feature of the British employment scene for many years, so these small but significant changes indicate an increasing awareness of grievance procedures and a willingness to use them, rather than simply a rise in race discrimination itself.

Resort to legal and other means to secure a measure of racial justice must be seen against a backdrop of increasing change and differentiation among minority communities. Changing patterns of employment show, on the one hand, an encouraging increase in skilled and non-manual employment in certain sections of the Indian, Afro-Caribbean and 'East African' Asian communities. But on the other hand, both unemployment and employment in the lowest-paid service and manufacturing industries remain worryingly high in the Pakistani and Bangladeshi communities, and among some sections of the Afro-Caribbean community (Jones, 1993).

For the former, equal opportunities policies face the challenge of breaking down institutional barriers to the employment of Asian and black people across the spectrum of jobs in industry, and particularly to their promotion in management structures in the private sector. There is also the challenge of pay inequalities between black and white employees who are performing comparable roles or doing similar work, although the evidence to date is unclear about how much pay inequality exists and what impact equality policies have had upon black–white pay inequalities.

For the latter, that is, Asian people predominantly from the Pakistani and Bangladeshi communities who are without work or who are clustered in low-paid occupations, equal opportunities policies face an even more serious challenge. It is important not to compound stereotypes, and a significant proportion of people of Bangladeshi and Pakistani descent are succeeding in the British context, whether in education, gaining access to non-manual jobs and the professions, or in business. However, whether they are relatively successful or not, people in these minorities are likely to see equal opportunities policies as an irrelevance. This suggests that in the future, whatever legislative framework exists for equal opportunities policies, a much tougher approach will be called for if the creation of a permanent rift or gulf between these minority communities and the majority is to be avoided.

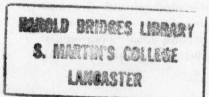

6
DISABLED PEOPLE AND
EQUAL OPPORTUNITIES

Introduction

This chapter is concerned with the subordinate social position and lack of equal opportunities faced by disabled people in Britain. It explores the foundations of existing inequalities, and examines in particular the principles behind the employment legislation that have been in force since the end of the Second World War. More recently, pressure for change has been augmented by a new understanding of disability fostered primarily by disabled people themselves. In this light, we examine recent legislative proposals brought to Parliament by both the Conservative Government and the Labour Opposition, and the analysis is set in its international context by a review of different approaches to equal opportunities using examples drawn from the United States and Sweden. The chapter ends with a discussion of possible ways forward for disabled people in Britain.

In few areas of contemporary life do disabled people enjoy equality of opportunity with their non-disabled counterparts (Oliver, 1985; Barton, 1989; Barnes, 1990; Drake, 1992; Morris, 1993). Their disadvantage is in part a result of the way in which disability is defined and understood. Until very recently the world of medicine has enjoyed unchallenged dominion over this area of policy so that disablement has been portrayed as an individual 'tragedy' arising from accident or disease. Now however, disabled sociologists and radical disabled people, many of them supporters of the Disabled People's Movement (Shakespeare, 1993; Hasler, 1993), have proposed an alternative *social* model. According to this disability is a product of the physical configuration of the built environment, and it is bolstered by prevailing social norms, values and beliefs (Finkelstein, 1980; Abberley, 1987; Swain et al., 1993). From this point of view, people are disabled not by their impairments, but by the contours and attitudes of society at large. As Leach (1989: 66) has noted: 'In redefining the nature of disability, disabled people are asserting that they are a disadvantaged or oppressed minority group whose unequal economic and social position stems from discrimination and lack of access to power.'

In Britain disability has long been regarded as a non-political subject and the exclusion of disabled people from decision-making processes remains the norm (Oliver, 1990; Drake and Owens, 1992; Drake, 1994). Many are disenfranchised, either because they do not appear on electoral registers or because they do not receive necessary information in appropriate formats to enable them to make an informed choice in casting their votes (Fry, 1987). They also have a less secure foothold in local politics (Croft and Beresford, 1989). Indeed, within the public sector, disabled county and district councillors and senior council officers are extremely rare and even those local authorities concerned to promote equal opportunities concentrate their efforts largely upon race and gender rather than disability. Leach (1989) has shown that within the public sector, Social Services Departments perform most poorly of all in the employment of disabled people, failing to meet even the 3 per cent quota established in the 1944 Disabled Persons Employment Act.

Both the level and the duration of unemployment among disabled people have been consistently higher than those experienced by non-disabled people (Townsend, 1979; Lonsdale, 1986; Hirst, 1987; Clark and Hirst, 1989; Glendinning, 1991). Martin, White and Meltzer (1989) have shown that in Britain less than a third of the 2 million disabled people of working age have jobs, and Barnes's (1991) evidence suggests that even those who do have employment are less likely than their non-disabled counterparts to occupy well-rewarded posts. Just 12 per cent of disabled workers (as against 21 per cent of non-disabled employees) are in managerial or professional grades. The average weekly wage of disabled male workers represents only 81 per cent of the average enjoyed by non-disabled males (*Hansard*, 6 June 1989, Col. 69) and Berthoud et al. (1993) highlight a direct connection between the severity of impairment and the level of unemployment.

It has come to be thought of as 'natural' that due to their impairments many disabled people cannot work and so must depend upon state benefits for their income, and because the medical model of disability has been prominent in shaping social security in Britain, disabled people's access to benefits is filtered not only by financial but also by medical criteria (Barton, 1986).

Schalock and Kiernan (1990) have challenged the prevailing view that disabled people are unable to work and have cited as evidence pilot programmes in the United States, Canada and Australia in which even people with severe impairments are employed. These programmes are based on the assumption that if they receive the necessary training and support, disabled people can be productive and integrated members of the community. König and Schalock (1991) discuss a variety of changes to the work environment which, once implemented, help to overcome the social and environmental barriers faced by disabled people who wish to work. These changes may include structural reconfiguration of the work setting, personal aids provided through new technology, flexible work time and, where necessary, the encouragement of attitudinal changes among fellow (non-disabled) workers.

Traditional ways of seeking to help disabled people into jobs have involved special or ameliorative forms of intervention often referred to as 'rehabilitation'. Vocational training of this kind has frequently been matched by special pleading on behalf of disabled people (in the main by non-disabled professionals) and by the lure of financial subsidies for prospective employers.

However, as we indicated at the beginning of the chapter there has been, of late, a significant challenge to received wisdom concerning the nature of disablement itself and the role of disabled people in the workplace. One manifestation of this new thinking has been the growing pressure for civil rights legislation. Since 1979 opposition parties have introduced over a dozen Bills into the British Parliament. Their aim has been to bring on to the statute books laws based upon a fundamentally new set of assumptions about the causes of disability. One recent attempt, the Civil Rights (Disabled Persons) Bill (1994), sought to guarantee equality of opportunity and the rights of full citizenship. Within such a framework, disabled people might secure employment, not through charitable benefaction, but as a result of fair competition in a non-discriminatory marketplace. For commentators such as Barnes (1991) and Bynoe et al. (1991) the introduction of anti-discrimination legislation was therefore crucial, not only as a means to combat widespread discriminatory employment practice but also as a way for disabled people to escape dependency upon private or public philanthropy.

Discrimination: an historical overview

Before examining these issues further, it is important to set the debate in its historical context and, in particular, to seek to explain how it came about that disabled people were divorced from the world of work.

Finkelstein (1981) nominates the Industrial Revolution as the period which first detached disabled people from access to employment and from society at large. He argued that in a rural, agrarian Britain, those who survived physical impairment, either at birth or through injury, would have lived as disabled people within their communities. There would be a constant and unbroken proximity between disabled and non-disabled people in the family, the village, the church congregation, and on the farm. In a harsh life for all, the position occupied by disabled people would have seemed little worse than and little different to the majority of the community. Disabled people would have carried out genuine social roles and domestic duties such as looking after children, cooking, cleaning, spinning and weaving.

While Finkelstein's view of disabled people in pre-industrial Britain may seem somewhat cheery, the inherent sense of belonging forms a stark contrast with the subsequent progressive disengagement of disabled people from social and economic life. The Industrial Revolution brought fundamental changes in the fabric of the community itself and in the demands and structures that shaped people's working lives. The ability of disabled people to participate in work was fundamentally undermined by these changes so that when families could no longer cope with them, vulnerable members would have been reduced to begging or to the protection of the church, or to the cruel regime of the workhouse. Since disabled people would have had great difficulty working large looms and other industrial equipment, one can see that the advent of manufacturing represented a key factor in the diminution of their social and economic status. Not only did factory work militate against their employment, new physical impairments were actually caused by these enterprises. The tendency of capitalism to sift out the infirm from the able bodied started with the requirements of large scale manufacturing and the production of goods in bulk for sale in the market place (Morris, 1969; Topliss, 1979; Ryan and Thomas, 1980).

According to Finkelstein, the Industrial Revolution separated disabled people from a viable and integrated way of life within the community, it removed them from social intercourse, withheld the dignity of work, and so rendered them *dis*-abled. 'Able bodiedness' became established as the norm for productive and socially integrated living. In a climate of great productive activity, those who did not work were regarded with abhorrence and were held to be responsible for their own poverty. Social policies at this time were based upon the central belief that individuals were entirely responsible for the circumstances in which they stood. However, Ditch (1991) reminds us that the respectable Victorian middle classes were anxious to be seen to be fair, so that they attempted to segregate the deserving from the undeserving poor. Charity was provided for those who warranted it: groups like the disabled, the widows and the orphans. The idea that there was an obligation to these blameless unfortunates was boosted subsequently by both the First and the Second World Wars, which manufactured their own disabled populations in huge quantities.

War placed disabled people under the hegemony of an increasingly powerful and respected medical profession. With ever greater precision, medicine linked disability to individual impairment. Disability was identified as personal incapacity, and was seen neither as a product of the way society was organised, nor as a result of the built environment. Disabilities could be categorised, counted, and ultimately reified to the extent that today's official statistics concentrate upon the typology and prevalence of disease and handicap, rather than the pertinence of these to the lives of those upon whom they impinge.

Piecemeal measures: disablement legislation in Britain

The foundation of the post-war welfare state is attributed in large measure to the work of Sir William Beveridge. In his report *Social*

Insurance and Allied Services, Beveridge argued that a system of social security should meet needs caused by 'Disability, that is to say, the inability of a person of working age, through illness or accident, to pursue a gainful occupation' (Beveridge, 1942: 124).

Whether resulting from chronic disability, physical disease or incapacity, Beveridge believed that the right way to meet needs was through the provision of disability benefits and industrial pensions, and by (domiciliary and institutional) medical treatment within a comprehensive health service supplemented by postoperative rehabilitation. Beveridge argued that the working population should contribute towards national insurance and social assistance schemes, which would support 'persons incapacitated by blindness or other physical infirmity' whether they had contributed or not (Beveridge, 1942).

In addition to the provision of benefits and health care, further provision was made through the 1944 Disabled Persons Employment Act, which sought to help those disabled people seen as capable of work actually to gain employment. The plight of injured servicemen and women returning from the carnage of war would have made disability a sensitive subject at this time, and the Act sought to ensure that at least some proportion of disabled people would be able to get work.

The 1944 Act defined a 'disabled person' as 'a person who, (on account of injury, disease, or congenital deformity), was substantially handicapped in obtaining or keeping employment'. The expression 'disease' was construed as including a physical or mental condition arising from 'imperfect development of any organ'. The Act set in place a number of innovative measures including the introduction of vocational training courses and industrial rehabilitation programmes. A register of disabled people was created and firms with more than 20 staff had to employ a quota of those registered. Though the proportion was set at just 3 per cent, the quota has been widely flouted throughout its history, with 80 per cent of employers failing to achieve the minimum requirement. Exemption permits have been handed out *en masse* and only ten prosecutions have ever been brought; none at all during the past twenty years (Gooding, 1994).

The Act also allowed for the introduction of regulations by which certain jobs could be reserved solely for disabled people. These tended to be low-grade occupations such as lift monitor and car park attendant. The Act, together with a later amendment Act of 1958, also provided for the setting up of special sheltered workshops and companies such as Remploy.

These schemes have provided work but not necessarily a substantial or even a living wage. Dutton et al. (1989) have shown that the pay of most disabled people in sheltered employment is very low. In 1989, the average wage of workers on the shop floor at Remploy was just £90 per week, at the same time the average remuneration for non-disabled people stood at between £200 and £249 per week (Prescott Clarke, 1990). Moreover, the highest salaries went, by and large, to the 80 per cent of Remploy managers who were not themselves disabled (Dutton et al., 1989).

Both the Beveridge Report and the 1944 Act were predicated upon the belief that disabled people were prevented from working by their medically defined, physical or cognitive impairments. The 1944 Act was intended to introduce positive steps to compensate people for their misfortune by providing some access into the lower end of the job market and by creating segregated settings, some of which in the event involved genuine labour but many of which were given over to artificial occupations intended to be therapeutic rather than productive.

In essence, the underlying assumption was that disabled people were unable to work due to chronic incapacity, accident or personal tragedy. Consequently it was not appropriate to regard them as mainstream members of the working population, but as deserving recipients of social security benefits and special employment subsidies and quotas.

The extent of disablement in contemporary Britain is difficult to gauge. In the 1991 census (Office of Population Censuses and Surveys, 1993) 6 675 000 people declared that they had a 'long-term illness'. Of these 3 064 000 respondents were of working age. While these figures offer some idea of scale, we must acknowledge that the concept of long-term illness may overlap, but not necessarily coincide, with the notion of disability.

Other prevalence measures are provided by the annual digest of social security statistics (Department of Social Security, 1994). Here, the medically oriented approach to welfare benefits is revealed in the specification of several distinct categories of disablement used to distinguish those claimants who qualify for particular types of allowances (see *Social Security Statistics*, Department of

Table 6.1   Sickness, invalidity and disablement benefits, 1993

Benefits	Total claimants	Claimants of working age
Sickness or invalidity benefits	2 114 000	1 826 000
Severe Disablement Allowance	316 000	261 000
Disability Living Allowance	1 308 000	946 000
Disability Working Allowance (as at 31 January 1994)	3 673	3 673

Source: Department of Social Security, 1994.

Social Security, 1994, Table D1.01: 163). The numbers of claimants for sickness and disability benefits are given in Table 6.1.

Supporters of a social model of disability argue that the medical classification of disabled individuals can tell us nothing at all about the social and physical barriers which serve to *disable* them, and the collection and use of such data epitomise the focus of British legislation hitherto, which has concentrated almost wholly upon the impaired individual, rather than upon the disabling effects of the environment in which he or she lives.

Over the years the portfolio of state benefits has widened, but access to this help has always been controlled not only by financial criteria determined by successive governments, but also by judgements made by medical panels about the circumstances of individual claimants. Some social security benefits are means-tested, for example the premiums or additions to basic levels of Income Support and the Disability Working Allowance. The DWA has generally been regarded as a disappointment in that only 11 per cent of applicants have been successful in obtaining favourable decisions, and in any case the criteria for payment entail that recipients still remain on very low levels of pay (*Hansard*, 27 October 1992, Col. 71). Non-means-tested benefits include the Invalidity Pension, Severe Disablement Allowance, Attendance Allowance and the Disability Living Allowance which includes a mobility component.

In summary, if the legislation as a whole was intended to provide disabled people with a route to employment then it has failed signally. To compound matters, disabled people are still largely denied access to public transport, many leisure facilities, some public buildings and to many parts of the education system. Lack of mainstream education has in turn prevented a high proportion of disabled people from gaining academic and professional qualifications.

Social expectations concerning disabled people, the inaccessibility of many buildings, the design of work settings, overt discrimination by employers and educational disadvantage have led disabled people either to command lower wages than those enjoyed by non-disabled counterparts, or to have no work at all (Barnes, 1991; Oliver, 1991). Current British legislation fails to provide equality of opportunity for disabled people in many areas of daily life, whether they are actually at work or wish to obtain work. All of this has led Scott (1994) to conclude that existing remedies are 'untenable, disjointed and unenforceable'.

The social model of disability and the search for change

Disabled people have increasingly questioned the assumptions upon which work, social welfare and social security are based. The Disabled People's Movement acknowledges that individuals may have physical or mental impairments, but argues that it is not these impairments which render people disabled. Rather, social attitudes and institutions, by their very nature, serve to *dis-able* people (Brisenden, 1986). As we mentioned in our introduction to the chapter, this new understanding constitutes a social model of disability. If we apply the model to employment, we see that some people are disabled by managers unwilling to offer them work they could do as well as any non-disabled person; they are refused employment simply because they have an impairment that may be of no relevance to their carrying out the tasks involved (Barnes, 1991). Again, some disabled people are precluded from applying for jobs because they are unable to reach the workplace. Most buses are so poorly designed that wheelchair users cannot enter them, and even where a person has his or her own car, it may be that a flight of steps and the lack of a ramp at the entrance to a building is sufficient to prevent access. Finally, viewed through this 'social model' lens, the benefits system takes on a very different cast, social security becomes a compensatory device intended to mitigate the exclusion of disabled people from the community in general and from paid work in particular.

In recent times, disabled people have formed their own pressure groups (Pagel, 1988; Morris, 1991; Hasler, 1993). They have done this partly to respond to the kinds of exclusion outlined above, but also to argue that policy-makers must abandon the idea that disability is best tackled by intervening in people's lives, categorising them, and producing palliative and segregational support structures. Instead, disabled people are seeking changes in society itself so that they have a fair chance of gaining mainstream, ordinary work, judged solely upon their ability to do the job. Accordingly, they demand better access to higher and vocational education, use of public transport, the appropriate telecommunications equipment and other 'opportunity equalising' modifications in towns, cities and workplaces.

To ensure the removal of existing barriers disabled people have demanded equal opportunities backed by anti-discrimination legislation, and the focus of debate has now clearly moved away from the incapacity of the individual towards the disabling propensities of (non-disabled) society.

In Chapter 3 we discussed a range of approaches to equal opportunity policies that we characterised as minimalist through to maximalist. These ideas are helpful in assessing recent attempts to introduce legislation for disabled people in Britain. The rights-based approach of the disabled people's movement was reflected in the drafting of the Civil Rights (Disabled Persons) Bill introduced late in 1993 by a Labour member of Parliament, Dr Roger Berry. Although the Bill was ultimately lost, it deserves our attention as a model of the maximalist position, exemplifying the kind of legislation that would accord with the precepts of a social account of disability, using a legal framework to ensure equal opportunities for disabled people. The government's own Disability Discrimination Bill, introduced early in 1995, more closely reflects a minimalist stance in which potential rights are hedged about with qualifications, limitations, and 'escape clauses' for employers and others, and in which exhortation replaces compulsion as the main tool of implementation.

In essence, the government based its objection to Dr Berry's Bill upon the findings of a cost compliance analysis carried out by civil servants from a variety of government departments. The document contained an estimate of the non-recurring costs of the Bill of some £17 billion, with a further £1 billion per annum in recurring costs. However, it was acknowledged in the analysis that some figures were 'speculative guesstimates' and others had been rounded up. The 'Rights Now' Campaign criticised the compliance cost analysis in that it contained no assessment of the benefits and savings that might accrue from disabled people gaining work. For example, there was no assessment of potential savings in social security benefits. Nor did the assessment take into account the fact that many buildings were already fully or partially accessible, and required no modification (Gooding, Hasler and Oliver, 1994).

At the heart of the Bill stood provisions for the setting up of a Disability Rights Commission which would have performed several duties. First, it would have worked towards the elimination of discrimination against disabled people by ensuring general compliance with the Act. It would also have investigated complaints, provided assistance to disabled people in pursuit of their new legal rights, advised the Secretary of State about the working of the Act and published a code of practice explaining the requirements of the Act.

Having set in place a regulatory and inspectorial mechanism, other clauses of the Bill specified measures to make it unlawful for any employer to discriminate on the grounds of disability against a person qualified to do a job. Broadly, the legislation would have covered such matters as job application procedures; the hiring, promotion or dismissal of employees; employee compensation; training; and other terms and conditions of employment. An employer would have had to 'make reasonable accommodation', that is, make facilities used by employees readily accessible to, and usable by, disabled people. If necessary an employer would have had to engage in job restructuring, including the modification of work schedules. Restrictions would also have been placed upon employers concerning the circumstances in which they could require a candidate to undergo medical examinations or enquire of applicants as to whether they were disabled.

Other sections of the Bill were concerned with disabled people as consumers, and these clauses would have made it illegal to deny them goods and services, including such items as hotel accommodation, education, facilities for banking or insurance, places of entertainment, transport by land, sea or air, telecommunications and the services of any profession or trade.

The Civil Rights Bill set out to change significantly the environment in which disabled people live, and the implications will be discussed farther after consideration of the government's own response, produced under considerable pressure from all sides. The government issued a consultation document setting out its own thoughts in July 1994 and presented its Disability Discrimination Bill (Great Britain, House of Commons, 1995) to Parliament in January 1995. Measures elaborated in the Bill fell far short of the kind of anti-discrimination laws desired by the opposition. First, the Bill as initially published defined disability in narrow terms such that many disabled people might be excluded from its provisions. Whereas the proposed Civil Rights Bill encompassed people with a physical or mental impairment, or those *reputed* to have such an impairment, the government Bill included only people with physical or mental impairments so severe that they had 'a substantial and long-term adverse effect on [a person's] ability to carry out normal day-to-day activities'. Secondly, in connection with employment, companies with less than 20 employees were exempted altogether from the 'duty not to discriminate' and the quota scheme was to be repealed in its entirety.

In respect of employment, the government's Bill heavily restricted disabled people's ability to pursue cases of unlawful discrimination through the courts. Cases would instead be heard by industrial tribunals. Thirdly, the government's Bill offered no guarantee of access to public transport or to places of education, and allowed a variety of circumstances in which disabled people's access to goods and services could be restricted or denied. Finally, the proposed 'National Disability Council' would lack the powers envisaged in the regulatory and investigative Disability Commission described in the opposition's Bill: powers currently enjoyed by both the Equal Opportunities Commission and the Commission for Racial Equality.

As we write, the government (mindful of its threadbare parliamentary majority, and under sustained pressure from the opposition parties), has intimated a willingness to give ground in some areas of the Bill, including the clauses concerned with access to public transport and with the definition of disability. However, the final shape of the legislation remains, as yet, unclear. For disabled people the government's Disability Discrimination Bill poses a dilemma. Disabled people's own groups have said that they will boycott the National Disability Council, but others stand ready to take whatever money and influence may be on offer. As K. Milne (1995: 27) has put it, 'It does not take a futurist to see recriminations ahead.' The Disability Movement can hardly feel like compromising its objectives having come this far, and its members remain determined, as the motto on their T-shirts testifies: 'To boldly go where all others have gone before'.

The opposition's Civil Rights Bill held out the prospect that disabled people might use a substantial body of new law to combat discrimination against them, whether it be in the workplace, the high street, or the community at large. It was a Bill which responded to the notion that disability has social rather than physiological causes, and its locus for change was environmental rather than individual. The government's response, while not denying the broader ramifications, sought to minimise the impact upon social and economic institutions by promoting the medical model of disability. A tight definition of disability couched wholly in terms of individual impairment, would allow the government heavily to circumscribe the scope of the Bill and as a consequence to moderate the effects of any movement towards equal opportunities, for example by allowing employers to reject, on a variety of grounds (including costs), 'unsuitable' individuals who applied for work. The opposition's Civil Rights Bill sought to promote the rights of disabled people as a group of (hitherto) disadvantaged citizens. The government's Bill aimed to help individual disabled people to 'overcome their disabilities' by adjoining modest environmental changes to existing programmes of welfare-based intervention. The relative merits of these two approaches are echoed in a wider, international debate, and it is to this context that we now turn.

Comparative approaches to overcoming discrimination

We continue our consideration of maximalist and minimalist approaches to equal opportunity policy by comparing the experiences of disabled people in Sweden, the United States and Australia. The reader will see that (although on a much grander scale) Swedish welfare programmes designed to assist individuals through specific forms of intervention accord more closely with the British Conservative Government's (minimalist) concept of targeted help for disabled people. On the other hand, the American and Australian rights-based approach has clearly informed the (maximalist) stance taken by the British Labour Party in the Civil Rights Bill.

Welfare approaches: the Swedish model

The Swedish approach to disabled people and work may be described as essentially compensatory or ameliorative. Ginsburg (1983) identified what she calls 'a staggering array' of selective policies targeted to overcome the problem of unemployment faced by specific groups in particular regions of the country. Gould (1988) has argued that the commitment of successive social democratic governments to full employment left relatively few people dependent upon social assistance, and claimants needed help only for relatively short periods of time. The main body concerned with the formulation and implementation of policy is the National Labour Market Board (Arbetsmarknadsstyrelsen, or AMS) which draws its membership from government, management and workforce.

To ensure full employment the AMS has pursued a strongly corporatist and interventionist approach to industrial policy and the labour market. Disabled people were not excluded from such aims and even the generous levels of disability pensions were not intended as a substitute for work, which was considered a necessary element of integration into society (Gould, 1993).

The principal approach of the Swedish system has been to use a variety of techniques designed to fit people to jobs. People have been helped even where extensive preparation was required before they could commence work. Gould (1988: 35) quantified this investment in support structures by highlighting the dramatic increase in welfare staff. In 1960 only 4500 social workers were employed by social services, compared with 25 000 by 1980. Likewise, the number of psychologists and related professionals increased from 7000 to 25 000. Ronnby (1985) recorded an increase in the total number of welfare workers from 35 000 in 1960 to over 160 000 by 1975.

Ginsburg (1983) and Gould (1993) describe the use of several kinds of mechanisms for the maintenance of high rates of employment and for worker protection. These have included on-the-job training, new recruitment grants, job placement, new vacancies information, career guidance, vocational training, mobility allowances, regional allowances and subsidies. Workers receive advance warning of redundancies, and unemployment is cushioned through high levels of benefit. To assist those without jobs, rehabilitation and training measures are provided by the Labour Market Institutes located in every region. The main purpose of these centres is to improve the physical, mental and social functioning of their clients. Since neither rehabilitation nor occupational training necessarily lead to a job, the state has also provided grants, subsidised employment and other measures including sheltered employment and relief work. Gould (1993) traced an increase in the number of subsidies to employers taking on disabled people from 48 000 in 1979 to 79 000 in 1988.

In Sweden 'Adjustment Groups' have the task of devising practical ways to help disabled people to get and keep jobs, and to promote positive attitudes towards them. The groups also advise on changes to the work setting in order to offset a person's impairment. Measures specific to work are supported by other interventions in housing, transport and social services. New buildings are made accessible and grants are available for remodelling existing dwellings. Until all public transport is made accessible, disabled people receive subsidies to use taxis. Notwithstanding all these efforts, disabled people who lack employment still face a difficult time. Swedish employers remain reluctant to appoint disabled people, usually citing profitability or lack of suitable work as the reason. Given the choice, companies are wont to select the non-disabled. Gould argues that disabled people are particularly hard hit during economic recession, and even during economic recovery they stand at the end of the line and can be bypassed as long as there is a ready source of non-disabled workers from other areas.

How long Sweden may be able to continue with its high level of welfare provision and supportive intervention is now in question. As unemployment moved ahead of 10 per cent (Savill, 1994) and total government debt in 1994 amounted to 80 per cent of gross domestic product, the newly elected Social Democrat Prime Minister, Ingvar Carlsson warned of deep cuts to come in welfare spending (Isherwood, 1994).

The Swedish approach has its critics. For example, Ronnby (1985) has argued that the Swedish state apparatus is designed to serve the interests of modern capitalism and the managerial class. One consequence of the extent of welfare support is that employers may more freely discard people in the knowledge that they will be 'patched up' by the system. Since the state provides income support, employers do not have to worry about the effects of redundancy upon their former staff. Sjostrom (1984) concurs with Ronnby's view, arguing that social work provides, in effect, 'janitorial' services: that is, for Sjostrom, surplus labour can be maintained on welfare until economic conditions allow for re-engagement in the workforce. Likewise, Ronnby believes that it is in the interests of the state to care for disabled people, since by doing so it releases non-disabled family members (carers) for work. Both Ronnby and Sjostrom see welfare as structurally subordinate and suppliant to capitalism.

Notwithstanding such criticisms, the welfare approach, based upon interventions aimed at the integration of disabled people into society at large, has gained broad support across the international community. König and Schalock (1991) report that disabled people have insisted on equal opportunities in education, employment and social life and have found their concerns reflected in international standards. 'For example, the International Labour Organisation (ILO) Vocational Rehabilitation and Employment (Disabled Persons) Convention, 1983 (No. 159) requires that appropriate vocational rehabilitation measures be made available to all categories of disabled people'; and the ILO Vocational Rehabilitation and Employment (Disabled Persons) Recommendation, 1983 (No. 168) calls for 'research and the possible application of its results to various types of disability in order to further the participation of disabled persons in ordinary working life'. Such aims were pursued during the United Nations Decade of Disabled Persons (1983–92). Momm and König (1989) describe the adoption of a community-based rehabilitation approach both in the UN's World Programme of Action for Disabled People and in the initiatives of the International Labour Organisation. Momm and König highlight the work of the ILO in Indonesia, the Philippines, Zimbabwe, Ethiopia, Malawi, Tanzania, Lesotho, Swaziland, Zambia and Kenya. Many of these community-based rehabilitation projects have involved the training and rehabilitation of disabled people. However, all of them have lacked:

> an essential element to which the United World Programme of Action and particularly organisations of disabled people around the world have drawn attention: rehabilitation efforts need to be complemented by what has been called 'equalisation of opportunities . . .
>
> In fact the essential part of the process falls largely outside the control of specialised rehabilitation programmes since successful integration depends mainly on the attitude of the community and its institutions and their acceptance of the idea that disabled people should not be marginalised or segregated but should be offered equal opportunities. (Momm and König, 1989: 505–6)

It is in the light of this understanding that other states have adopted a fundamentally different approach to disabled people's employment and citizenship. Their concern has been to eradicate discrimination and to establish civil rights and equal opportunities for disabled people.

Civil rights approaches: America and Australia

The contemporary approach in the United States has differed markedly from that in Sweden. The rights of disabled people as full citizens have been enshrined in the United States with the Americans with Disabilities Act of 1990. The Act resulted from more than 20 years of powerful lobbying by disabled people and their allies (De Jong, 1979, 1983; Anspach, 1979). Using a broad definition of disability, the Act has accorded extensive rights to disabled people under five main sections or titles.

Title I of the Act outlaws discrimination against disabled people in public and private sector employment. Those disabled people who could perform the 'essential functions' of a job qualified for protection under the legislation. Any employer with 15 or more staff is required not to discriminate against such candidates and must make 'readily achievable' and 'reasonable' accommodations to the workplace to facilitate disabled employees.

Title II dealt with public services and transport. Public bodies have to make 'reasonable' changes to rules, policies or practices and remove physical barriers, or provide auxiliary aids, to render their services usable by disabled people. The Act covers all government facilities, services and communications. Any newly purchased public service vehicles must be accessible, and from 1996 coaches and trains will be included in these requirements. Titles III and IV required the accommodation of disabled people in educational, recreational and leisure facilities such as schools, cinemas and shops. Phone companies had, within three years, to provide TDD relay (a specialised telecommunications system) for persons with hearing impairments. Lastly, title V set out the enforcement structure of the Act and the avenues of redress available to disabled people where employers or service providers failed to comply with the law. The Act is enforced by an Equal Employment Opportunities Commission and by designated state agencies.

One of the main strands of argument against the introduction of similar legislation in Britain has been the fear of the cost of implementation. However, Scott (1994) cites data from America which show that implementation of the Americans with Disabilities Act did not lead to excessive expenditure, litigation or commercial bankruptcies. All but 1 per cent of accommodations made for disabled employees cost less than $5000 (about £3300). Furthermore, by making businesses more accessible to disabled people, sales of goods and services increased. Scott quotes the example of a Pizza Parlour that introduced a TDD telephone system for customers with hearing impairments. The deaf community boosted the sales of the outlet by 80 per cent within three months of the new equipment being installed. The National Federation of Small Business Owners acknowledged that the Act became a goldmine for them. The economic arguments against the Act were further undermined by the fact that, as President Bush stated in a speech at the White House in July 1990, 'When you add together state, local and private funds, it costs almost $200 billion annually to support Americans with disabilities, in effect to keep them dependent.'

The further criticism, that disabled workers were less reliable than non-disabled personnel, was effectively refuted by the results of a survey taken over three decades by DuPont in Washington which found that 97 per cent of disabled workers were average or above average in terms of job safety; 86 per cent were average or above average on attendance; and 90 per cent were average or above average on general job performance (Scott, 1994: 22).

The civil rights-based approach extends beyond the United States. Both Canada and Australia have adopted similar measures. Tucker (1994) draws parallels between the Americans with Disabilities Act and the Disability Discrimination Act passed in Australia in 1992. Though having different antecedents, the Australian legislation also postulates the issues in terms of civil rights, and sees enforcement as being a matter of law. Even the terminology is similar: employers must make 'reasonable accommodations' to allow disabled employees to perform the 'essential functions' of the job. Again, the Australian Disability Discrimination Act provides that all facilities available to the public must be accessible to disabled people. This includes services such as banking, insurance, transport, travel and telecommunications.

Conclusions: disabled people and equal opportunities

Our analysis has shown that legislation for disabled people has been formulated according to one of two main kinds of approach. First, we have seen welfare-based measures aimed at individual intervention, composed within a medical understanding of disability. Secondly, there have been rights-based initiatives aimed at producing change in the social and physical environment so as to remove sources of discrimination. Oliver (1991) has argued that welfare-based attempts to improve the employment prospects of disabled people have failed because they focus almost entirely upon labour supply. Their aim has been to make individual disabled people suitable for work but, while they may succeed in individual cases, such programmes *ipso facto* allow employers to assume that disabled people may not be effective employees: why else would they need training, rehabilitation, and special bidding undertaken by non-disabled people on their behalf? As Lunt and Thornton (1994) observe, the individual is presented as 'in some way less than whole and as deficient, and thus the employer requires compensation in order to employ him/her'. Erlanger and Roth (1985) therefore propose that what is required is more intensive action on the demand side of the economic equation. They recommend alterations to the organisation and conduct of work itself through the removal of architectural barriers, the introduction of flexible timetables and so forth. Oliver concludes that role-related government policies aimed only at the labour supply are unlikely to improve the social and economic position of disabled people. Further, he argues that government policy has never provided incentives to promote 'barrier-free work environments'. Indeed, the unemployment of disabled people and their institutionalisation have 'performed a particular ideological function, standing as visible monuments to the fate of others who might no longer choose to subjugate themselves to the disciplinary requirements of the new work system' (Oliver, 1991: 139). 'Individuality can be seen as the dominant discourse and is suggested as the commonsensical [sic] way to understand the area. This precludes recognition and discussion of a number of other positions, including structural disadvantage' (Lunt and Thornton, 1994: 225).

Hitherto then, the more typical response of policy-makers has been to 'individualise' the problem of unemployment among disabled people. Employers have been encouraged to take on disabled people in return for government subsidies. As has been seen, the social model of disability implies an entirely different foundation for policies concerned with the employment of disabled people. From this perspective, since all people have rights accorded to them as citizens, it is appropriate that work environments should be constructed, in so far as is possible, to accommodate all categories of people. Such a theory leads to a policy of alleviation rather than compensation (Oliver, 1990). It entails the redesign, reframing, reconstruction and reconstitution of work through inclusionary policies, and work itself requires redefinition so as to encompass all people of all abilities (Lunt and Thornton, 1994).

Gooding (1994) warns against too stark a polarisation in any analysis of 'welfare' versus 'rights' approaches to equal opportunities. Whilst acknowledging the welfare-inspired orientation of existing law, Gooding perceives in British social policy since 1970 'scattered glimpses' of a rights-based approach. She cites as evidence the desegregation envisaged in the 1981 and 1993 Education Acts and the removal of environmental barriers presaged by the 1970 Chronically Sick and Disabled Persons Act, amended in 1976 to include places of employment within its scope. However, Gooding acknowledges that the new discourse of rights is only feebly present in these pieces of legislation (Gooding, 1994: 129–32). For example, Topliss and Gould (1981) have argued that subsequent case law has heavily favoured employers, and has discouraged local authorities from taking action under the Chronically Sick and Disabled Persons Act.

Several pressures militate for anti-discrimination legislation. First, the lobbying power of disabled people has grown enormously as they have developed a collective call for citizenship and equal rights. Through use of current (albeit imperfect) law, and through direct action and even civil disobedience (Crow, 1990; Shakespeare, 1993), disabled people have brought their claims to political and public attention.

Secondly, the nature of work itself is changing. Heavy industry and manufacturing has declined, to be replaced by jobs in new technology and computing: jobs which many disabled people are able to perform perfectly well. The workplace is also changing, for in many of these new jobs, the employee works from home.

Thirdly, there are significant economic arguments. If disabled people are employed, benefit payments are reduced. Disabled people are also important as consumers, spending some £33 billion per year. Accordingly, anti-discrimination legislation has received support from surprising quarters such as the Employers Forum and the House of Commons Employment Select Committee (Gooding, 1994). Fourthly, a significant number of British companies have declared themselves to be in favour of strong disability rights legislation (Trapp, 1995).

Finally, formidable support has built up across the political spectrum in recent years. Roger Berry's Civil Rights (Disabled People) Bill was reintroduced into Parliament by another backbench Labour MP (Harry Barnes) early in 1995. The Civil Rights Bill was a landmark in that it proposed measures congruent with the social rather than the medical model of disability, and it responded to pressures applied by disabled people themselves. To achieve full participation both in employment and in society as a whole, they sought to replace charity and state philanthropy with anti-discrimination legislation. The Disabled People's Movement has never denied that individual impairments constrain people in what they can do, but its fundamental goals are access, work, mobility and equality of opportunity. Anti-discrimination legislation is a mechanism central to the fulfilment of these aims. Social security benefits might still be needed by disabled people whose impairments prevent them from working even in the most accommodating environment, but the Disabled People's Movement argues that these benefits should stem from the rights of citizenship, rather than the benefaction of state patronage.

7
AGE AND EQUAL OPPORTUNITIES

Introduction

Equal opportunities policies can be portrayed as strategies de-signed to work for various minority groups – for a marginalised 'them' rather than 'us' – even though effective equal opportunities policies are arguably in the interests of the community as a whole. The example of age discrimination challenges these assumptions. Barring fatal accidents or premature deaths from illness, we all grow into later life. Therefore preventing discrimination on grounds of age potentially has a universal application in a way that other equal opportunities causes do not.

As ageing is an inescapable part of the human condition it is all the more surprising to find that, in western cultures at least, attitudes towards ageing and older people are often ambivalent and negative. One would have thought that, on grounds of self-interest alone, equal opportunities throughout the life course would have been made more of a priority than they are. Everyone, one assumes, hopes to have some choice in their teens, twenties or sixties about what kind of work they would like to do, whether they wish to work part-time or full-time, and when they would like to leave the labour force.

In the United Kingdom, however, age stands out as the major social division side-stepped by anti-discriminatory legislation. At the time of writing anti-discriminatory legislation on disability is being introduced (see Chapter 6) and legislation against race and sex discrimination now has a relatively long history. But the present government has set its face against proposed age equality legislation, favouring persuasion and a policy of mildly exhorting employers to stop discriminating on grounds of age.

We do not wish to imply by these opening remarks, however, that the experience either of being an older worker or of old age itself (post-retirement) need be negative. Not all older employees are pushed aside by younger workers, sidetracked into less valued roles or made redundant before they are ready to leave the work-force. As with race, gender and disability, age inequality is either reduced or increased by a range of social and individual circum-stances: for instance, social class and economic assets, family cir-cumstances, individual abilities. Just as we cannot use a blanket explanation of 'sexism' to account for the varied experiences of women and men in the labour market, neither can 'ageism' be deployed as a catch-all term to compare older and younger workers' experiences. If older workers are unemployed, the rea-sons may lie elsewhere than in age discrimination. If they are employed and relatively well-off, we might conclude that age dis-crimination is either non-existent or is working in a positive dir-ection for the older worker.

The main aim of this chapter is to evaluate as objectively as possible what the employment outcomes have been for both youn-ger and older people. How far is age 'the unrecognised discrimina-tion' (McEwen, 1990) and is there a case for a much tougher approach towards guaranteeing workers' rights in this field, and especially for older workers? Before we examine the evidence, however, some clarification of what is meant by ageism and age discrimination is necessary.

Age discrimination

Put simply, age discrimination refers to differential treatment on grounds of chronological age rather than merit, ability or other individual characteristics. Age-based judgements may be based on knowledge of birth-dates or ages on application forms or other records, or they may be inferred from appearance ('She looks too young for that position' or 'He looks like he's past it – shouldn't somebody younger be doing that job?').

Age discrimination in recruitment is legal in the United King-dom and quite common in job advertisements. Quoting an Equal

Opportunities Commission survey of over 11 000 advertisements for instance, Laczko and Phillipson note that over a quarter stated an age preference; two-thirds of these asked for applicants aged under 35 (1990: 88). A glance at any 'situations vacant' column of a newspaper will confirm this, though with a clustering of age preferences in secretarial and administrative posts (and sometimes combined with covertly expressed gender preferences), as the following examples show:

Receptionist
for Fine Art Publishers, established in 1880, at prestigious Chelsea Head Office. Age 25–50. Smart appearance with good wordprocessing skills.

Marketing sec
Incredibly fast and able secretary. 20s . . . with minimum 50 wpm, in young and growing Retail Marketing Co . . . Variety, pressure and never a dull moment. Call Vanessa . . .

Journalists
We are looking for young English mother tongue journalists with experience . . .
Please give full details of age, education . . .

Chairman's PA
Major Covent Garden PR Consultancy seek a PA for their dynamic Chairman . . . This confidential role involves assisting with his vested interests . . .
Ideally aged in your late 20s . . .

(Source: Guardian, 20 March 1995: 34–7)

Job advertisements which specify age show only part of the picture, and it is likely that more unstated age discrimination exists in initial selection, interviews and subsequent processes such as promotion or redundancy. While many advertisements now encourage applications from other traditionally excluded groups such as gay and lesbian people, disabled people and those from minority ethnic groups, positive encouragement to underrepresented age groups is conspicuous by its absence.

Job advertisements also illustrate the point that negative age discrimination is experienced by younger as well as older applicants or employees, and typically both the youngest and the oldest in the workforce experience the most discrimination. For instance, two of the examples given above discourage applicants in their late teens or early twenties.

Rates of redundancy (the numbers of workers made redundant for every 1000 employees) confirm that the oldest and youngest age groups are most affected. For instance in Spring 1994 male employees aged over 50 were the most likely to have been made redundant (14.5), although it is worth noting that in Spring 1991 the youngest groups (age 16–24) had the highest rates at 29 and 18 per thousand for men and women respectively (see Table 7.1). Rates of unemployment, however, seem to show that it is the youngest group which experiences exclusion from the labour force most frequently (see Table 7.2).

However, comparisons of unemployment between age groups are complicated by the fact that there is a considerable amount of 'disguised unemployment' among older workers. This stems partly

Table 7.1   Redundancy rates by age and gender, Great Britain (redundancies per '000 employed)

Age	Men		Women		All	
	1991	1994	1991	1994	1991	1994
16–24	29	14	18	8	24	11
25–49	21	12	8	5	16	9
50+	23	15	9	8	18	11

Note: Rates have been rounded to the nearest whole number.
Source: Employment Gazette (1995: 25), adapted from Table 7.

Table 7.2   Claimant unemployment by selected age groups in the UK, October 1994 (percentages[a])

	18–19	20–24	30–39	50–59	All ages[b]
Men	22	21	13	13	13
Women	15	11	4	5	5
All	19	16	9	9	9

Notes:
[a] Percentages have been rounded;
[b] Also including age groups not listed in this table.
Source: Employment Gazette, 1994b. Adapted from Table 2.15, S32.

from the government's decision to reclassify the status of unemployed men aged over 60 in 1983 (Laczko and Phillipson, 1991: 50), which had the effect of reducing the unemployment rate by gradually removing them from the unemployment register. From 1983 they no longer had to register as unemployment claimants to make sure that contribution credits to their retirement pensions were being made. By October 1994 only 2.3 per cent of those over 60 were counted as unemployed, compared with a rate of 9.4 per cent for the UK workforce as a whole (*Employment Gazette*, 1994b: S32). Throughout the twentieth century the proportion of older workers participating in the labour force (and therefore counting as unemployed if not in work) has declined dramatically, especially as far as men are concerned – a trend to which we will return below.

Many unemployed men in their fifties are 'discouraged workers'. They are significantly more likely than the younger unemployed to face long-term unemployment and a significant number give up seriously looking for work. There is also a contrast with a lower rate of unemployment among women, many of whom are economically active in their forties (see Table 7.2).

However, a growing tendency for women to also exit early from the workforce (in their fifties) should not be overlooked. As Ginn and Arber put it, 'A key concern is to understand why women's employment declines so dramatically in their fifties, prior to the state retirement age, when employment is at a high level for women in their forties' (1995: 80). They conclude that this trend is particularly paradoxical in view of the freedom from childrearing responsibilities most women in mid-life have, though family and caregiving responsibilities play a part in decisions to leave paid employment. Among the women in their fifties surveyed by Ginn and Arber, however, age-related attitudes to the undesirability of staying on in paid work and expectations of discrimination seemed to play the most significant part.

Why have these drastic transformations in the labour market occurred, and why have both older men and women been increasingly expected to exit from the workforce at ages well below the official or traditional retirement age? And if there are systematic patterns of discrimination against older workers, both male and female, what rationales or beliefs underpin such actions?

One set of explanations is provided by critical social and psychological theories of the ageing process in western countries

(Minkler and Estes, 1991). There are many variants to these ideas, but they all lead in the same direction. They suggest that ageist beliefs and myths about older people, far from being diminished by advances in both health and scientific understanding of ageing, are still very much with us and tend to reinforce discrimination in the workplace.

Age, ability and work

Perhaps the most significant and damaging set of myths are those which reinforce prejudices about the supposed efficiency of younger as compared with older workers. Younger workers are more readily portrayed as dynamic, adaptable, energetic, creative and intelligent. Job advertisements again provide illustrations of this way of thinking. As one advertisement (from the same source as those cited above) put it, the applicant sought would be working for a 'dynamic team of senior (*but young*) managers' (our italics).

However, there is no conclusive evidence that the productivity or contribution of employees declines with age; rather, experience may enhance skills and judgement in certain respects. As Bromley points out, 'the age factor in occupational performance and re-training is often less important than intelligence, motivation, attitude and education' (1988: 182). This is not to deny that, as we age, both physical and mental changes occur or that there are some losses of capacity or ability to work in certain ways. Before the traditional retirement age of 60 or 65, however, these changes are relatively insignificant. As Bromley and others stress (see for example Kimmel, 1980: 351–63), they can also be ameliorated or compensated for by a progressive approach to retraining and by a positive view of the valuable contribution older employees can make.

Psychological research comparing younger with older groups of people has focused on several important dimensions: for instance, intelligence, memory and learning capacity, and creativity and thinking skills. As far as intelligence or intellectual performance is concerned, some tests appear to support the 'gradual deterioration with age' view. However, there are problems with these findings. One problem is that psychologists disagree about what intelligence tests actually measure, and whether it is safe to combine scores from one type of test with another in order to generalise about the effects of ageing. For instance, some research seems to show that 'the mental abilities involved in untimed verbal tests are maintained quite well as age advances whereas the mental abilities involved in the timed performance tests are not' (Bromley, 1988: 219). However, we must remember that, even if they are valid, such results are based on tests which closely examine individuals' performance in rather unfamiliar ways. Psychological testing in 'laboratory conditions' may well turn up evidence of mental change and perhaps some losses of capacity from the optimum, but in an everyday work setting it is much less likely that such changes would be observable or significant.

Another problem of interpretation is the cohort effect, which results from comparing any sample groups of different ages. By comparing, say, a group of 20-year-olds with a group of 60-year-olds, one may not be identifying the effects of the *ageing* process as much as the historical and educational experiences of each age-cohort. For instance, the educational opportunities of the older group may have been limited, and this may affect both the attitudes respondents have towards intelligence tests (including confidence) and their actual abilities in the test. By the time the 20-year-old group reach *their* sixties, performance levels of older workers in intelligence tests may well have changed. The cohort effect is likely to affect other kinds of comparison between age groups, and also needs to be borne in mind when observations are made about age and memory, or creativity and innovativeness.

Negative views of old age make it easy to blame memory failures on the ageing process, and from mid-life onwards people are apt to refer to their own lapses in this way. Similar memory lapses in younger adults will typically be ascribed to other reasons than ageing.

However, there is some evidence that younger people find it easier to use their short-term memories, and that older people sometimes find it harder to retrieve numerical information (Bromley, 1988: 209–10). There is also evidence to support the view that older workers will need more time to learn new skills than younger workers. However, the capacity to learn seems to be largely unaffected if motivation is high. Much seems to depend on the range and quality of opportunities available for older workers to receive training and to upgrade their skills. Though performance in memory and learning tests does tend to decline gradually with age, it is relatively insignificant in the 45–65 age band and does not justify unwillingness to invest in appropriate training for older workers.

Negative views of ageing also surround ideas about creativity and thinking skills. Older workers are often supposed to be more conservative and rigid in their outlook, the young more adaptable and innovative. The assumption is that, if an organisation wishes to be forward-looking and in tune with its markets or with rapidly changing social trends, ways must be found to make the middle-aged and older step aside in favour of the younger people with the ideas.

A major problem with this assumption is that it is not necessarily *age* which tends to make people cautious or conservative in organisations but *responsibility*. Risk-taking and innovative or 'debunking' behaviour is difficult if one is a staff supervisor, a chief, a manager or even someone responsible for a small team's work and livelihoods.

Traditionally, it is the older employees who have occupied the more responsible roles, whether in non-manual or manual employment. But if career-striving younger people occupy such roles it is quite likely that they too will adopt appropriately cautious behaviour. Quips about younger colleagues being 'old before their time' or being 'about 40 since she/he was 18' illustrate how people tend to associate mid-life with caution, and how they find humour in what seems to be age-inappropriate behaviour in a younger employee. Equally there may be reluctance in managerial or professional fields to envisage older colleagues in challenging or 'rebel' roles – unless, of course, there is a desire to sidetrack them into tangential activities.

Japanese culture and management experience provide an interesting example to question the idea that greater age cannot be associated with creativity and innovation. As Fogarty suggests, 'Japanese management practice offers some particularly interesting lessons in how to balance together the contributions of young and old in a management structure' (1975: 226). Since Fogarty wrote that observation, Japan continued to lead the world in economic growth and in successfully matching new products to changing trends in consumer demand. Involving older employees – sometimes very senior colleagues – in management has certainly not stood in the way of Japanese success. More positively, it is likely that the experience and imaginativeness of older employees have played key roles in making sure that Japanese businesses have addressed the broader and more fundamental questions about where they were headed, or what strategic decisions needed to be made.

In sum, there is inconclusive evidence about the effects of ageing on cognitive skills and mental functions during people's working lives. Some differences between age groups have been observed, but how far the ageing process itself is responsible is still uncertain. Cohort effects might explain some differences and lack of opportunities to upgrade skills among older workers may explain others.

The case is stronger, however, for linking ageing with lowered ability or productivity in certain *physical* tasks at work (Meier and Kerr, 1976; Charness, 1985). There is evidence that older manual workers can be somewhat less able to perform repetitive and strenuous work or to work as well in adverse conditions as younger workers, although this depends on the nature and level of work in question. Again, cohort effects may be playing a part if older workers have been subject to historically specific hazardous conditions, or have suffered industrial injury or impairment at rates which no longer prevail.

However, as we saw in Chapter 2, less skilled work requiring a lot of physical strength has declined dramatically in the past few decades. Where age and productivity may be more significant, perhaps, is in the area of monotonous semi-skilled factory work often performed by women, for example in food-processing. But this in turn raises equal opportunities questions about the design of such jobs: should the older worker be replaced by someone younger, or should the nature and pacing of the work be changed? Fogarty (1975: 146) gives examples of the features of certain kinds of work that call for re-design – for instance continuous heavy work in hot environments.

Early exit: a case of discrimination?

So far we have explored the idea that ageist assumptions and negative views of the capabilities of older workers underpin age discrimination in employment. This is not the whole story, however, and the trend towards early exit from the workforce cannot be explained entirely in terms of perceptions and prejudices. Perceptions do not exist in a vacuum, and to fully explain discrimination against older workers – and thus to be aware of the task facing equal opportunities policies – the economic or labour market context must be taken into account.

Some commentators, for example Phillipson (1982) and Estes (1991), suggest that capitalist market economies tend to exploit the social divisions of age to manage the supply of labour. In times of labour shortage such as the 1940s and early 1950s, attitudes favouring the employment or re-engagement of older workers were promoted by the civil service and other employers, whereas when there is a need to restructure the labour force and to shed industrial workers, the burden of redeployment and redundancy falls disproportionately on older workers. Contrasting trends may even occur within a decade, according to Laczko and Phillipson, who suggest that the 1980s were marked at the beginning by exhortations to older workers to leave the workforce as soon as possible 'to cope with high unemployment and large numbers of school leavers' and towards the end by 'calls on older workers to remain in employment as long as possible' (1990: 84).

Evidence to support the political economy thesis can be found in the initial creation of a phase of life seen as a 'pensionable age' (in the United Kingdom this was age 70 when the first state retirement pension was introduced in 1908), followed by the gradual extension of the idea that older people should not work during that final phase. At the end of the nineteenth century, for instance, two-thirds of men who survived to age 65 continued of necessity to work beyond that age (Laczko and Phillipson, 1991: 10), despite greatly increased risks to their health. However, as Laczko and Phillipson point out, the proportion of men over 65 in employment had fallen to a third by the mid-twentieth century and now only a few per cent of men over 65 continue to work.

In the post-war welfare state, receipt of the state retirement pension was conditional upon giving up work. It was only relatively recently (1989) that this retirement condition was waived. As Walker puts it, by then 'in practice . . . the damage was done' (1990: 61). The notion that old age is a 'pensioned off' workless phase had been firmly implanted. Summing up the impact of retirement policy from a political economy perspective, Walker concludes that

The long-term decline in the participation of older people, particularly older men, in the workforce cannot be attributed to . . . changes in the individual characteristics of older people . . . nor . . . simply on the basis of the preferences expressed by older workers. In Britain and other industrial societies, retirement policies have been used . . . to reduce and restructure workforces in response to both the constant pressure to increase productivity and cyclical change in the demand for labour. Thus, retirement may be seen as an age discriminatory process designed to exclude older people *en masse* from the workforce. (1990: 59)

These comments about the social and economic role of retirement for the over-sixties can now be applied to the 55–9 age category. Early exit has begun to play a similar function for the economy in terms of restructuring and 'downsizing'. As we saw in Chapter 2, the proportion of men who are economically active has fallen in all age groups over the past two decades. However, 'this fall was particularly large for men aged 55 and over' (Central Statistical Office, 1995: 66) – see Table 7.3. The table shows just how significantly economic activity among men aged 16–19, 55–9 and 60–4 declined between 1976 and 1993. Among women in the same age groups economic activity rates stabilised and the projections in Table 7.3 for older women offset somewhat Ginn and Arber's (1995) concerns about a steep rise in early exit among this group.

Table 7.3 Civilian labour force economic activity rates by gender and age in Great Britain (estimates/projections; percentages)

	16–19	20–4	25–34	35–44	45–54	55–9	60–4	All 16+
Men								
1976	71	86	95	96	96	92	80	79
1986	73	86	94	95	92	81	54	74
1993	64	84	93	94	91	75	52	72
1996	58	81	93	94	90	74	50	71
2006	56	78	93	94	89	74	46	69
Women								
1976	68	65	54	67	67	54	27	47
1986	70	71	64	72	71	52	19	50
1993	64	71	71	77	75	55	25	53
1996	61	69	73	79	76	55	26	54
2006	59	69	81	85	78	57	27	56

Note: Percentages have been rounded.
Source: Adapted from Central Statistical Office (1995: 66), Table 4.4.

Now that the economic activity rate among men aged 55–9 has fallen to about three-quarters of that group (from nine-tenths in 1976), the assumption is that it too will stabilise because the number of younger people entering the labour force has declined and will continue to do so. The labour force aged under 24 is projected to fall by half a million between 1993 and 2006. Over the same period the proportion of over-45s in the labour force will increase from 33 to 36 per cent (Central Statistical Office, 1995: 65). Thus the labour force is gradually ageing, and although competition among older workers for employment will increase, competition from younger workers will decrease slightly as their numbers fall and substantial proportions go into further and higher education. This may have some implications for equal opportunities and a swing back to more positive attitudes towards older workers, although it is also likely that the long-term decline in manufacturing and semi-skilled jobs will continue to depress opportunities for older men.

Thus the political economy approach seems to have a great deal of explanatory power. Attitudes to older workers and readiness to employ them are clearly linked to both demographic and labour market trends. The positive side to this, as far as older workers are concerned, is that although ageist views are widespread they are not immutable. If vacancies are hard to fill, particularly when part-time workers are needed to work flexible hours, then employers seem ready to suspend their prejudices.

However, as with any model or theory, the political economy approach to age and the employment market distorts reality if it is taken too far. Though valuable at a macro-level, it may need readjustment or qualification in a number of ways. First, the theory in broad outline seems to explain the experience of older men much better than older women. As Table 7.3 shows, economic activity among older women has increased, not decreased, and it may even do so in the future (though Ginn and Arber, 1995, provide evidence to throw doubt on this). Thus the question 'why does the capitalist market economy exploit divisions of age to make older people redundant?' seems rather irrelevant to women, and a more appropriate question might be 'why has the capitalist market economy facilitated a rise in women's labour market participation (at least in their forties) but not men's?' (see Chapter 4 for further discussion of gender and employment).

A second limitation of the political economy approach is that it may overemphasise both the value of staying in employment in later life and the notion that all who exit early from the workforce do so on unfavourable terms. Walker, for instance, seems to discount the possibility that either choice or the changing characteristics of older workers play a significant part in the trend towards early exit (see above quotation, 1990: 59). But does the theory that retirement policies are used primarily to manipulate or restructure the workforce entirely account for rising demand for early exit among at least some groups? Withdrawal from the labour market can take place on terms which are favourable to former employees and relatively costly to employers. Not all older workers are 'thrown on the scrap heap' with only small redundancy or severance payments, and for some – albeit a fortunate minority – an affluent 'third age' of leisure, possibly with part-time work supplementing income from an occupational pension, is a reality. A counter theory, therefore, is that the trend to early exit has in part been fuelled by union pressure and by changing social aspirations which reflect new attitudes towards later life and leisure.

However, we suggest that the phenomenon of affluent 50-somethings qualifies rather than undermines the political economy perspective. Although some employees win better redundancy or early retirement arrangements than others, they are still in the minority. McKay's survey of pensioners' assets, for instance, showed

> the relative unimportance of income from savings and from occupational pensions for all except the best-off third or so of the pensioner population, despite the rapid rise in the average income from this source in the 1980s. (1992: 8)

And though carrots as well as sticks are used to induce early exit, this does not invalidate the basic idea that it is the market economy which defines the working age and its limits.

This is why the term 'exit' is preferred to 'retirement'. The latter suggests a voluntary withdrawal from the labour market and stresses the passivity of older people once they have 'retired'. The former allows us to recognise that older workers are sometimes ejected from the workforce against their will, or that they would still wish to work if working conditions or wages were different.

Thus the distinction between 'voluntary' and involuntary redundancy or early retirement is rather questionable. People who are not made redundant overnight and who appear to exercise some choice over when to leave the labour force might nevertheless be much swayed by social or normative pressures as well as financial ones. Feelings that one is out of place or obstructing opportunities for a younger employee can erode the self-confidence or self-esteem of older workers.

However, the voluntary/involuntary distinction is also questionable if those who 'decide' to leave the workforce early are pressured to do so either because their earnings are relatively low or because of illness and the effects of arduous work on health. International evidence shows that 'high rates of unemployment in industries with physically and psychologically onerous work increase the probability of early retirement' (Møller, 1987: 427). Discussing Denmark's government-sponsored early retirement scheme in comparative context, Møller concludes that

> The degree to which a wage-earner's retirement is either voluntary or compulsory may be of individual and psychological interest . . . however there is overwhelming evidence both from within Denmark and elsewhere that the poorer the working conditions, the stronger the probability of early retirement. (1987: 433)

This brings us back to questions of equal opportunity. How far do pressures to take early retirement represent unfair discrimination against older workers? Or is there, on the other hand, a genuine ethical point that, as older workers have already enjoyed the opportunity to work, it is only right that they should allow younger or relatively workless people to have a share?

Three conflicting principles are at work here. The first is the idea of equal treatment (see Chapter 3) and of giving people opportunities chiefly on grounds of *merit*, irrespective of age. Neither younger nor older workers have any special claim to work. If an older worker can work more effectively than a younger worker then he or she has the stronger case, but must make way for a younger worker if there is a choice to be made and the younger employee proves to have greater merit or ability.

As we saw in Chapter 3, however, the idea that merit gives an unchallenged right to work can be questioned. First, there are problems about the ways in which 'merit' is defined – in recruitment or promotion, for instance, selection criteria might unfairly discriminate against older workers. Secondly, there are questions about the design of work itself and the conditions under which jobs are carried out. When assessing merit or ability to work effectively is it fair to assume, for instance, that older employees 'cannot work fast enough' without first looking at the way that work is organised, or how working conditions might be improved for workers of all ages?

The second principle to bear in mind is that of *need* for work. In Chapter 3 we discussed the example of a job applicant who had been unemployed for a considerable time and whether this applicant should be given priority, even though his or her merits or qualifications did not quite match those of another applicant who already had another job. Similarly the need principle can be applied to the debate about competition between older and younger people for work. While a man in his fifties may still have both financial and psychological needs to carry on working, arguably a younger man in his early twenties and who has never had the opportunity to work has yet greater needs.

There is also an element of justice on the younger people's side in the notion that 'it's our turn now'. Is there any justice in the principle that older workers should enjoy greater job security than younger employees simply because they got there first? Furthermore, a society in which a rising proportion of young men can see no clear route to secure employment and to which they feel little commitment is increasingly felt to be jeopardising social stability.

Conversely, however, there is a third principle to apply to consideration of early exit versus continuing in work. Crudely it might be expressed as 'wait your turn' rather than 'it's our turn now' – a principle of *queueing for work*. One way of resolving competition for a scarce supply of work is to delay entry to the workforce and to give priority to older rather than younger workers. This way, younger people would find competition for jobs (other than short-term or part-time) even stiffer than it has been to date, but with the compensation that when they reach mid-life it will be their turn. They will be given greater consideration and better employment opportunities.

There are already traces of this pattern. An increasing proportion of younger people are going into higher education or as a result of unemployment are being forced to delay entry to the labour force (see Table 7.3). Also women have traditionally tended to leave paid work during a phase of childrearing in their twenties or early thirties, re-entering the labour force later (see Chapter 4). Women's roles are changing, and delayed or postponed entry to employment will not be as significant in the future as it has been to date if increasing numbers of younger women stay in paid work throughout the childrearing phase. However, to the extent that the traditional pattern continues to exist it does lessen inter-generational competition, especially between older and younger women for part-time jobs.

In practice all three of the above principles enter discussions about work and how it should be shared out between the generations. However, Bytheway's research on large-scale redundancy in South Wales (1986, 1987) suggests that, of the three, older workers (aged over 55) came closer to accepting the second principle – that is, accepting the needs of younger people for work – than either of the other two.

This was largely because, in this example, the redundancy scheme settled upon the workers by the British Steel Corporation made a clear distinction between those aged below and above 55. The over-55s were encouraged by the scheme's Readaptation Benefit (which gave workers *up to* 90 per cent of their earnings in the first year after redundancy, 80 per cent in the second year) not to look for work. For many there was little financial incentive to do so, as finding another job meant loss of the Readaptation Benefit. However, as Bytheway points out, not all the redundant steelworkers aged over 55 in this example did well out of the scheme. Some had not worked for the Corporation for many years, did not receive particularly high redundancy payoffs or works pensions and so were financially in need of another job. But in a tightly-knit industrial community, the redundancy scheme had 'created a certain moral obligation on older workers not to seek work – to do so, it was argued, would deprive younger unemployed men to whom work would bring greater financial advantage' (Bytheway, 1995: 102).

Although this is but one example, similar effects may be observed in wider policy initiatives on early retirement. For example, the UK government's job release scheme (JRS), which operated between 1977 and 1988, applied the 'younger people must be given a chance' principle. Introduced primarily to reduce the unemployment rate, the JRS offered workers who took early retirement an allowance which, at least in the case of unskilled and semi-skilled workers, provided relatively full replacement of earnings (Laczko and Phillipson, 1991: 81). The government stipulated that employers who took advantage of the scheme to restructure their workforces had to replace retirees with younger unemployed workers, though surveys of the JRS showed that over two-fifths of replacements were over the age of 26. Nevertheless the JRS proved to be effective in replacing older workers with younger ones. As a relatively modest scheme, however, it did not make much impact on unemployment as a whole. In a peak year (1984), for example, fewer than 100 000 replacements were created by JRS when the total unemployed stood at over 3 million (Laczko and Phillipson, 1991: 92).

The abandonment of JRS is also significant. There is a growing conflict of interests between government and employers on the subject of early retirement. From the point of view of government, too much early retirement puts additional strains on public expenditure: for example by demand for schemes to subsidise early retirement, retirees' claims on government benefits of various kinds and loss of income tax revenue from older workers who leave the workforce. On the other hand, employers seek to use early retirement schemes to rationalise and shed labour.

This conflict of interest is well illustrated by the French experience of government policies towards early retirement and rights to work in later life (Guillemard, 1985). In the 1960s an interventionist government promoted policies to keep older workers in the labour force, refusing to lower the official pensionable age and subsidising efforts to integrate older employees in the workplace. The main unions opposed this policy, however, seeking change on the grounds that earlier retirement would benefit many of their older members and release jobs for the younger. Employers' associations, as in Britain, also sought support for early retirement schemes to facilitate flexibility and restructuring. Thereafter, as Guillemard explains,

> arguments and viewpoints began . . . converging. Under pressure from the economy and owing to the new line-up of political forces, all actors agreed, for various reasons, on a policy of literally 'unemploying' older workers. The rapid expansion of this policy has plunged French old-age policy not only into a financial crisis, as these . . . 'pre-retirement' schemes ate up more than

half the unemployment fund in 1984, but also into a crisis of legitimacy and motivation. (1985: 381)

Thus conflicts and dilemmas in early retirement policy pose interesting questions for what the definition of equal opportunities in mid-life and later life might be:

- Should 'equal opportunities' for older workers entail protection of the right to 'retire' early, or to have the choice to move into part-time or less physically demanding work on the grounds that, as employees age, they have rather special needs and different capacities – or are these *protective* assumptions ageist?
- Should the emphasis in equal opportunities be placed on *anti-discrimination*, aiming to establish older workers' rights to either stay or take on work for as long as they wish or are able to demonstrate that they can do the job?
- Or should equal opportunities policies on age aim to be *developmental*? This would entail focusing on the nature of work that has to be done and whether beneficial cost-effective changes can be made. It would also regard older employees as a resource to be developed, identifying both the training needs of older employees and the contribution they themselves might be able to make to further development and transmission of skills (see Chapter 8 for a discussion of 'managing diversity').

Age, equal opportunities and the policy agenda

In the United Kingdom and other industrial countries a protective ideology has affected thinking on age and work far more than awareness of the problem of age discrimination. Anti-discriminatory and developmental thinking lags behind. Where legal rights for older workers have been established, for example rights in Belgium, France, Germany and Sweden to training and educational leave programmes at any age (Fogarty, 1975: 226), they tend to be undermined by 'protective' policies such as encouragement of early exit or the introduction of flexible pension schemes.

Only in the United States is there legislation to deal comprehensively with age discrimination in employment. In other countries where there is any legislation, such as France, coverage is usually restricted to matters such as banning age requirements in job advertisements.

A survey by the Employment Department (Moore et al., 1994) found considerable variation among 22 countries in policies on the employment of older workers, ranging from legislation against age discrimination, policies to retain older workers, and policies on equality in early retirement schemes and in pension schemes. Some countries (for instance Japan, Austria and Germany) use state subsidies to promote the recruitment of older workers while others (for example the Scandinavian countries) concentrate on 'health at work' schemes aimed at older workers. The Employment Department report concludes that, despite the range of provisions and policies tried in different countries, nowhere have outcomes been significantly changed in terms of providing suitable jobs for older workers.

Even in the United States, where an Age Discrimination in Employment Act was passed in 1967, the impact of an anti-discriminatory philosophy has been slight. American law forbids age discrimination against people aged 45–64 in recruitment and promotion, and in providing training and other benefits.

According to Laczko and Phillipson, the main reason for the Act's muted impact has been the unwillingness of either government or employers to take the legislation seriously or to publicise it effectively; consequently many employees are simply unaware of their rights, or of how they might establish a case of age discrimination (1991: 120). They also mention the negative impact legislation may be having on the willingness of employers to hire older workers protected by anti-discrimination legislation, although presumably if the legislation were properly enforced it would have the opposite effect, encouraging employers to act fairly in recruitment processes to avoid charges of age discrimination. Whatever the causes of the United States' weak implementation of age discrimination laws, the end result has been much the same as in other industrial countries, in terms of a trend towards early retirement and the lay-off of workers in their fifties.

Not surprisingly perhaps, policy-makers and politicians in the United Kingdom have tended to use the limitations of whatever legislation has been introduced in other countries to justify the case for not introducing age discrimination laws. The case for improving on others' legislative efforts, or of putting age discrimination on the same footing as sex or race discrimination, is rarely explored.

For instance, in reply to a call for an age discrimination law an Employment Minister, Ann Widdecombe, gave a written answer to the House of Commons (*Hansard*, 18 October 1994, Col. 197) which pointed out that 'this Government has no intention of introducing legislation on age discrimination; it would be ineffective . . .'. The minister went on to argue how additional legislation would burden employers and how a persuasive approach would bear more fruit. The assumption was that though some injustice exists, the needs of older workers can be met through existing channels or by encouraging employers to be less discriminatory on grounds of age.

How the government can argue this, however, is not clear, given lack of evidence about whether existing institutions meet the challenge of age discrimination in any way. For instance in reply to another Parliamentary question (20 April 1994) on 'how many UK employees have (a) won and (b) lost an appeal against unfair dismissal on age grounds', the same government minister admitted that there is no way of knowing. At present, the Industrial Tribunal Central Office does not collate information on age discrimination in an easily accessible way (*Employment Gazette*, 1994c: 139).

Despite the absence of specific legislation on age discrimination, though, it is worth noting that the industrial tribunal system can at least be used to challenge unfair dismissal when age has been used as the sole criterion. For example in Birmingham in 1992, an industrial tribunal awarded a total of £40,000 compensation to three taxi drivers who had been dismissed simply because their employer had chosen the age of 60 as a yardstick to decide who should be made redundant (EOR, 1994e: 12).

Some employers are at least aware of the problem of age discrimination and have incorporated statements about it in their equality and management policies. The Littlewoods organisation, for instance, launched a 'dignity at work' policy in 1994 which included advice on how to counter age discrimination. In doing this, Littlewoods went beyond any current legislative requirements. Over 50 employees have been designated as investigators who have the brief to provide assistance in cases of alleged discrimination or victimisation, including age discrimination (EOR, 1994f). Other employers have also been cited as moving towards some recognition of age discrimination and the need to counter it in selection and training policies: for example National Westminster Bank, Nationwide Building Society, Sainsbury's, South Yorkshire Police, Unigate and Waverley District Council (EOR, 1994e: 12).

In addition to these initiatives there is evidence that, despite ruling out legislation on age discrimination, the government itself has at least begun to consider the issue more seriously than in the past. An advisory group was set up by the Employment Department (chaired by Ann Widdecombe) and, in a paper entitled *Getting On* (see EOR, 1994g: 12), government has urged employers to take five steps to counter age discrimination. These are to

- select and promote employees on grounds of merit or ability and regardless of age;
- remove age bars, or references to age limits, in job advertisements, the selection process and in advice to recruitment agencies. The 'date of birth' section should be removed from official forms (though, as noted by the EOR, 1994a: 12, the Civil Service routinely continues to request dates of birth on application forms);
- positively welcome applications from older workers;
- consider how to introduce flexible working arrangements that facilitate retention of older workers;
- be prepared to invest in all workers regardless of age. The productivity benefits of employing and retaining older workers are specified: for example lower staff turnover and increased customer satisfaction.

Conclusion

In sum, however, the above advice comes closer to symbolic policy-making than a genuine programme of change. Government has reacted to increasing public awareness of age discrimination but rather than leading opinion or forging policy it seems more likely that the *Getting On* report will echo similar previous government exhortations to value older workers, which have appeared from time to time (Phillipson, 1982).

The crucial test of government concern is willingness to introduce anti-discriminatory legislation, and at the time of writing there are no plans for this. Interestingly the Social Justice Commission, set up to advise the Labour Party on a range of social policy questions, does advocate a toughening of all anti-discrimination laws and the inclusion of legislation on age discrimination (see EOR, 1994h: 2). However, the Labour Party will not be bound by the Social Justice Commission's recommendations and it remains to be seen whether this development will have any impact.

In support of the case for not introducing age-related anti-discrimination legislation we might conclude that it is rather difficult, looking at international evidence, to measure the outcomes of such legislation or to anticipate what its impact might be in countries where there is currently no legislation, such as the United Kingdom.

First, there is the danger of a backlash against older workers. Admittedly this problem is always mentioned when anti-discrimination laws are proposed, but in this case there is some evidence from the United States that age equality laws might disadvantage some older job applicants rather than protect them. Secondly, there is no clear evidence that outcomes, as shown by the participation rate of older workers in the labour force, are any different in countries which have some anti-discrimination legislation compared with those which do not (EOR, 1994i). As with gender inequalities and the rate of women's participation in the labour force, outcomes seem to be affected to a much greater extent by the supply of work, and in particular by the availability of part-time jobs.

However, as we have pointed out, there are serious and widespread problems of age discrimination in industrial countries. In response to rapid economic change and the need to restructure the workforce, both employers and governments have colluded in (though sometimes conflicted over) the task of putting substantial numbers of older workers outside the labour force. Given the profound nature of these changes, it is hardly surprising that the mild forms of age-related anti-discriminatory legislation to be found around the world have not made much difference.

Therefore the case for anti-discriminatory legislation and other measures on age inequality could only be properly assessed if a tougher approach were to be tried. In the meantime, though, we should not forget that *some* positive outcomes have been observed even where legislation on age equality is not particularly demanding or wide-ranging. In parts of Australia, for instance, there have been significant increases in the numbers of employees aged over 60 recruited into government agencies since 1991. There is also evidence from the same country and from the United States that employers have begun to make significant changes in job descriptions and evaluations, bearing the need to avoid age discrimination in mind (EOR, 1994i: 9).

Finally, we should not forget the 'backstop' role of equal opportunities legislation, which we discussed in Chapter 4 with regard to protecting gains in gender equality. While it may be an uphill struggle for equal opportunities policies to generate new opportunities or expand horizons for excluded groups, policies which include government legislation may be able to play a vital role in safeguarding the labour market position of employees who fall into vulnerable categories, such as older workers. For example in the United States (EOR, 1994c: 12) there is evidence that some older workers were protected by age equality legislation from job losses. But for legislative protection, losses would have been even more severe during the 1980s period of labour market restructuring and 'shake-outs'.

8
MANAGING EQUAL
OPPORTUNITIES

Introduction

In the preceding pages we discussed the changing context (Chapter 2) and different models and concepts of equality policies (Chapter 3) while the main part of the book has concentrated on equality outcomes for a range of groups. An understandable response to all this might be, 'theories and information are fine, but what about equal opportunities in practice?' How may we explain different modes of implementation of equality policies, and how much difference does the adoption of one kind of strategy make as opposed to another?

Accordingly, in this penultimate chapter we aim to draw upon the ideas and examples discussed in previous chapters to examine the *management* of equality strategies and how earlier modes of management or implementation are being superseded by a 'managing diversity' approach.

'Management' refers to a host of functions and tasks in a wide range of organisations and industries. Therefore we first need to discuss management and implementation in a little more detail, and consider the relationship between management strategies and equal opportunities.

Although managers are by definition interested in implementation and in how to apply ideas to real situations, this does not mean that they are always concerned with one narrow reality, nor that they are impervious to fads and fashions in management thinking. This applies to equality and diversity in the workforce as much as it does to any other management concern. Ideas about the way equality strategies might be harnessed to business competitiveness have become increasingly noticeable (see, for example, Kandola et al., 1995), and these ideas have emanated from the world of management and business rather than from government or social policy.

However, there is no single 'business case' for or against equality policies resting on one set of economic realities or business objectives (Dickens, 1994). Private sector companies and public sector organisations will have rather different views on the business case for equal opportunities. To accommodate these the Commission for Racial Equality (1995), for instance, distinguishes between a 'business case' for equal opportunities in the private sector and a 'quality case' in public bodies. There will also be different views among different kinds of industry or organisation. The nature of the workforce in terms of levels of pay and valued skills, for instance, suggest themselves as important factors affecting the ways in which equality policies are regarded, or whether managers think they should be woven into business or management objectives.

Thus rather than contrasting a complicated world of theories and models of equality policy with a 'nitty gritty' but relatively simple world of hard-headed managers driven by practical considerations, it would be nearer the truth to see the latter world as equally complicated. There are many rival ideas about what the best approaches to management might be (see for example Peters, 1989) and, in the real world, competing models of management practice.

There are three general points to consider before we examine the models in more detail. First, how central are equality policies in the worlds of public and private sector management? On the one hand, for example, the Commission for Racial Equality has found that almost all employers in a wide-ranging survey of 168 of the largest UK companies and their subsidiaries have made a commitment to (racial) equality policies (Ollerearnshaw and Waldreck, 1995). But on the other hand, of these only half had begun to translate their publicly stated commitment into any kind of action.

How can such apparent management conservatism, or resistance to equality policies, be explained? Previous research suggests that institutional discrimination is primarily responsible. Better awareness through training, combined with a degree of law enforcement, are usually recommended as the main strategy to deal with the problem.

While such strategies have some impact, however, progress in racial equality (see Chapter 5) and in other fields has been relatively slow. In coming to terms with this the CRE and other bodies such as the Equal Opportunities Commission have begun to ask whether a better response from employers and managers might be elicited by showing how equality policies can improve employee initiative, effectiveness and productivity. As Ollerearnshaw and Waldreck put it,

> The commission has decided that, while law enforcement remains a priority . . . it must engage more people in taking action for racial equality and better human relations. And it must get them to do so not because the CRE tells them to, but because they want to – because they understand that implementing . . . equality measures. . .is of direct benefit to themselves. (1995: 24)

The second major question is whether a managing diversity approach will succeed in these aims where previous equal opportunities policies have either failed or had limited success. Does 'managing diversity' represent a genuine step forward which will accelerate the adoption of equality and diversity targets, or is it a form of rhetoric which, in attempting to 'sell' equality to managers, will only succeed in softening or weakening equality policies?

Also, we need to be aware of the scale and significance of changes sweeping through the world of management. As we saw in Chapter 2, these changes are manifesting themselves in a number of ways: for instance, both public and private organisations are increasingly tending to contract out their work to smaller groups, companies or individuals, leaving smaller 'core function' groups to be managed; in the Civil Service, health service and other public agencies, restructuring and privatisation have been accompanied by significant changes towards a managerialist and market-oriented approach to administration; and again in both public and private sectors 'delayering' of management has been increasingly advocated.

A third question, then, is whether flatter management structures and the changes in organisational culture now expected to accompany them will put equality strategies at the core of business objectives. Or will decentralisation and delayering do the opposite, with greater power at the local level leading to more appointments being made arbitrarily, to greater scope for favouritism in staff promotion, and to the erosion of company-wide equal opportunity standards?

This is a question we introduced in Chapter 2, and it is worth returning to now to consider contemporary thinking in management on the issue. Among management gurus such as Peters (1986, 1989) there is a rather optimistic view of 'change as a positive challenge'. Consider these comments by Nixon for example:

> There is now a wide measure of agreement in management literature that the organisations which survive and prosper . . . will have an attitude of welcoming change; constantly searching for improvements; being close to and responsive to their customers; and being innovative, creative and flexible. They will recognise the importance of empowering people at every level, so that they show initiative and see to it that everything goes well . . . . They will be moving away from patriarchy, control, dependency and compliance towards community, partnership, autonomy and a sense of shared ownership. (1995: 36)

To say that these are normative or somewhat idealistic statements is not to conclude that they are necessarily wrong. There may well be some evidence that rapid economic and organisational change could, even as a by-product, encourage the promotion of equality and the shedding of hide-bound attitudes towards hierarchies in management – although as will be recalled, the evidence to date is rather mixed (see Chapter 2 and Mason and Jewson, 1992).

'Management talk' is often designed to be idealistic and inspirational rather than sceptical or realistic. The opposite case, that human beings often take refuge in conservative opinions and prejudiced attitudes when technological and economic changes threaten their security, also needs to be considered (Schon, 1971). In other words, we need to keep an open mind about whether business success is associated with profound cultural changes in organisations in the ways identified by management specialists, and in turn whether the kinds of cultural change envisaged do actually lead to greater equality.

The management response to equal opportunities

In Chapter 3 we identified a spectrum of equal opportunities policies from 'minimalist' to 'maximalist'. In the world of management these developments have been increasingly recognised in recent years, so that as noted above most leading companies now have at least a basic or minimalist policy. Managers now seem to distinguish between:

1. 'First generation' equal opportunities policies;
2. 'Second generation' positive or affirmative action;
3. The managing diversity approach.

Equal opportunities

While formal policies to promote equal opportunities have often been put in place, the experience hitherto has been that companies are usually lukewarm in their response and unwilling to integrate an equality strategy into the cultural heart of their businesses.

Behrens and Auluck (1993) have argued that both public and private sector employers have long acknowledged the importance of the principle of equality of opportunity and fair treatment for employees at work. In the 1960s and 1970s this was seen primarily as a question of raising awareness, so creating a sense of social responsibility. But as overall equality aims were not necessarily tied to specific employment opportunities, early initiatives remained unfocused and non-strategic. The approach sought to change people's attitudes about the world in general rather than their behaviour in the workplace in particular. As initiatives were unrelated to corporate strategy they were often met with scepticism from senior managers.

Several authors have described early resistance to the introduction of equal opportunity policies in practice. Hunt (1975) demonstrated that male managers did not believe it would be 'a good thing' if more women occupied senior posts, and they had serious reservations about equal pay. Rose and Deakin (1969) identified a perception among managers that customers might object to interacting with employers who were not white, male and 'able-bodied'. Managers argued that they were not free agents, and had to take into account the attitudes of others. Carby and Thakur (1977) drew attention to the potential for 'backlash' from existing employees, where equal opportunities overrode previous 'perks', privileges and practices. Wrench (1987) highlighted the ambivalence of many trade unions and pointed to a 'noticeable gap between formal policy and practical action'.

Adjustments (re-entry to work after childbirth, child care, flexible working arrangements) were seen very often as the responsibility of the individual employee rather than the employer. Hunt's study of 223 employers in 1973 found managers blaming a lack of career-consciousness and the break in women's working lives as major reasons for the absence of women in senior positions. However, only a small minority of employers made arrangements to take account of the different patterns of women's working lives (Hunt, 1975). More recently, Cameron (1993) finds that equal opportunities policies still fail to deal with the underlying causes of discrimination, and in management terms have often been reactive and expensive attempts at 'quick-fix' solutions which are unrelated to the needs of businesses and people. She also argues that such policies were unbalanced because they excluded men – 'the other 50 per cent of the equality equation' (1993: 19).

Positive or affirmative action

In Chapter 3 we showed how, partly as a result of the perceived failure of earlier equal opportunities policies, a number of nations began to develop the idea of affirmative action. This strategy, it will be recalled, seeks to introduce an element of preference to support individuals from disadvantaged or previously excluded groups over individuals from other groups.

From her review of the experience of women in business and industry, Heilman (1994) concluded that those who were perceived to have gained some advantage through affirmative action were more likely to have negative evaluations made of them by their peers. She called this effect 'the stigma of incompetence'.

Heilman's conclusions are similar to the sceptical views of positive action found among many managers. There is a general belief that the stigma associated with affirmative action could fuel rather than debunk stereotypical thinking and prejudiced attitudes:

> The impression that one is left with is that the overriding con-
> cern is not about fairness or equal opportunity, but about im-
> proving the numbers. This may be fine if you are a member of
> the targeted groups, but extremely unfortunate if you are not.
> (Kandola et al., 1995: 32)

Further criticism has been levelled by Small (1991), who has argued that positive action may yield nothing more than tokenism:
the assumption by organisations that once they had achieved an
acceptable number of recruits from previously excluded groups –
usually in single figures – they need look no further. Woo (1990)
has provided examples from some American universities where
admission targets have been used to restrict, rather than enhance,
the numbers of students from disadvantaged backgrounds.

Behrens and Auluck (1993) identify three kinds of failure on
the part of public policy-makers to convince managers and employers of the case for adaptable or business-friendly equality policies. First, the failure of supporters of affirmative action to identify
it as an historically located tool of policy development rather than
an end of policy in itself. Secondly, the failure to identify what the
goals of policy are and what a diverse public service or private
sector company should look like. And thirdly, the failure made by
proponents of equal opportunities in assuming that the focus of
change is the historically disadvantaged groups themselves rather
than the organisation, its external and internal environments and
all its human resources. In line with this thinking, Behrens (1993)
suggests that, from his own experience, merely providing training
opportunities for black people (for example) sets them up to fail
because it does not change the environment and culture in the
workplace where discrimination occurs. Managers are required to
give the lead by giving more attention to their own behaviour at
work, together with a more imaginative approach to equality strategies which is coupled with genuine consultation.

Managing diversity

For Behrens and Auluck (1993), Kandola et al. (1995) and others,
the relative failure of both equal opportunity and affirmative action strategies to translate to the business or management world
leads to a new approach: 'managing diversity'. For these authors,

equal opportunities in the workplace become a human resource management issue. Equal opportunities at work should be part of a broader cultural change in organisations.

What then is 'managing diversity'? Kandola et al. (1995: 31) suggest that a variety of definitions of diversity have been produced, but that there are certain key features:

● Diversity and differences between people can, and should, if managed effectively, add value to the organisation.
● Diversity includes virtually all ways in which people differ, not just the more obvious ones of gender, 'race' and ethnicity, disability, etc.
● Diversity has as its primary concern issues of organisational culture and the working environment.

As Kandola et al. point out, one of the main implications of this approach is that 'managing diversity is not just about discrimination' and a 'focus on those areas covered by anti-discrimination legislation':

> In contrast, managing diversity has a more positive starting point, whereby the message that valuing people and enabling them to work to their full potential will make the workplace more inviting and also benefit the long-term vitality and profitability of the organisation. (1995: 31)

Whether these assumptions have foundation and whether, as Kandola et al. believe, managing diversity represents a significant yet 'evolutionary' step in equal opportunities strategy remains to be seen. We return to an assessment of managing diversity in the conclusion.

For Behrens (1993), however, managing diversity does attempt to address the needs and aspirations of all employees, not just those groups traditionally targeted by equal opportunities policies. Any targeted positive action should be set in the broad context of strategic action both to change the workplace culture and to reduce discrimination. Such change requires that managers should periodically stop to challenge the assumptions under which they are proceeding. For example, they should check to see whether all employees are 'invited into the club' (Copeland, n.d.). Unwritten organisational rules may need to be changed to nurture and appreciate diversity and to develop sensitivity to individual differences.

A primary aim of a managing diversity approach is to improve the skills of all staff so that they can contribute to business efficiency through their own personal development. The challenge is first to develop human resources across a broad front, not just those groups which are marginalised or underrepresented. Traditionally, managers have looked upwards to ascertain what is expected of them. Managing diversity asks them to look down and across as well. A second strategic aim is to construct a workforce which seeks to represent in all ways and at all levels the diverse community served by the organisation, and from which its customer base is drawn.

Two additional points can be made about managing diversity: the first is that its supporters do not claim that a diversity strategy will be *entirely* different from other equal opportunities approaches. Kandola et al. maintain that 'although the breadth of focus is quite different . . . they do in fact have many initiatives in common' (1995: 34).

Differences between managing diversity and equal opportunities policies

Managing diversity
- seeks to ensure that all employees maximise their potential and their contribution to the organisation;
- embraces all employees and potential employees. No one is excluded;
- concentrates on the culture of the organisation, and the meeting of business objectives;
- does not rely on positive action or affirmative action;
- is the concern of all employees, especially managers.

Equal opportunities approach
- is perceived as an issue for disadvantaged groups such as women, ethnic minorities and disabled people;
- is treated as an issue to do with personnel and human resource practitioners;
- offers less of an emphasis on culture change;
- concentrates on issues of discrimination;
- relies on positive action.

(Adapted from Kandola et al. (1995: 31))

A second point is that its proponents do not claim that managing diversity is a panacea for every business or organisational problem. Again, Kandola et al. distinguish between what they see as the 'proven benefits' of a managing diversity approach supported by evidence, and more debatable or indirect benefits. Among the former are claims that a diversity approach reduces turnover and absenteeism, makes it easier than before to recruit scarce labour, and enhances employee flexibility or transfers within organisations; among the latter are claims that it improves innovation, decision-making and problem-solving, and that it indirectly improves morale, job satisfaction, productivity and public image.

Implications for management

So far we have summarised the distinctions made by management researchers and advisers between three models of equality strategy. The latter model, managing diversity, emphasises incentives and benefits to managers and employers. The 'carrot' for managers is a perception of equality as 'good for business' (Dickens, 1994: 5). On the other hand equality strategies which developed earlier seemed to rest on the expectation that managers use various kinds of 'sticks' rather than carrots.

Jewson et al. (1990: 9) identify a number of management initiatives that were associated with equal opportunities in the past:

- A legalistic approach by managers which emphasised 'compliance with perceived legal requirements and Codes of Practice'.
- Managerial initiatives which are built upon models of 'good practice' and which, through training or other channels, attempt to persuade employees of the value of equality measures.
- A 'coercive' strategy based on the organisation's own rules (rather than laws or external regulation) and the specification of procedures to be followed to achieve defined outcomes.

Based on studies of a wide range of organisations, Jewson et al. confirm the picture of reluctance among managers to develop any of these strategies much beyond a token effort. They report that management initiatives on equal opportunity are widely regarded, especially by line managers, as being outside the legitimate sphere of management intervention. There is 'universal awareness' that anti-discrimination laws exist and that companies or organisations are often vulnerable to legal action, but

> Among managers at all levels, including among Personnel, there were a great many basic errors and misunderstandings concerning the requirements of the law, the recommendations of Codes of Practice, the functions of statutory bodies, the contents of company policies and initiatives, and the meanings of terms such as positive action and positive discrimination. (Jewson et al., 1990: 10)

Our view is that this state of affairs is only partly explicable in terms of cost constraints or inertia: that is, the costs of time and effort in diverting managers to what is often a rather unfamiliar set of activities. More fundamentally in an individualistic, pro-business management ethos, 'equal opportunities' suggests an image of grey levellers rather than optimistic or positive achievers.

If this is the case, the attempt to 'sell' managing diversity to managers is understandable. Perhaps the managing diversity approach has some strengths as a critique of what has often been passed off as 'equal opportunities' before, even if the outcomes of this approach have yet to be fully demonstrated and assessed.

But as we asked at the beginning, what differences are there likely to be if one approach is tried rather than another? How are specific management functions likely to be affected, for example in recruitment and selection, training and career development? We will now explore each of these functions in more detail, beginning with the implications of a 'diversity' approach for planning the basic or initial framework for equality in the organisation.

Strategic and operational planning

A strategic approach to managing equal opportunities policies is often conspicuous by its absence. Whether you are an employee, manager or student, or have been in any of these roles, we suggest that it would be illuminating to think about an organisation or educational institution you are familiar with, or where you may have worked in the past.

For instance, if there is/was an equal opportunities policy, do you/did you know how it operates? What are/were the stated or published aims of the policy and who is responsible for implementing each part of it? The harder it is to discover basic information on these points, either from people at the office/shop-floor level or from management, the more likely it is that a strategic approach has not been considered or applied.

Many private companies and public or voluntary sector organisations have now taken some steps towards becoming non-discriminatory employers, but it is likely that these steps will have been rather hesitant and directionless. Change is of a 'disjointed incremental' nature (Ham and Hill, 1984) as well as minimalist in equal opportunities terms.

The following thumbnail sketch illustrates the disjointed incremental approach. It is based on key findings of management observers such as Kandola et al. (1995), O'Neilly (1995) and Auluck and Iles (1989), and upon the consultancy work of Behrens (see note at the end of this chapter).

□   □   □   □   □

1. There is a well-produced statement (probably on glossy paper) of company/institutional policy on equal opportunities. It is apparently comprehensive, claiming to counter discrimination on grounds of gender, race and ethnic or religious background, and disability (but probably not age or sexual orientation). There is an accompanying leaflet on sexual and racial harassment, and some idea is given of who to consult if there are harassment problems.

2. The company/organisation has contacted advisory groups and support networks such as Opportunity 2000 and the Employers' Forum on Disability, though no one can point to any tangible outcomes from this contact.

3. Access for disabled people to buildings, and to (most) facilities inside them, has recently been improved. However, there are few signs of change to the working environment, and few disabled employees in evidence.

4. Your enquiries are dealt with by a manager in 'human resources' or a similar department or team. It turns out that he/she and perhaps one or two other colleagues are solely responsible for the entire equal opportunities programme. However, equal opportunities is only a relatively minor part of their brief.

No concrete advice has been given to them about how to coordinate equality or diversity goals either vertically (between top management/board level and individual teams or units) or horizontally (for example between training and personnel functions). Top management does not seem to 'own' any equality initiatives and has not signalled that equal opportunities are a serious priority.

5. The organisation/company does more than many others in collating information relevant to equal opportunities. Not only is recruitment monitored by gender, ethnic group, disability and age, but also similar patterns in promotion and transfer, and in turnover and exit from the organisation. Data are also easily available, though have not been collated, to measure outturns by grade and function of all employees according to gender, ethnic group and disability.

Though some work has been done to gather information, however, no attempts have been made to analyse what the data mean. Outturns are not compared and contrasted with any overall objectives, either in terms of equality objectives or the wider goals of the company/institution.

6. In one department you discover a team in which very good practices exist as far as the integration of disabled with able-bodied employees is concerned. Unusually, there are five or six disabled employees working in a team of twenty or so. The working atmosphere is friendly and relaxed, and some of the able-bodied employees report on the positive gains they have made (for example in training and extra resources) from the addition of disabled colleagues to the team.

Good practice in this case has been pushed forward by an understanding and imaginative manager who knows a lot about disability and how to deal with resistance to the idea of employing disabled people. However, he is rather embarrassed about the team's achievements in this direction and does not want them to be publicised or spoken of widely in the company.

7. In general, attitudes on the office/shop floor towards the equality policy are either hostile or indifferent. Even if some employees' attitudes are more favourable than this, 'equal opportunities' are seen as something which is in the province of middle or senior managers, or personnel management

functions, rather than affecting the day-to-day work experience or the individual's role in the organisation.

□   □   □   □   □

Having a more coherent and comprehensive equality strategy than this means more than being able to coordinate a range of separate 'equal opportunity' activities. According to a managing diversity perspective, it entails a strategic vision of where the organisation is headed (Kandola et al., 1995: 34). Thus it is argued that equality and diversity goals must be incorporated into the main vision or mission of the organisation – a statement of 'what the company or organisation is all about'.

Once an overall strategy has been clarified, a number of 'substrategies' – key activities and targets – can emerge. These may include, first, a strategy for *bringing top management on board*. All of the management studies mentioned above identify this as a crucial first step. Top management backing can be affected by

1. the persuasiveness of change agents (whether external advisers or managers from inside) and their ability to put the case for an equality strategy which enhances, rather than conflicts with, either a business ethos or other organisational objectives (for example commissioning social services);
2. vulnerability to litigation, especially in a period when redundancies are on the increase, can also sharpen top management receptiveness to an equality strategy;
3. and public image, either of the company or organisation, or of important departments within it, can prove to be a competitive spur among senior managers to adopt equality measures. Publication of an 'equality index' or league table comparing progress among rival departments, for instance, though in danger of trivialising the issues may have quite a significant effect on senior managers.

Secondly, a strategy for *monitoring progress and outcomes* which goes beyond a descriptive or statistical approach to include investigation of employees' *lived experiences* of the workplace and their position in the organisation.

O'Neilly (1995) gives a good example of the importance of this in a study of a large commercial organisation ('Shop Inc.'). This company had gone to considerable efforts to monitor statistically the representativeness of its workforce in terms of gender,

ethnic group, etc. A 'committed top management team' had introduced a forward-looking equal opportunities policy which included thorough and clear publicity to all staff and appropriate
training to middle managers.

The results, however, were disappointing. People from minority ethnic groups, for instance, continued to be seriously underrepresented, even in areas with sizeable black and Asian
communities. The underrepresentation of Asians at the managerial level was particularly worrying because of the evident expertise in surrounding Asian communities in similar retail outlets.
As O'Neilly puts it, 'We were faced by a conundrum – good policies, apparently faithfully followed, had not prevented some form
of discrimination taking place' (1995: 34).

It was only when O'Neilly and colleagues began to investigate
more closely the lived experiences of both white and minority
ethnic group staff of Shop Inc. that they began to find out why the
existing policies had not been working. White staff, it appeared,
usually had decisive advantages over minority staff in the amount
of informal knowledge they were able to gain about how the promotion system actually worked, how to gain experience ahead of
formal interviews for promotion, and how to influence supportive
networks in the company.

Therefore, while an 'equal opportunities audit' is a necessary
ingredient of strategic and operational management, an audit
which is limited to statistical analysis may be of limited value and
may even be misleading. A 'managing diversity' approach would
suggest that listening to employees at all levels is vital if a strategic
approach is to include effective plans for corrective action. Just as
top management should be brought on board so should employees, including those who work in a predominantly white or
predominantly male environment.

Thirdly, a strategy for building up a *critical mass of expertise* on
equality issues. An *ad hoc* or incremental approach to lack of expertise might involve either the hiving off of responsibility to a team or
division which takes on special responsibility for equal opportunities, or to individual line managers throughout the organisation. There are two dangers here: the first is that, if equality
specialists are scattered throughout an organisation, they tend to
lack 'clout' because they cannot as easily act as a concerted group;
also, relatively isolated specialists can either become demoralised

or identify more with the department they are placed in than with the equality strategy as a whole. However, a second danger is that, if expertise resides in a single united team or group, that group as a whole will tend to be marginalised. Equal opportunities will 'belong' only to that group.

This is not to suggest that a core group of managers willing to promote equality should not be formed. In fact it is difficult to see how any progress could be made without such a group, although it could exist as a network rather than as a team in one place or department. The point is that a strategic approach towards building a critical mass of expertise involves devolution of responsibility and the spread of expertise to a wide range of functions, so that the many rather than the few are required to take equality concerns into account in their work. Some examples would be bringing equality dimensions into training on customer relations, or on interviewing and how to conduct staff appraisals.

Finally, a strategic approach involves, above all, clear *communication* of an *attainable set of equality targets*. 'Targets' could include any of the objectives mentioned above: for instance finding out about employees' opinions and experiences of selection, promotion and appraisal procedures in the organisation and providing an action report by a certain date, or identifying which key personnel will receive training on particular equality or diversity issues.

There now seems to be consensus among management advisers that if 'targets' are narrowly defined in numerical terms, as having to reach proportionate numbers of minority or excluded groups in the organisation, they will easily be misunderstood as 'quotas' and will therefore be resisted by employees. This represents another distinction between earlier equal opportunities thinking and more recent 'diversity' approaches. Equality targets, according to the latter approach, must be defined by a broader strategy for equality which is both accepted and widely understood by the majority. Cameron concludes that 'low-key, systematic long-term change' is much more likely to produce 'concrete, credible results' (1993: 20) than numerical targets which are imposed from above.

Recruitment and selection

Thus one of the sharper differences of emphasis between a managing diversity approach and affirmative action affects recruitment

and selection most of all. The diversity strategy stresses the importance of selecting people for a job or for internal promotion on the
basis of their *individual* characteristics or talents, whereas affirmative action is portrayed, perhaps unfairly, as a strategy which sees
candidates as members of certain categories first (gender, 'race',
etc.) and as individuals second.

The object of the diversity approach is to value everyone's individual contribution and potential, whether he or she is a member of
the majority culture or not, and this must be reflected in the selection process. For example, it will be important to listen to views from
the group with which the appointed candidate will be working, and
to find out which candidate's abilities or potential could best fit with
the group's development needs. Kandola and Fullerton (1984) use
the analogy of a mosaic to illustrate the diversity strategy, and as far
as selection is concerned this implies that individuals' distinct differences must be recognised so that single pieces, as it were, can be
chosen to complement one another in a pattern.

Having said that, there is however considerable overlap between managing diversity and other equal opportunities approaches to selection. First, best practice in any strategy would
include the all-important objective of ruling out any irrelevant or
discriminatory selection criteria. Coussey and Jackson (1991: 76–
91), for instance, present a useful check-list of selection procedures which call for close scrutiny on this count:

- How the skills or requirements for the job are identified, and
  how these are communicated in advertisements and translated
  into appropriate selection criteria.
- The way candidates' educational qualifications and experience are assessed.
- How interviews are planned, whether interview questions are
  screened for bias, and how reviews of interview performance
  are managed.
- The design of application forms and aptitude tests.
- The shortlisting procedure, and whether it is examined for
  bias or discrimination against certain categories of applicant.
- How the quality and effectiveness of selection procedures are
  monitored.

Throughout, Coussey and Jackson stress not only objectivity in
the selection process and avoidance of discrimination, but also a

flexible approach which includes an element of positive action. For instance, they suggest that educational requirements need to be looked at carefully:

> It is assumed that a general educational level indicates good reasoning ability, and that particular experience brings relevant knowledge and skills. Often this is true, but not always. Many candidates with the ability and skills to do the job will not have the qualifications and experience specified; they may have left school early; have been denied a chance to follow your favoured career path; and may have gained the skills you need in other ways. (1991: 78)

Similarly, with reference to interviewing or assessing aptitudes, the authors draw attention to the need to be broad-minded about cultural differences and the factors which often exclude applicants from minority or disadvantaged backgrounds.

In these respects not a great deal separates equal opportunities or affirmative action strategies from a managing diversity approach. Coussey and Jackson are reminding those who design and operate selection processes that candidates come from diverse backgrounds and that to ascertain their merits and qualities objectively means paying attention to variety and individual difference. Thus affirmative action can be interpreted to mean something quite close to a diversity approach, despite the supposed danger of slipping into selection by category ('race', gender, etc.) rather than by individual merit.

Another way in which managing diversity and other equal opportunities approaches share common ground is in terms of adopting flexible and open-minded approaches to selection. Neither equal opportunities nor affirmative action should require the slavish adoption of selection or recruitment procedures which have to be applied uniformly throughout an organisation. Justifiable criticisms of equal opportunities policies have been made by proponents of managing diversity, because there are examples of management in which successful outcomes have been confused with conformity to procedures or with efforts to reach targets in narrowly defined ways.

Liff (1989) describes such shortcomings, but also shows that implementation of an equal opportunities strategy can be imaginative and flexible. She cites the example of a food company which brought about better outcomes (a rise in appointments of women from minority ethnic groups, positive feelings about equal opportunities among all staff) by deciding *not* to alter or review methods of selection and recruitment within the company. Instead, the company decided to review its contracts with staff recruitment agencies and to explore ways of requiring them to recruit more widely than before.

Thus, in this case, keeping successful outcomes clearly in mind defined the approach to selection. Again it shows that equal opportunities practices can resemble a managing diversity approach quite closely. Managing diversity has been defined as 'meeting business objectives . . . [which] means that any action should lead to perceived benefit and the outcome of the action should be evaluated . . .' (Kandola et al., 1995: 32). In Liff's example of equal opportunities, these objectives were met.

In other respects, however, managing diversity has brought a marked shift in objectives and in attitudes towards the goals of equality strategies, including approaches to selection. For instance, in its more radical guise, managing diversity raises questions about the predominant culture and values of an organisation. Is the company run as a 'men's club' at certain levels, for example, so that activities associated with women's roles, or perceived to be 'feminine', are stigmatised? Or in ethnic or religious terms, is an organisation perceived to belong to one particular group?

Managing diversity approaches seek to value personal qualities and cultural attributes that have been downgraded in the past. Thus the emphasis might be less on selection procedures (as illustrated in Coussey and Jackson's check-list, above) and more upon raising questions about the organisation's culture which candidates are being asked to join: how diverse is it, and how might it, and the image it projects, be changed so as to improve the selection of talented candidates?

Dickens suggests, though, that while managing diversity expresses significantly different goals, 'some reservations can be expressed about the practical, as opposed to the theoretical distinctiveness of this approach and its potential to deliver' (1994: 9). It is not yet clear what valuing individual difference and diversity practically means as far as selection and recruitment are concerned, and nor has a convincing case yet been built up to demonstrate that employees will react more positively to diversity criteria of appointment than to affirmative action criteria. 'X can't do the job, she was only appointed because she's different!' might become as much of a slur as 'X was only appointed because she's a woman/from a minority group, etc.'.

Finally, the practical consequences of managing selection or recruitment in small firms or organisations must be considered. Applying standard equal opportunities criteria to small businesses is hard enough, mainly because small businesses are highly concerned to preserve what they see as group harmony and good relations between employer and employees. In such situations, 'acceptability' criteria often predominate over 'suitability' criteria (Jenkins, 1986: 27). Introducing objective and impartial methods of selection can be extremely difficult in family-sized workplaces or where vacancies are usually filled by applicants who hear of jobs by word of mouth. However, the practicalities of applying diversity criteria to small firms, or to small decentralised teams in larger organisations, may be even more difficult to work out and justify on the ground.

Training and career development

Training which either promotes or is relevant to equality concerns can take many forms, for instance:

- training for recruiters;
- awareness training which highlights problems of discrimination and provides knowledge of the law;
- positive action training which aims to upgrade the confidence and skills of employees who belong to groups which are under-represented at certain levels in the organisation;
- developmental training, for example traineeship schemes or management training schemes, which might be part of an accelerated development programme targeted at particular groups (for instance to foster the careers of younger black men in management).

There is now awareness among management advisers that any of the above kinds of training can be counterproductive unless they are integrated into a wider equal opportunities plan (Coussey and Jackson, 1991: 108). Also, the dangers of restricting 'positive action' training to women, black people and other groups are now widely understood (Behrens and Auluck, 1993) and recall the flaws of the 'individual' and 'role-related' models of change discussed in relation to gender in Chapter 4. Some targeted training may well be effective, but only if wider training needs involving the workforce as a whole are addressed simultaneously.

Therefore, as with selection processes, differences between a managing diversity approach and a 'traditional' equal opportunities approach to training are not necessarily all that great. In the past, much awareness training for instance earned a bad name for overreliance on a confrontational and authoritarian style. Participants were often expected to assume guilt for patterns of inequality and discrimination over which they had no control or very little influence. Such training, far from changing attitudes in a positive direction, was in danger of stimulating resentful 'backlash' attitudes towards the idea of equal opportunities.

For these reasons also, Coussey and Jackson note, 'positive action training exclusively for ethnic minority people has rarely been used' (1991: 126), as senior managers worry that resentment and divisiveness will occur if particular categories of employees appear to be given special or exclusive training. Acceptance of women-only positive action training seems to be higher, however, and some training agencies (for example the Civil Service College) now provide a substantial menu of courses which are targeted at women in employment, as well as other groups such as disabled employees, i.e. courses which enhance life and business skills, career planning and assertiveness.

Consequently, there is more of a convergence of managing diversity and equal opportunities approaches to training than a sharp division between them. If there are differences, they are more of emphasis and style than of basic approach.

Managing diversity initiatives are attempting to push equality-relevant training out of what might seem to be an equal opportunities ghetto by linking concepts of individual need and diversity to training. Rather than assuming that women or disabled employees, say, tend to have similar training needs or are 'coming from the same direction' in their attitudes to careers or work, diversity approaches suggest that everyone's training needs should be assessed and responded to individually.

This is not too far from Parekh's (1992) argument (discussed in Chapter 3) that positive discrimination should not entail an unthinking policy of proportionality or of placing women and minority group employees in positions because of their gender or minority status. Individuals must be given the opportunity to make their own choices, and presumably this would apply to training opportunities as well as promotion or transfer.

Another difference of emphasis that managing diversity approaches would stress is in bringing equality-relevant objectives to *all* training. Rather than packaging 'equality' into equal opportunities or positive action training of various kinds, and running the risk of marginalising the issue, the suggestion is that the content and aims of every training course are revised with diversity in mind. Thus whether the training is in safety, handling new equipment or technical processes, or in selling to a new overseas market, the idea would be to incorporate course elements that would develop previously underutilised skills and potential, and include a greater diversity of participants than hitherto.

A skills audit, for instance, might show that employees who belonged to a particular minority ethnic community spoke the language of the country to which a firm was hoping to mount an export drive; inclusion of those employees in a training programme to enhance their contribution to product development could pay considerable dividends and allow the firm to capitalise on previously untapped skills or insights.

With regard to both including as wide a group of employees as possible in training, and taking equality or diversity into as many training opportunities as possible, equal opportunities strategies were already beginning to move in the direction now being pioneered by managing diversity. However, the managing diversity approach gives stronger impetus to a focus on behaviour at work. Where behaviour falls short of expectations which have been widely disseminated, management sanctions are available and can be used. Thus in contrast with early equal opportunities training, which often had rather broad and unspecified objectives, a managing diversity approach to training encourages the adoption of specific and measurable objectives to change behaviour.

A similar theme emerges in connection with supervision, appraisal, performance monitoring and career development in general. Iles and Auluck have argued that in order to consolidate changes brought about by training, an organisation's appraisal and reward system should be closely tied to equal opportunity requirements. They suggest that criteria for employee appraisal might include: the worker's own contribution to the equality or diversity strategy and 'fulfilling staffing targets, establishing monitoring systems, and non-discriminatory selection procedures' (1989: 27). They add that 'Rewards and sanctions need to be tied to evaluation of performance in such areas, including promotion, transfer, involvement in more interesting work, recognition and sanctions for harassment or policy violations' (1989: 27).

This is significant because Iles and Auluck's views show how managing diversity can be used to sanction employees as well as reward them. Although, as Dickens (1994) points out, managing diversity is associated with 'carrots' rather than 'sticks', it is possible that an equality or diversity strategy could be perceived by a majority of non-managerial employees simply as a new way of exercising managerial control: a policy of sticks for the workers and carrots for the managers.

Therefore, to be seen as fair, equality strategies must include not only rewards for employees who are shown to help the process in their work, Iles and Auluck argue, but also monitoring of the performance of managers, and of the company or organisation itself. As Cameron concludes, a genuine 'personnel and line partnership' must be forged so that all employees, irrespective of level, gender or other divisions, begin to 'own the strategy' and share responsibility for making it work (1993: 20).

Conclusion

There is no lack of ideas about how the implementation of equal opportunities policies can best be managed in either the private or public sectors. In practice, however, managerial implementation has been patchy and limited. There are islands of good practice, for example in some of the larger private companies, banks and building societies (Coussey and Jackson, 1991), but they are surrounded by a sea of token adherence to equal opportunity.

A number of reasons have been identified for the lack of centrality of equal opportunities in the world of management: ingrained patterns of institutional discrimination; organisational cultures which are swamped with economic and technological change and which cannot cope with yet more changes such as equal opportunity initiatives; and a clash between individualistic, competitive business values and a perception of equal opportunities as a soft-hearted social justice issue.

We suggest, however, that two other reasons stand out as being particularly important because they relate directly to the everyday realities of managers. The first is the economic or cost-benefit factor. As Dickens observes, 'some organizations will benefit from the *absence* of equal opportunities'. For example 'Organizations can, and do, obtain cost-benefits from the non-recognition (but utilisation) of women's skills, the undervaluing of women's labour, and from the exploitation of women as a cheap, numerically flexible . . . workforce' (1994: 13).

The second reason for the patchy and incremental implementation of equal opportunities, at least in the United Kingdom, lies in the minimalist requirements of the law and government. Where laws are tougher, as in the United States, equality strategies are taken seriously by private sector management (see Chapter 2). Also, in the United Kingdom itself, equality and diversity strategies are more apparent in local government than in the private or voluntary sectors because, under the Race Relations Act and Sex Discrimination Act, local authorities face statutory requirements to implement equal opportunity policies.

It remains to be seen whether European Union legislation will make a significant difference to British management resistance to equality strategies. There are some signs that European laws will toughen the 'negative' or anti-discrimination side of equal opportunities, as evidenced already by rulings on the unfair dismissal of pregnant women (see Chapter 2). However, there are few signs that the more 'positive' or active promotion of equality strategy will be strengthened by European legislation.

In view of the slow progress made by earlier equal opportunities strategies in management practice, we also asked at the beginning of the chapter whether the more recent managing diversity perspective will make a difference and overcome the obstacles outlined above.

Our summary of managing diversity attempted to show that, as a set of ideas, it has a genuinely 'radical' potential as a programme for change. Managing diversity cannot be written off simply as a 'repackaging' of earlier equal opportunity concepts or as a 'soft sell' approach to otherwise unpalatable policies. If fully implemented, managing diversity requires a complete overhaul of the way organisations are structured.

Paradoxically, perhaps, a radical approach to managing diversity would not be too far from the ideas of Parekh (1992), a supporter of radical maximalist strategies. For example, he advocates the need to question established definitions of merit (see Chapter 3) and, by implication, this means a broad-minded recognition of the diversity of talents and abilities in an organisation. As mentioned above, Parekh's views on choice and the right of individual employees either to strive for higher positions or to decline them also chimes in with the managing diversity philosophy.

The first two approaches we discussed in this chapter (equal opportunities and affirmative action) tend to focus on equal opportunities as a set of specialised activities run by personnel departments or specialist advisers. Managing diversity, on the other hand, asks *all* managers and other employees to incorporate equality and diversity concerns in their work. Also, if combined with existing reward and sanction systems, it holds the promise of bringing about effective change.

All these points, however, are still largely theoretical. Managing diversity is a relatively new approach, in the United Kingdom if not in the United States and other countries. More comparative research is needed to find out whether managements which do or do not adopt it have significantly different outcomes, in terms of either equality and diversity, or productivity and other aspects of the 'business case'.

In practice, though, there are already signs that managing diversity will not revolutionise management equality strategies. One reason is the cost-benefit constraint. Just as earlier equal opportunities policies are perceived as potentially damaging to profits, so too may managing diversity approaches seem costly or inappropriate to many employers. Where a firm is desperate to find and retain high-calibre and skilled staff, one can see the argument that a diversity approach, with its emphasis on flexibility and informality, would be appealing; but where a firm relies mainly on low-paid, semi-skilled and part-time workers who are required to perform routine tasks, ideas of managing diversity seem rather remote.

Dickens sees a pattern emerging in Britain whereby companies will tend to adopt selected parts of the managing diversity strategy rather than the entire approach. For example, they are likely to target career development and career-break schemes on high-flyers and women with 'management potential' rather than making them available to all women in the organisation (1994: 14).

There is something of a contradiction in the managing diversity strategy's emphasis on the 'business case'. It is held that a diverse organisation, when compared to a monocultural one, will have greater openness, a commitment to valuing every employee and more innovative ideas: all these things will lead to greater productivity.

Is this a hard-headed business case, however? Many of the positive changes and benefits to which advocates of managing diversity refer are of a qualitative, hard-to-measure nature. In some ways the managing diversity literature seems to be as full of exhortation as earlier social justice models of equal opportunity were. There is an equal emphasis, though in different language, on transforming the culture of individuals and organisations through training and persuasion. The contradiction, then, is that managing diversity has opted to stand or fall by the business argument, but the substance of the business case itself is as yet rather debatable.

Finally, we recalled at the beginning of the chapter that all innovations in managing equal opportunities must be seen against the background of profound changes in the nature of work, and of the social and economic context (see Chapter 2). The managing diversity message of valuing every employee will be particularly hard to put into practice in an era of 'downsizing', and where the equal opportunity dilemmas are as often to do with whom to make redundant as with whom to hire.

A key question emerges from the above analysis. To achieve greater equity, should management efforts be aimed predominantly at the workforce or more in trying to redesign the nature and processes of work itself? All three of the approaches discussed in this chapter (equal opportunities, affirmative action and managing diversity) ultimately focus on the individual employee, either as a member of a disadvantaged group (in the first two) or as a person with a distinct identity in the organisational 'mosaic'. It is true that the managing diversity approach is predicated upon changes in the culture of the work setting, but even here the primary focus remains that of managing individual people rather than the transformation of work.

Up to now, equal opportunities policies have been concerned primarily with fitting 'unusual' or previously excluded groups or individuals into antithetical corporate organisations. However, recent trends in employment (see Chapter 2) suggest that in future workers are likely to be in smaller, perhaps more specialised groups, sometimes with more autonomy over their working relations.

In this context, it is important to remember that even the latest development in equal opportunities thinking, managing diversity, has emerged from a corporate world which is rapidly becoming dated. Thus it is difficult to anticipate appropriate management strategies for the future, though perhaps the bulk of the excluded and disadvantaged will be found, as now, in those parts of the service sector which are arduous and low-paid. In the next chapter we will turn to these questions and to the ways in which a more structural, work-centred view of equality strategies might be developed.

□   □   □   □   □

NOTE: The thumbnail sketch of a typical approach to equal opportunity is partly based on a synthesis or range of impressions gained by R. Behrens (Civil Service College, Sunningdale, United Kingdom) in extensive and wide-ranging consultancy work. However, it is not based on the example of any particular organisation or company.

9
CONCLUSION

We began with a central question: What difference, if any, do equal opportunities policies make? Related to this key question are others: How justifiable are equality policies even if they do make a difference? What public images do they convey, and are negative images likely to replace positive ones? Will there be any public support for equality policies in the future?

In order to draw together some conclusions about these questions, we will first review some of the more important lessons to be learned from the outcomes of equal opportunity policies as they have developed so far. Secondly, we will discuss the prospects for further development, highlighting the key factors and trends in employment which we think will have the greatest impact.

Outcomes in perspective

In this section we do not intend to summarise or review all the main outcomes discussed in the book from Chapter 5 through to Chapter 8. The aim rather is to put outcomes into perspective. What, in retrospect, do the various outcomes of equality policies tell us, and how are our interpretations of outcomes affected by expectations and political perspectives?

As we suggested in our opening paragraphs, it is not very difficult to find negative images of equal opportunities policies or pessimistic conclusions about outcomes. Imagine a discussion among critics of equal opportunities policies. A dyed-in-the-wool socialist, for whom class is the fundamental and overriding social division which explains all other inequalities, might decry equal opportunities policies as a diversion from the 'real' business of class conflict or trade union politics. A business leader bent on maximising profits and slimming down the workforce might regard them as expensive and unproductive. A radical feminist or black community activist would see equality strategies as yet another government ploy to buy off the leaders of their movements and to co-opt them into the establishment. A right-winger who supports the free market and a libertarian who champions individual freedom would both oppose equal opportunities policies because they seem to represent gross interference with personal choice and the private life of the citizen.

These are, of course, oversimplified and stereotypical examples of views or ideologies. In this book we have shown how at least some business or management thought, for instance, has embraced and tried to develop equality strategies rather than reject them. Similarly, not all egalitarians would wish to oppose all equal opportunities strategies. The examples of Swedish and European Union policies to reduce sex discrimination, the latter relatively limited in their impact, nevertheless demonstrate the partial commitment of feminist, radical and social democratic lobbies to equal opportunities.

Thus in reality it is possible to find mixed views on the successes and limitations of equal opportunities policies, and certainly some less pessimistic or hostile conclusions than those of our imaginary discussion.

Where disappointment with outcomes does occur, it may stem from overambitious expectations of equal opportunities policies. But anti-discrimination legislation and equality strategies in the workplace will not change the world. They were never designed to do so. In the United Kingdom for example, none of the provisions of the 1975 Sex Discrimination Act nor the 1976 Race Relations Act move very far beyond a minimalist approach towards equality and discrimination; a certain limited amount of positive action is encouraged, but the policies were designed to win majority consent rather than to force change (see Chapters 5 and 6). The enormous task of diminishing social divisions, class inequality and poverty could only ever be realistically addressed by economic and social policies which operate on a much broader front: for instance taxation, social security and education policy.

As these truths have dawned, proponents of equal opportunities strategies have replaced the somewhat moralistic and utopian aims of earlier policies – in particular the rhetoric which accompanied equal pay and anti-discrimination legislation of the 1960s and 1970s – with more cautious and pragmatic goals. There is now widespread acceptance, for instance, that equality strategies which are based upon attempts to change employees' views of the world will usually be counterproductive. As we showed in Chapter 4, best practice in managing equal opportunities now emphasises change in behaviour in the workplace rather than conversion of employees' minds to a particular world view.

A more pragmatic assessment of equality strategies would suggest that such policies may help to diminish discrimination and open up opportunities, but that they cannot exert a purely independent influence. Sloane and Jain's (1989) survey of the first wave of 1960s and 1970s legislation on race and gender equality, for instance, indicated that growth in demand for labour and other economic changes at that time were probably more significant as causes of growing opportunity than equal opportunity legislation itself. In the main, significant improvements in wages and labour market position occurred for minorities and women *before* the implementation of equality legislation (though see discussion in Chapter 5).

However, equal opportunity policies do not have to be a prime cause of change to be regarded as significant for equality or the reduction of discrimination. In particular, we suggest that one of the main roles of equality policies and legislation is that of *opportunity protection*, much as health and safety policies have a preventive or protective role.

If this is the case, the image that best portrays equality policies is that of a ratchet-wheel rather than an engine of change. After any turn of the wheel in favour of previously excluded or underrepresented groups (perhaps as a result of demand for labour or other economic and social factors), equality policies may be able to prevent the wheel from slipping backwards. This is not to say that it is impossible to find instances in which a legislative programme or policy has been a prime agent in bringing change; however, on balance, we conclude that equal opportunity policies in employment tend to protect or consolidate gains rather than cause them.

The benefits of equality legislation and policies are often more apparent when a group is deprived of them, or where they may be diluted or withdrawn. In Chapter 6, for example, we referred to worries in the race relations field about the harmonisation of social legislation in the European Union, and the possibility that Britain's race equality legislation will be weakened or reduced to the lowest common denominator. The major West European countries do not have equality laws which are specifically addressed to race relations, as Britain does. Those who had been critical of Britain's race relations legislation for its apparent limitations are now arguing that it is better than nothing, and that it does make a difference.

Another illustration is in the field of opportunities for disabled people. The Sex Discrimination Act and Race Relations Act, despite their limitations, do represent the beginnings of an equality strategy and official recognition that problems of discrimination must be addressed. This is the kind of acknowledgement disabled people would have been glad of much earlier, and which they are now seeking in improved civil rights laws (see Chapter 7).

Gains or achievements are also evinced by many other outcomes, none of which are examples of sweeping change but which show that the grass is not growing over equality policies and laws. For instance, in this book we have referred to the gradual rise in the number of race and sex discrimination cases heard by industrial tribunals, and the recent rise in the proportion of cases with successful outcomes. In some instances, for example where women in the armed forces lost their jobs when they were pregnant, tribunal rulings are not only benefiting the individuals concerned (amounts of compensation are no longer kept below a specified limit) but are also helpful to others who have been similarly discriminated against. European legislation on sex discrimination has proved to be genuinely liberating to women in a number of ways, not simply in terms of access to work or wrongful dismissal but also with regard to social security and pension rights.

In sum, any conclusions about outcomes are bound to depend upon expectations and political perspectives and the way these affect interpretations of the facts. Our view is that equal opportunities policies are more accurately seen as examples of piecemeal social reform than radical visions (or nightmares) of egalitarian social engineering. Progress towards more fully representative numbers of women, black people, and other minority groups in every occupation has proved to be disappointingly slow; it is also the case that the incidence of sexual harassment and racist attack or abuse has shown little sign of reduction (although recognition of the problem and procedures to deal with it may be prompting more victims to report incidents that previously would have been unreported).

Gradually, however, even piecemeal reform can achieve change. For example, as we showed in Chapter 4, the numbers of women in certain professional and managerial positions may still be low (and there is little or no improvement at the top of the management tree), but where equality strategies have been introduced there have been demonstrable changes.

These conclusions seem to be backed up by those with expertise in managing or implementing equality policies. For instance Cameron (1993), it will be recalled, advocates the gradual and cumulative adoption of equality strategies (see Chapter 4). Unless all employees can see the benefits of such strategies, and unless the majority are brought into the process of developing and implementing them, equality policies are likely to be disowned and derailed. Sustained change towards greater equal opportunity and diversity, according to this view, is achieved through experimentation, learning from mistakes and a succession of limited changes.

Thus a certain amount of change in organisational cultures towards acceptance of equality policies is detectable. For instance some kinds of discriminatory language and attitudes are no longer as acceptable as they were (though this depends on the industry or workplace in question, and whether those who are discriminated against are in an isolated minority). Many would argue that this represents a largely cosmetic change because racism, sexism and other forms of discrimination have merely been driven beneath the surface of everyday life. However, it seems unlikely that even surface change is unaccompanied by at least some substantial long-term change. Paradoxically, the 'backlash' attitudes to which we referred at the beginning of this book are a sign of this. In a way, resentment of, or resistance to, equality policies are a sign that they are beginning to bite. Purely cosmetic policies would excite little interest or controversy.

Prospects

Two banks of cloud obscure the horizon of equal opportunities policies and make it especially difficult to assess prospects. The first concerns the degree of opposition to equality policies that might be generated, and whether any backlash might be sufficiently strong to neutralise or even reverse existing policies.

Much depends upon whether equality policies are seen as divisive or not. The managing diversity approach (see Chapter 4) identifies earlier equal opportunities strategies as divisive because they appear to be targeted upon minorities: positive action in recruitment of people from minority groups, special forms of additional training for women, and so on. Where there is no impact, equal opportunity issues are marginalised; where there is impact, injustices to the majority are perceived as outweighing whatever benefits are being gained by minority employees or women (though even supposed beneficiaries may be resentful of equal opportunities policies).

The above critique, found for example in the work of Kandola et al. (1995), correctly identifies some of the pitfalls of earlier policies. Doubts remain, though, about whether the managing diversity strategy will actually be adopted in a way which encompasses all sections of the workforce, and whether it will succeed in convincing both employers and employees that greater diversity is in the common interest.

Even if the prospects for the dissemination of managing diversity strategies are relatively rosy, however, there are further questions about whether the philosophy itself dodges thorny issues and weakens earlier commitments to equality. Managing diversity stresses integration and the harnessing of individual differences to a common effort. However, this model, in the end, seems to stress individual rather than structural change: the emphasis is still upon changing outlook and individual behaviours, not upon a complete overhaul of the systems of power and status which underpin discrimination and patterns of blocked opportunity. This reveals a fundamental dilemma of equal opportunities policies: are they in existence to change individuals and possibly to 'compensate' for earlier disadvantages, or is their object to challenge the definitions of normality or acceptability which are so often used to exclude women, black people, people with the 'wrong' accents or with working-class backgrounds, disabled people, and so on?

In some circumstances widening opportunities for some unavoidably means reducing them for others. In other words, genuinely effective equality policies may have to hurt. Continual improvements in productivity and renewal of technology in the workplace mean that better-paid and relatively secure jobs are in ever shorter supply. Challenging institutionalised inequalities in access to these positions is bound to cause conflict and resentment at times, and it seems to us that the managing diversity philosophy underplays this.

However, it would be unfair to conclude that managing diversity will always weaken or dilute equality strategies. Employees or their representatives might in some circumstances be able to turn the rhetoric of equality back onto their managers, possibly exploiting the language of empowerment and cooperation in order to obtain their demands. Leading management experts (see, for example, Peters and Waterman, 1982) advocate willingness to respond flexibly to conflict and a listening approach by managers to employees' concerns. Thus equality concerns (for example introduction of greater flexibility in working hours for parents) could benefit. As we noted in Chapter 4, however, these prospects very much depend upon the status of the employees in question, and the perceived value of the work they do.

This brings us to the second cloud of uncertainties surrounding the prospects for equal opportunities: the rapidly changing nature of work. In Chapters 2 and 4 we paid particular attention to the possible impact of trends in organisational change upon equal opportunities. Decentralisation of operations and 'delayering' of management were identified as changes which could seriously weaken centralised or standard equal opportunity strategies.

Again, however, parochial views should be avoided. Although there is a global dimension to these changes in the organisation of work, marked differences are still evident. The United States and to a lesser extent the United Kingdom stand out as countries which are leading the way in terms of deregulation of the economy, privatisation of public sector activities and restructuring of the workforce. Therefore we may expect any influences upon equality policies, positive or negative, to be particularly marked in these countries.

In Japan, on the other hand, competitiveness has been built upon 'a management system that was dependent on co-operation between employers and employees to attain a common purpose' (Yuzawa, 1994: 13). Interestingly, Yuzawa concludes that although widespread concern was expressed in the 1990s about the continued success of the Japanese economy, this concern is rather overdone and that 'the fundamental structures which have been driving the Japanese economy over the last three decades appear to be unchanged' (1994: 18). Consequently, although questions are increasingly asked in Japan about some of their traditional approaches to work such as 'groupism' and commitment to lifetime employment, the essential principle of valuing their workforces will be retained.

The significance of this goes beyond Japan itself, or its importance as a comparative contrast to American-style management, which is based on more overtly capitalist relations and market principles. This is because, in addition, Japanese management provides a model within the countries to which Japanese companies have transferred or developed branches – especially, in the European context, the United Kingdom (White and Trevor, 1983). Although the effects should not be overestimated, Japanese influences on management practice and cultivation of good employee relations may offset some of the negative influences on equal opportunities policies mentioned above. The possible marriage of Japanese paternalism in industrial relations and existing equal opportunity policies certainly seems to be a subject worthy of more extensive investigation.

Finally, and beyond these international differences in the organisation of work, our discussion of the prospects for equal opportunities prompts the question: What are the prospects for organising work itself so that it responds to the needs of human beings rather than as at present, seeing equal opportunity policy as something which intervenes mainly to render people both suitable for, and subservient to, work?

This idea is not as odd as it may first appear. To begin with, writers, artists, researchers and inventors have to some extent already been able to create the nature or process of their work as well as its products. Also, in the equal opportunities field, there are structural perspectives on the nature of social divisions which suggest that full equality entails changes in the nature and organisation of work, rather than changes in the characteristics of the employee (for example through additional or compensatory training). For instance, research on older workers suggests that for them to compete on an equal footing with younger workers, especially where physical work is involved, the working environment and the nature of work itself may need to be changed (Fogarty, 1975). Similarly, structural perspectives on gender inequality suggest that both paid work processes or routines and families need to change to recognise the shared responsibilities of men and women to paid work and domestic work (see Chapter 5).

There have in recent times been profound changes in what constitutes work. Current trends are towards homeworking, telecottaging and flexible time working. On most production lines in richer industrial countries one will find robots at the workbench rather than people.

In thinking about the focus of concerns about equal opportunities, the common picture is of large companies employing few staff from disadvantaged or excluded groups. Hitherto, equal opportunities policies have been concerned primarily with fitting 'unusual' groups or individuals into antithetical corporate organisations. However, the trends mentioned above suggest that in future workers are likely to be in smaller, perhaps more specialised groups, which in many cases will have greater autonomy over their work contracts and ports of entry to work, if not the work itself.

The challenge for equal opportunities may therefore change from lack of access to the corporate workplace to lack of the training, information and knowledge needed for (home-based) technological or communication work in settings such as the information superhighway, World Wide Web (Internet), virtual reality technology, and so forth. In this context, not only is it difficult to anticipate equal opportunity prospects, but also to define 'management' itself in a high technology future.

However, there is the possibility that many of the highly charged and visible social criteria or labels which now form the basis of discrimination in work settings (for instance disability, age, gender, race and ethnicity) may become increasingly unimportant for the growing proportion of people who do not work in the same physical space or meet at a central office or factory.

These topics are still remarkably absent from most equal opportunity or managing diversity strategy discussions. There is now a huge English language literature on equal opportunities, but in most research studies and other sources, the focus is on equality strategies in isolation from the work that people actually do.

Comparison of pay levels, inequalities in working conditions and in access to the more skilled or responsible positions are of course much-discussed subjects. However, the results of interaction between different equal opportunities strategies on the one hand and, on the other, technological change, work cultures and relationships between employees in specific industries are all, as yet, relatively undeveloped subjects – they represent a major challenge for future equal opportunities research.

BIBLIOGRAPHY

ABBERLEY, P. (1987) 'The concept of oppression and the development of a social theory of disability', *Disability, Handicap & Society*, 2 (1), pp. 5–19.

AMERSFOORT, H. VAN (1982) *Immigration and the Formation of Minority Groups: The Dutch Experience 1945–75*, Cambridge: Cambridge University Press.

ANSPACH, R. (1979) 'From stigma to identity politics', *Social Science and Medicine*, 134, pp. 765–73.

AULUCK, R. and ILES, P. (1989) 'From racism awareness training to strategic human resource management in implementing equal opportunity', *Personnel Review*, 18 (4), pp. 24–32.

BARNES, C. (1990) *Cabbage Syndrome: The Social Construction of Dependence*, Basingstoke: Falmer.

BARNES, C. (1991) *Disabled People in Britain and Discrimination: A Case for Anti-Discrimination Legislation*, Belper: British Council of Organisations of Disabled People.

BARRY, B. (1988) 'Equal opportunity and moral arbitrariness' in Bowie, N. (ed.) *Equal Opportunity*, Boulder: Westview Press, pp. 23–44.

BARTON, L. (1986) 'The politics of special educational needs', *Disability, Handicap & Society*, 1 (3), pp. 273–90.

BARTON, L. (1989) *Disability and Dependency*, Lewes: Falmer.

BASSET, P. (1994) 'OECD says jobs depend on adapting to change', *The Times*, 8 June, p. 29.

BEHRENS, R. (1993) 'Managing diversity', *Viewpoint: The Magazine for Benefits Agency Managers*, 8 (Summer), p. 19.

BEHRENS, R. and AULUCK, R. (1993) *Action Planning for Diversity Management: A Comparative Perspective*, (no place): Southern Africa Development Unit, United Kingdom Civil Service.

BERTHOUD, R., LAKEY, J. and McKAY, S. (1993) *The Economic Problems of Disabled People*, London: Policy Studies Institute.

BEVERIDGE, SIR W. (1942) *Social Insurance and Allied Services*, Cmd. 6406, London: HMSO.

BLAKEMORE, K. and BONEHAM, M. (1994) *Age, Race and Ethnicity*, Buckingham: Open University Press.

BOWIE, N. (ed.) (1988) *Equal Opportunity*, Boulder: Westview Press.

BRADSHAW, J. (1972) 'The concept of social need', *New Society*, 30, pp. 640–3.

BRAHAM, P., RHODES, E. and PEARN, M. (eds) (1981) *Discrimination and Disadvantage in Employment*, Milton Keynes: The Open University Press.

BREWSTER, C. and TEAGUE, P. (1989) *European Community Social Policy: Its impact on the UK*, London: Institute of Personnel Management.

BRISENDEN, S. (1986) 'Independent living and the medical model of disability', *Disability, Handicap & Society*, 1 (2), pp. 173–8.

BROMLEY, D. B. (1988) *Human Ageing – an Introduction to Gerontology*, Harmondsworth: Penguin.

BROWN, C. (1984) *Black and White Britain: The Third PSI Survey*, London: Gower/Policy Studies Institute.

BROWN, L.D. (1983) 'Managing conflict among groups' in D. Kolb et al. (eds) *Organisational Psychology: An Experimental Approach*, New Jersey: Prentice Hall.

BYNOE, I., OLIVER, M. and BARNES, C. (1991) *Equal Rights for Disabled People: The Case for a New Law*, London: Institute for Public Policy Research.

BYTHEWAY, B. (1986) 'Making way: the disengagement of older workers' in Phillipson, C., Bernard, M. and Strang, P. (eds) *Dependency and Interdependency in Old Age: Theoretical Perspectives and Policy Alternatives*, London: Croom Helm, pp. 315–26.

BYTHEWAY, B. (1987) 'Redundancy and the older worker' in Lee, M. (ed.) *Redundancies, Lay-off and Plant Closures: Causes, Character and Consequences*, London: Croom Helm, pp. 115–26.

BYTHEWAY, B. (1995) *Ageism*, Buckingham: Open University Press.

CABLE, V. (1994) 'Wrong readings of the chapter', *The Independent*, 7 June, p. 19.

CAMERON, I. (1993) 'Formulating an equal opportunities policy', *Equal Opportunities Review*, 47 (January/February), pp. 16–20.

CAMPBELL, D. (1994) 'Minorities shy away from police career', *The Guardian*, 14 July, p. 5.

CARBY, K. and THAKUR, M. (1977) *No Problems Here? Management and the Multi-Racial Workforce including a Guide to the Race Relations Act, 1976*, London: Institute of Personnel Management.

CASTLES, S., with BOOTH, H. and WALLACE, T. (1984) *Here for Good: Western Europe's New Ethnic Minorities*, London: Pluto Press.

Central Statistical Office (1994a) *Social Trends 24*, London: HMSO.

Central Statistical Office (1994b) *Regional Trends 29*, London: HMSO.

Central Statistical Office (1995) *Social Trends 25*, London: HMSO, p. 66.

CHARNESS, M. (ed.) (1985) *Aging and Human Performance*, New York: Wiley.

CHOTE, R. (1994) 'A woman's work is rarely equal', *Independent on Sunday*, 22 May, p. 8.

CLARK, A. and HIRST, M. (1989) 'Disability in adulthood: ten year follow up of young people with disabilities', *Disability, Handicap & Society*, 4, pp. 271–83.

COHEN, N. and BORRILL, R. (1993) 'The new proletariat', *Independent on Sunday*, 16 May, p. 19.

COLLIER, R. (1995) *Combating Sexual Harassment in the Workplace*, Buckingham: Open University Press.

COLLINS, D. (1991) 'Digest: social charter', *Journal of European Social Policy*, 1 (1), p. 59.

COLLINSON, D.L., KNIGHTS, D. and COLLINSON, M. (1990) *Managing to Discriminate*, London: Routledge.

Commission for Racial Equality (CRE) (1985) *Positive Action and Equal Opportunity in Employment*, London: CRE.

Commission for Racial Equality (CRE) (1991) *Second Review of the Race Relations Act 1976*, London: CRE.

Commission for Racial Equality (CRE) (1995) *Racial Equality Means Business: A Standard for Racial Equality for Employers*, London: CRE.

Commission of the European Communities (1992) *Employment in Europe, 1992*, Brussels: EC Commission.

Commission of the European Communities – Eurostat (1991) *A Community of Twelve: Key Figures*, Brussels: Commission of the EC.

COOKSEY, B. (1986) 'Policy and practice in Tanzanian secondary education since 1967', *International Journal of Educational Development*, 6 (3), pp. 183–202.

COOPER, R. (1994) 'Fair employment priorities', *Equal Opportunities Review*, 53 (Jan/Feb), pp. 17–18, London: Industrial Relations Services.

COPELAND, LENNIE (n.d.) *Learning to Manage a Multicultural Workforce*, (no place): K.E.P.T. Classroom Trainers' Workbook.

CORFIELD, K. (1994) 'Women in Lucas project', *Equal Opportunities Review*, 54 (March/April), p. 17.

COUSSEY, M. and JACKSON, H. (1991) *Making Equal Opportunities Work*, London: Pitman/Longman.

COUSSEY, M. and WHITMORE, J. (1986) *Jobs and Racial Equality*, (no place): British Institute of Management.

COYLE, A. (1989) 'The limits of change: local government and equal opportunities for women', *Public Administration*, 67, Spring, pp. 39–50.

COYLE, A. and SKINNER, J. (eds) (1988) *Women and Work*, London: Macmillan.

CROFT, S. and BERESFORD, P. (1989) 'User-involvement, citizenship and social policy', *Critical Social Policy*, 26, pp. 5–18.

CROW, L. (1990) *Direct Action and Disabled People: Future Directions*, Manchester: Greater Manchester Coalition of Disabled People.

CUNNINGHAM, S. (1992) 'The development of equal opportunities theory and practice in the European Community', *Policy and Politics*, 20 (3), pp. 177–89.

DANIEL, W. (1968) *Racial Discrimination in England*, Harmondsworth: Penguin.

DE JONG, G. (1979) *The Movement for Independent Living, Origins, Ideology and Implications for Disability Research*, Michigan: University Centre for Rehabilitation.

DE JONG, G. (1983) 'Defining and implementing the independent living concept' in N. Crewe and I. Zola (eds) *Independent Living for Physically Disabled People*, London: Jossey-Bass.

Department of Social Security (1994) *Social Security Statistics 1994*, London: HMSO.

DEX, S. and SHAW, L. (1986) *British and American Women at Work*, Basingstoke: Macmillan.

DICKENS, L. (1994) 'The business case for women's equality: is the carrot better than the stick?', *Employee Relations*, 16 (8), pp. 5–18.

DITCH, J. (1991) 'The undeserving poor: unemployed people then and now', in M. Loney, R. Bocock, J. Clarke, A. Cochrane, P. Graham and M. Wilson (eds) *The State or the Market*, London: Sage.

DOYAL, L. and GOUGH, I. (1991) *A Theory of Human Need*, Basingstoke: Macmillan.

DRAKE, R.F. (1992) 'Consumer participation: the voluntary sector and the concept of power', *Disability, Handicap & Society*, 7 (3), pp. 301–12.

DRAKE, R.F. (1994) 'The exclusion of disabled people from positions of power in British voluntary organisations', *Disability & Society*, 9 (4), pp. 463–82.

DRAKE, R.F. and OWENS, D.J. (1992) 'Consumer involvement and the voluntary sector in Wales: breakthrough or bandwagon?', *Critical Social Policy*, 33, pp. 76–86.

DUTTON, P., MANSELL, S., MOONEY, P., EDGER, M. and EVANS, E. (1989) *The Net Exchequer Costs of Sheltered Employment*, Sheffield: Department of Employment, Employment Services.

EDWARDS, J. (1987) *Positive Discrimination, Social Justice and Social Policy*, London: Tavistock.

ELSON, D. and PEARSON, R. (eds) (1989) *Women's Employment and Multi-Nationals in Europe*, London: Macmillan.

Employment Gazette (1994a) 'Ethnic groups and the labour market', *Employment Gazette*, 102, 5 (May), pp. 148–53, London: Employment Department.

Employment Gazette (1994b) 'Claimant unemployment: rates by age', *Employment Gazette*, 102, 9 (Sept), pp. 301–36, London: Employment Department.

Employment Gazette (1994c) 'Parliamentary questions: age discrimination', *Employment Gazette*, 102, 5 (May), p. 139, London: Employment Department.

Employment Gazette (1995) *Employment Gazette*, 103, 1 (Jan), p. 25, London: Employment Department.

EOC (Equal Opportunities Commission) (1994) *Labour Market Structures and Prospects for Women*, London: EOC.

EOR (*Equal Opportunities Review*) (1993) 'Action for race equality: an EOR survey of employer initiatives', *Equal Opportunities Review*, 48 (Mar/April), pp. 14–19, London: Industrial Relations Services.

EOR (*Equal Opportunities Review*) (1994a) 'Taking the cap off discrimination awards', *Equal Opportunities Review*, 57 (Sept/Oct), pp. 11–13, London: Industrial Relations Services.

EOR (*Equal Opportunities Review*) (1994b) 'Employment forecasts for women to the year 2000', *Equal Opportunities Review*, 56 (Jul/Aug), pp. 20–2, London: Industrial Relations Services.

EOR (*Equal Opportunities Review*) (1994c) 'Paternity leave', *Equal Opportunities Review*, 55 (May/June), pp. 14–28, London: Industrial Relations Services.

EOR (*Equal Opportunities Review*) (1994d) '£173,000 sex bias award', *Equal Opportunities Review*, 53 (Jan/Feb), p. 2, London: Industrial Relations Services.

EOR (*Equal Opportunities Review*) (1994e) 'Age legislation "a burden on business" ', *Equal Opportunities Review*, 55 (May/June), p. 12, London: Industrial Relations Services.

EOR (*Equal Opportunities Review*) (1994f) 'Littlewoods launches "dignity" policy', *Equal Opportunities Review*, 58 (Nov/Dec), p. 8, London: Industrial Relations Services.

EOR (*Equal Opportunities Review*) (1994g) 'Call for age discrimination law', *Equal Opportunities Review*, 58 (Nov/Dec), p. 10, London: Industrial Relations Services.

EOR (*Equal Opportunities Review*) (1994h) 'A family-friendly future', *Equal Opportunities Review*, 58 (Nov/Dec), p. 2, London: Industrial Relations Services.

EOR (*Equal Opportunities Review*) (1994i) 'International review of policies towards older workers', *Equal Opportunities Review*, 57 (Sept/Oct), pp. 8–9, London: Industrial Relations Services.

EOR (*Equal Opportunities Review*) (1995) 'Discrimination cases in tribunals: 1993–94', *Equal Opportunities Review*, 59 (Jan/Feb), p. 37, London: Industrial Relations Services.

ERLANGER, H. and ROTH, W. (1985) 'Disability policy: the parts and the whole', *American Behavioral Scientist*, 28, pp. 319–45.

ESTES, C.L. (1991) 'The new political economy of aging: introduction and critique' in Minkler, M. and Estes, C.L. (eds) *Critical Perspectives on Aging*, New York: Baywood Publishing, pp. 19–36.

EURAG (1987) *The Older Migrant*, The Hague: European Association for the Welfare of the Elderly.

Eurostat (1992) *A Social Portrait of Europe*, Luxembourg: Office for Official Publications of the European Community.

FEC (Fair Employment Commission) (1994) *Fair Employment Commission Fifth Annual Report, 1993–94,* London: HMSO.

FEINSTEIN, H. (1995) 'Wrong gender's agenda', *The Guardian,* 2 March, p. 14.

FINKELSTEIN, V. (1980) *Attitudes and Disabled People: Issues for Discussion,* London: Royal Association for Disability and Rehabilitation (RADAR).

FINKELSTEIN, V. (1981) 'Disability and the helper/helped relationship. An historical view' in A. Brechin, Liddiard, P. and Swain, J. (eds) *Handicap in a Social World,* London: Hodder & Stoughton, pp. 58–64.

FISHKIN, J. S. (1988) 'Do we need a systematic theory of equal opportunity?' in Bowie, N. (ed.) *Equal Opportunity,* Boulder: Westview Press, pp. 15–21.

FLORIG, D. (1986) 'The concept of equal opportunity in the analysis of social welfare policy', *Polity,* XVIII (3), pp. 392–407.

FOGARTY, M. (1975) *Forty to Sixty – How We Waste the Middle-Aged,* London: Bedford Square Press/National Council of Social Service.

FOMBRUN, C., TICHY, N. M. and DEVANNA, M. A. (eds) (1984) *Strategic Human Resource Management,* New York: John Wiley.

FORBES, I. (1989) 'Unequal partners: the implementation of equal opportunities policies in western Europe', *Public Administration,* 67, pp. 19–38.

FORBES, I. (1991) 'Equal opportunity: radical, liberal and conservative critiques' in Meehan, E. and Sevenhuijsen, S. (eds) *Equality, Politics and Gender,* London: Sage, pp. 17–35.

FRITCHIE, R. (1988) 'Positive action training in a cold climate', in Coyle, A. and Skinner, J. (eds) *Women and Work,* London: Macmillan.

FRY, E. (1987) *Disabled People and the 1987 General Election,* London: Spastics Society.

GINN, J. and ARBER, S. (1995) 'Exploring mid-life women's employment', *Sociology,* 29 (1), pp. 73–94.

GINSBURG, H. (1983) *Full Employment and Public Policy: The United States and Sweden,* Lexington: Lexington Books.

GLAZER, N. (1987) *Affirmative Discrimination: Ethnic Inequality and Public Policy,* Cambridge, Mass.: Harvard University Press.

GLAZER, N. and MOYNIHAN, D. (1975) *Ethnicity: Theory and Experience,* London: Harvard University Press.

GLENDINNING, C. (1991) 'Losing ground: social policy and disabled people in Great Britain 1980–1990', *Disability, Handicap & Society,* 6, pp. 3–19.

GLUCKLICH, P. (1984) 'The effects of statutory employment policies on women in the United Kingdom labour market' in Schmid, G. and Weitzel, R. (eds) *Sex Discrimination and Equal Opportunity,* Aldershot: Gower, pp. 107–31.

GOFFMAN, E. (1952) 'On cooling the mark out: some aspects of adaptation to failure', *Psychiatry,* 15 (November), pp. 541–63.

GOODING, C. (1994) *Disabling Laws, Enabling Acts: Disability Rights in Britain and America*, London: Pluto Press.

GOODING, C., HASLER, F. and OLIVER, M. (1994) *What Price Civil Rights?*, London: Rights Now Campaign.

GOULD, A. (1988) *Conflict and Control in Welfare Policy: The Swedish Experience*, London: Longman.

GOULD, A. (1993) *Capitalist Welfare Systems: A Comparison of Japan, Britain and Sweden*, London: Longman.

Great Britain, House of Commons (1995) *Disability Discrimination Bill*, London: HMSO.

Greater Manchester Coalition of Disabled People (1990) 'National campaign fund', *Annual Report 1989–1990*, Manchester: Greater Manchester Coalition of Disabled People, pp. 12–13.

GREGG, P. and MACHIN, S. (1993) *Is the Glass Ceiling Cracking? Gender Compensation Differentials and Access to Promotion among UK Executives*, Discussion Paper 94–5, London: Department of Economics, University College London.

GREGORY, J. (1987) *Sex, Race and the Law*, London: Sage.

Guardian (1994a) Comment: 'The wages of retreat', *The Guardian*, London: 21 December, p. 19.

GUILLEMARD, A. (1985) 'The social dynamics of early withdrawal from the labour force in France', *Ageing and Society*, 5 (4), pp. 381–412.

GUSTAFSSON, S. and JACOBSSON, R. (1985) 'Trends in female labor force participation in Sweden', *Journal of Labor Economics*, 3 (1), pt. 2, S256–S274.

HALSEY, A. H. (1978) *Change in British Society*, Oxford: Oxford University Press.

HALSEY, A. H. (1988) *British Social Trends Since 1900*, Basingstoke: Macmillan.

HALSEY, A. H. (1992) *Opening Wide the Doors of Higher Education*, Briefing Number 6, London: National Commission on Education.

HAM, C. and HILL, M. (1984) *The Policy Process in the Modern Capitalist State*, Hemel Hempstead: Harvester Wheatsheaf.

HARDING, N. (1989) 'Equal opportunities for women in the NHS: the prospects of success?', *Public Administration*, Spring, 67, pp. 51–63.

HASLER, F. (1993) 'Developments in the disabled people's movement' in Swain, J., Finkelstein, V., French, S. and Oliver, M. (eds) (1993) *Disabling Barriers, Enabling Environments*, London: Sage.

HAYEK, F.A. VON (1960) *The Constitution of Liberty*, London: Routledge & Kegan Paul.

HEATH, A. (1981) *Social Mobility*, London: Fontana Collins.

HEILMAN, M. E. (1994) 'Affirmative action: some unintended consequences for working women', *Research in Organisational Behaviour*, 16.

HENDRY, C. and PETTIGREW, A. M. (1986) 'The practice of strategic human resource management', *Personnel Review*, 15 (5), pp. 3–8.

HEVEY, D. (1992) *The Creatures Time Forgot*, London: Routledge.

HIRST, M. (1987) 'Careers of young people with disabilities between the ages of 16 and 21', *Disability, Handicap & Society*, 2, pp. 61–75.

HOCHSCHILD, J. L. (1988) 'Race, class, power and equal opportunity' in Bowie, N. (ed.) *Equal Opportunity*, Boulder: Westview Press, pp. 75–111.

HOLLAND, L. (1994) 'Positive action for race: madness, positive discrimination or a sound business approach?', *Equal Opportunities Review*, 58 (November/December), p. 48.

HUHNE, C. (1993) 'The EC must learn to live without walls', *Independent on Sunday*, 27 June, p. 21.

HUNT, A. (1975) *Management Attitudes and Practices towards Women at Work, An Employment Policy Survey carried out in 1973 by the Social Survey Division of the Office of Population Censuses and Surveys on behalf of the Department of Employment*, London: HMSO.

ILES, P. and AULUCK, R. (1989) 'From racism awareness training to strategic human resource management in implementing equal opportunity', *Personnel Review*, 18 (4), pp. 24–32.

Independent (1994a) Untitled article on the Stonewall riots, *The Independent*, 23 June, p. 23.

Independent (1994b) Editorial: 'The wrong way to attack racist crime', *The Independent*, 23 June, p. 19.

ISHERWOOD, J. (1994) 'Poll victor warns of "deep cuts" in Sweden', *Daily Telegraph*, 20 September, p. 13.

JACKSON, J. A. (1963) *The Irish in Britain*, London: Routledge.

JENCKS, C. (1988) 'What must be equal for opportunity to be equal?' in Bowie, N. E. (ed.) *Equal Opportunity*, Boulder, Col.: Westview Press, 47–74.

JENKINS, R. (1986) *Racism and Recruitment: Managers, Organisations and the Labour Market*, Cambridge: Cambridge University Press.

JENKINS, R. and SOLOMOS, J. (eds) (1989) *Racism and Equal Opportunity Policies in the 1980s* (second edition), Cambridge: Cambridge University Press.

JEWSON, N., MASON, D., WATERS, S. and HARVEY, J. (1990) *Ethnic Minorities and Employment Practice, A Study of Six Organisations. (Research Paper No. 76)*, Leicester: Department of Sociology, University of Leicester.

JONES, C. (1985) *Patterns of Social Policy: An Introduction to Comparative Analysis*, London: Tavistock.

JONES, T. (1993) *Britain's Ethnic Minorities*, London: Policy Studies Institute.

JONUNG, C. (1984) 'Patterns of occupational segregation by sex in the labour market' in Schmid, G. and Weitzel, R. (eds) *Sex Discrimination and Equal Opportunity*, Aldershot: Gower, pp. 44–68.

JOSEPH, K. and SUMPTION, J. (1979) *Equality*, London: John Murray.

KANDOLA, B. (1993) 'Managing diversity', *Viewpoint: The Magazine for Benefits Agency Managers*, 8 (Summer), p. 18.

KANDOLA, R. and FULLERTON, J. (1984) *Managing the Mosaic: Diversity in Action*, London: Institute of Personnel Management.

KANDOLA, R., FULLERTON, J. and AHMED, Y. (1995) 'Managing diversity: succeeding where equal opportunities has failed', *Equal Opportunities Review*, 59, Jan/Feb, pp. 31–6.

KANTER, R. MOSS (1976) 'The policy issues: presentation VI' in Blaxall, M. and Reagan, B.(eds) *Women and the Workplace: The Implications of Occupational Segregation*, Chicago: University of Chicago Press, pp. 282–91.

KELLY, J. (1993) *Barriers to Women's Development in the Workplace: Harnessing Wasted Talents*, Speech given at the 'Towards Diversity' Conference, Civil Service College, Sunningdale Park, Berkshire, 7 July.

KIMMEL, D. C. (1980) *Adulthood and Aging* (second edition), New York: Wiley.

KIRP, D. (1979) *Doing Good by Doing Little: Race and Schooling in Britain*, Berkeley: University of California Press.

KÖNIG, A. and SCHALOCK, R. (1991) 'Supported employment: equal opportunities for severely disabled men and women', *International Labour Review*, 130, pp. 21–37.

LACZKO, F. and PHILLIPSON, C. (1990) 'Defending the right to work: age discrimination in employment' in McEwen, M. (ed.) *Age – the Unrecognised Discrimination*, London: Age Concern England, pp. 84–96.

LACZKO, F. and PHILLIPSON, C. (1991) *Changing Work and Retirement*, Buckingham: Open University Press.

LANSLEY, S. (1994) *After the Gold Rush – The Trouble with Affluence*, London: Henley Centre for Forecasting/Century Books.

LASH, S. and URRY, J. (1987) *The End of Organized Capitalism*, Oxford: Blackwell.

LAWSON, R. (1990) ' "Social citizenship", work and social solidarity: historical comparisons between Britain and Sweden', Paper presented to the 85th Annual Meeting of the American Sociological Association, Washington, DC, 14 August.

LEACH, B. (1989) 'Disabled people and the implementation of local authorities' equal opportunities policies', *Public Administration*, 67 (Spring), pp. 65–77.

LEE, S. M. (1993) 'Racial classifications in the US Census: 1890–1990', *Ethnic and Racial Studies*, 16 (1), pp. 75–94.

LIFF, S. (1989) 'Assessing equal opportunities policies', *Personnel Review*, 18 (1), pp. 27–34.

LONSDALE, S. (1986) *Work and Inequality*, Harlow: Longman.

LUNDBERG LITHMAN, E. (1987) *Immigration and Immigration Policy in Sweden*, Stockholm: The Swedish Institute.

LUNT, N. and THORNTON, P. (1994) 'Disability and employment: towards an understanding of discourse and policy', *Disability and Society*, 9, pp. 223–38.

LUSTGARTEN, L. (1989) 'Racial inequality and the limits of the law' in Jenkins, R. and Solomos, J. (eds) *Racism and Equal Opportunity Policies in the 1980s* (second edition), Cambridge: Cambridge University Press, pp. 14–29.

MACLEOD, D. (1994) ' "Well presented" women winning graduate jobs', *The Guardian*, London, p. 4.

MCCRUDDEN, C., SMITH, D. and BROWN, C., with the assistance of KNOX, J. (1991) *Racial Justice at Work*, London: Policy Studies Institute.

MCEWEN, E. (ed.) (1990) *Age – the Unrecognised Discrimination*, London: Age Concern England.

MCKAY, S. (1992) *Pensioners' Assets*, London: Policy Studies Institute.

MAES, M.-E. (1990) *Building a People's Europe: 1992 and the Social Dimension*, London: Whurr Publishers.

MARSH, C. (1991) 'The right to work: justice in the distribution of employment' in Manning, N. (ed.) *Social Policy Review 1990–91*, Harlow, Essex: Longman, pp. 223–42.

MARSH, D. and RHODES, R. A. W. (eds) (1992) *Implementing Thatcherite Policies: Audit of an Era*, Milton Keynes: Open University Press.

MARSHALL, A. (1995) 'Rush to leave Britain explodes migrant myths', *Independent on Sunday*, 19 February, London.

MARTIN, J., WHITE, A. and MELTZER, H. (1989) *Disabled Adults: Services, Transport and Employment*, London: OPCS.

MASON, D. and JEWSON, N. (1992) ' "Race", equal opportunities policies and employment practice: reflections on the 1980s, prospects for the 1990s', *New Community*, 19 (1), pp. 99–112.

MAXWELL, P. (1989) 'The impact of equal value legislation in Northern Ireland', *Policy and Politics*, 17 (4), pp. 295–300.

MEEHAN, E. (1993) *Citizenship and the European Community*, London: Sage.

MEEHAN, E. and SEVENHUIJSEN, S. (eds) (1991) *Equality, Politics and Gender*, London: Sage.

MEEHAN, E. and WHITTING, G. (1989) 'Introduction: gender and public policy', *Policy and Politics*, 17 (4), pp. 283–5.

MEIER, E. and KERR, E. (1976) 'Capabilities of middle-aged and older workers: a survey of the literature', *Industrial Gerontology*, 3, pp. 147–56.

MIEKLE, J. and REDWOOD, F. (1994) 'The glass ceiling', *Guardian Education*, 31 May, pp. 2–3.

MILNE, K. (1995) 'Able to protest', *New Statesman & Society*, 10 February, pp. 25–7.

MILNE, S. (1995) 'Sex bias "destroyed" woman firefighter', *The Guardian*, 1 April, p. 6.

Ministry of Culture, Sweden (1992) *Act concerning Equality between Men and Women – the Equal Opportunities Act*, Stockholm: Equality Affairs Division, Ministry of Culture.

Ministry of Labour, Sweden (n.d.) 'Equality between men and women in Sweden: government policy to the mid-nineties' (unpublished background paper), Stockholm: Arbetsmarknadsdepartementet.

MINKLER, M. and ESTES, C. L. (1991) *Critical Perspectives on Aging: The Political and Moral Economy of Growing Old*, New York: Baywood Publishing Company.

MISHRA, R. (1986) 'Social policy and the discipline of social administration', *Social Policy and Administration*, 20 (1), pp. 28–38.

MØLLER, I. H. (1987) 'Early retirement in Denmark', *Ageing and Society*, 7 (4), pp. 427–43.

MOMM, W. and KÖNIG, A. (1989) 'Community integration for disabled people: a new approach to their vocational training and employment', *International Labour Review*, 128 (4), pp. 497–509.

MOORE, J. (1987) *The Welfare State – the Way Ahead*, London: Conservative Political Centre.

MOORE, J., TILSON, B. and WHITTING, G. (1994) *An International Overview of Employment Policies and Practices Towards Older Workers*, Sheffield: Employment Department.

MORRIS, A. (1994) 'Paying for the bill', 'Society' Supplement, *The Guardian*, 26 October, p. 7.

MORRIS, J. (1991) *Pride Against Prejudice: Transforming Attitudes to Disability*, London: The Women's Press.

MORRIS, J. (1993) *Independent Lives: Community Care and Disabled People*, London: Macmillan.

MORRIS, P. (1969) *Put Away*, London: Routledge and Kegan Paul.

MYLES, G. (1992) *EEC Brief – Volume Three*, Lisburn: Locksley Press.

NANTON, P. (1992) 'Official statistics and the problem of inappropriate ethnic categorisation', *Policy and Politics*, 20 (4), pp. 277–86.

NEWELL, S. (1992) 'The myth and destructiveness of equal opportunities: the continued dominance of the mothering role', *Personnel Review*, 21 (4), pp. 37–47.

NIXON, B. (1995) 'Training's role in empowerment', *People Management*, 9 February, pp. 36–8.

Office of Population Censuses and Surveys (OPCS) (1991) *Social Trends*, London: HMSO.

Office of Population Censuses and Surveys (OPCS) (1992) *1991 Census – County Report: West Midlands (Part 1)*, London: HMSO.

Office of Population Censuses and Surveys (OPCS) (1993) *General Household Survey 1991*, London: HMSO.

OLIVER, M. (1985) 'Discrimination, disability and social policy' in Brenton, M. and Jones, C. (eds) *The Yearbook of Social Policy 1984–1985*, London: Routledge and Kegan Paul.

OLIVER, M. (1989) 'Conductive education: if it wasn't so sad it would be funny', *Disability, Handicap & Society*, 4 (2), pp. 197–200.

OLIVER, M. (1990) *The Politics of Disablement*, London: Macmillan.

OLIVER, M. (1991) 'Disability and participation in the labour market' in Brown, P. and Scase, R. *Poor Work: Disadvantage and the Division of Labour*, Milton Keynes: Open University Press.

OLLEREARNSHAW, S. and WALDRECK, R. (1995) 'Taking action to promote equality', *People Management*, 23 February, pp. 24–9.

O'NEILLY, J. (1995) 'When prejudice is not just skin deep', *People Management*, 23 February, pp. 34–7.

Organisation for Economic Cooperation and Development (OECD) (1994) *The OECD Jobs Study*, Paris: OECD Publications Service.

PAGEL, M. (1988) *On Our Own Behalf*, Manchester: Greater Manchester Coalition of Disabled People.

PAREKH, B. (1992) 'A case for positive discrimination' in Hepple, B. and Szyszczak, E. M. (eds) *Discrimination: the Limits of Law*, London: Mansell Publishing, pp. 261–80.

PERSSON, I. (ed.) (1990) *Generating Equality in the Welfare State: The Swedish Experience*, Oslo: Norwegian University Press.

PETERS, T. J. (1989) *Thriving on Chaos – Handbook for a Management Revolution*, London: Pan/Macmillan.

PETERS, T. J. and AUSTIN, N. (1986) *A Passion for Excellence: The Leadership Difference*, London: Fontana.

PETERS, T. J. and WATERMAN, R. (1982) *In Search of Excellence*, New York: HarperCollins.

PHILLIPS, A. (1994) 'Worst off among equals?', *The Guardian*, 25 January, p. 15.

PHILLIPSON, C. (1982) *Capitalism and the Construction of Old Age*, London: Macmillan.

PILKINGTON, E. (1994) 'Winners and losers in sex bias cases', *The Guardian*, 11 August.

PITT, G. (1992) 'Can reverse discrimination be justified?' in Hepple, B. and Szyszczak, E.M. (eds) *Discrimination: the Limits of Law*, London: Mansell Publishing, pp. 281–99.

PRAGER, J. (1982) 'Equal opportunity and affirmative action: the rise of new social understandings', *Research in Law, Deviance and Social Control*, 4, pp. 191–218.

PRESCOTT CLARKE, P. (1990) *Employment and Handicap*, London: Social and Community Planning Research.

PURNELL, S. (1994) 'Whitehall's mandarins fight off reform', *The Daily Telegraph*, 28 June, p. 11.

RAPOPORT, R. and MOSS, P. (1990) *Men and Women as Equals at Work*, Thomas Coram Research Unit, Occasional Paper No. 11, London: Institute of Education, University of London.

REED, C. (1995) 'Good ol' boys get into a mean mood', *The Guardian*, 2 March, p. 12.

RONNBY, A. (1985) *Socialstaten*, Lund: Studentlitteratur.

ROSE, E. J. B. in association with DEAKIN, N. et al. (1969) *Colour and Citizenship: A Report on British Race Relations*, London: Institute of Race Relations, Oxford University Press.

ROUSSEAU, J. (1761) *A Discourse upon the Origin and Foundations of Inequality among Mankind*, London: Dodsley.

RUGGIE, M. (1984) *The State and Working Women: A Comparative Study of Britain and Sweden*, Princeton: Princeton University Press.

RUTHERFORD, F. (1989) 'The proposal for a European directive on parental leave: some reasons why it failed', *Policy and Politics*, 17 (4), pp. 301–10.

RYAN, J. and THOMAS, F. (1980) *The Politics of Mental Handicap*, Harmondsworth: Penguin.

SAVILL, A. (1994) 'Swedes cling to nanny state's apron', *The Independent*, 18 September.

SAYAL-BENNETT, A. (1991) 'Equal opportunities – empty rhetoric?', *Feminism and Psychology*, 1 (1), pp. 74–7.

SCARMAN, L. G. (LORD SCARMAN) (1982) *The Brixton Disorders, 10–12 April, 1981*, London: HMSO.

SCHAAR, J. (1967) 'Equality of opportunity, and beyond' in Pennock, R. and Chapman, J.W. (eds) *Equality: Nomos IX*, New York: Atherton Press.

SCHALOCK, R.L. and KIERNAN, W. E. (1990) *Habilitation Planning for Adults with Disabilities*, New York: Springer Verlag.

SCHON, D. (1971) *Beyond the Stable State*, London: Temple Smith.

SCOTT, V. (1994) *Lessons from America: A Study of the Americans with Disabilities Act*, London: Royal Association for Disability and Rehabilitation (RADAR).

SHAKESPEARE, T. (1993) 'Disabled people's self-organisation: a new social movement?', *Disability, Handicap & Society*, 8 (3), pp. 249–64.

SHER, G. (1983) 'Preferential hiring' in Regan, T. (ed.) *Just Business – New Introductory Essays in Business Ethics*, Philadelphia: Temple University Press, pp. 32–59.

SHER, G. (1988) 'Qualifications, fairness and desert' in Bowie, N. (ed.) *Equal Opportunity*, Boulder, Col.: Westview Press, pp. 113–27.

SJOSTROM, K. (1984) *Social Politiken*, Stockholm: Arbeterkultur.

SLOANE, P. J. and JAIN, H. C. (1989) *The Development of Equal Opportunities Policies in North America and Europe: An Overview*, Discussion Paper 89–03, Aberdeen: Department of Economics, University of Aberdeen.

SMALL, S. (1991) 'Attaining racial parity in the United States and England: we got to go where the greener grass grows!', *Sage Race Relations Abstracts*, 16 (2).

SOKOLOFF, N. J. (1992) *Black Women and White Women in the Professions*, London: Routledge.

SOLOMOS, J. (1989) *Race and Racism in Contemporary Britain*, London: Macmillan.

SPARROW, P. R. and PETTIGREW, A. M. (1988) 'Strategic human resource management in the UK computer supplier industry', *Journal of Occupational Psychology*, 61 (1), pp. 25–42.

STAMP, P. and ROBARTS, S. (1986) *Positive Action: Changing the Workplace for Women*, London: National Council for Civil Liberties.

Statistics Sweden (SCB) (1992) *On Women and Men in Sweden and EC*, Orebro, Sweden: SCB Publishing Unit.

STEELE, J. (1995) ' "Foreign" pawns in a presidential game', *The Guardian*, 25 April, p. 10.

SWAIN, J., FINKELSTEIN, V., FRENCH, S., and OLIVER, M. (eds) (1993) *Disabling Barriers, Enabling Environments*, London: Sage.

TITMUSS, R. H. (1963) *Essays on the 'Welfare State'* (second edition), London: George Allen and Unwin.

TITMUSS, R. H. (1976) *Commitment to Welfare* (second edition), London: George Allen and Unwin.

TOPLISS, E. (1979) *Provision for the Disabled* (second edition), Oxford: Blackwell.

TOPLISS, E. and GOULD, B. (1981) *A Charter for the Disabled*, Oxford: Basil Blackwell and Martin Robertson.

TORDAY, P. (1994) 'Record figures may spur new work policies', *The Independent*, 8 June, p. 9.

TOWNSEND, P. (1979) *Poverty in the United Kingdom*, Harmondsworth: Penguin.

TOYNBEE, P., OXFORD, E. and WARD, V. (1995) 'Beyond the ceiling, the sky's the limit', News Analysis: *The Independent*, 27 April, p. 17.

TRAPP, R. (1995) 'Employers argue for strong disability law', *Independent on Sunday*, Business Section, 3 September, p. 8.

TRAVIS, A. (1994) 'Axed gays may claim millions', *The Guardian*, 5 August, p. 1.

TUCKER, B. P. (1994) 'Overview of the DDA and comparison with the ADA', *Australian Disability Review*, 3–94, pp. 23–37.

WALKER, A. (1990) 'The benefits of old age? – Age discrimination and social security' in McEwen, E. (ed.) *Age – the Unrecognised Discrimination*, London: Age Concern England.

WALKER, M. (1995) 'Double blow for affirmative action', *The Guardian*, 13 June, p. 9.

WEBB, J. (1988) 'The ivory tower: positive action for women in higher education' in Coyle, A. and Skinner, J. (eds) *Women and Work*, London: Macmillan.

WESTERGAARD, J. and RESLER, H. (1976) *Class in a Capitalist Society*, Harmondsworth: Penguin.

WHITE, M. and TREVOR, M. (1983) *Under Japanese Management*, London: Heinemann.

WHITEHILL, A. M. (1991) *Japanese Management: Tradition and Transition*, London: Routledge.

WHITTING, G., MOORE, J. and WARREN, P. (1993) *Partnerships for Equality: A Review of Employers' Equal Opportunities Groups*, London: Department of Employment.

WILLMOTT, H. (1987) 'Racism, politics and employment relations' in Lee, G. and Loveridge, R. (eds) *The Manufacture of Disadvantage*, Milton Keynes: Open University Press.

WOO, D. (1990) 'The "over-representation" of Asian Americans: red herrings and yellow perils', *Sage Race Relations Abstracts*, 15 (2).

WRENCH, J. (1987) 'Unequal comrades: trade unions, equal opportunity and racism' in Jenkins, R. and Solomos, J. (eds) *Racism and Equal Opportunity Policies in the 1980s*, Cambridge: Cambridge University Press.

YUZAWA, T. (1994) 'Japanese business strategies in perspective' in Yuzawa, T. (ed.) *Japanese Business Success: The Evolution of a Strategy*, London: Routledge, pp. 1–22.

INDEX